# Impact maths 1 R

# About this book

Impact maths provides a complete course to help you achieve your best in your Key Stage 3 Mathematics course. This book will help you understand and remember mathematical ideas, solve mathematical problems with and without the help of a calculator and develop your mental maths skills.

Exercises you should try without the help of a calculator are marked with this symbol:

## Finding your way around

To help you find your way around when you are studying use the:

- **edge marks** shown on the front pages – these help you get to the right unit quickly

- **contents list** and **index** – these list all the key ideas covered in the book and help you turn straight to them.

- **links** in the margin – these show when an idea elsewhere in the book may be useful:

There is more about fractions on page 119.

## Remembering key ideas

We have provided clear explanations of the key ideas you need throughout the book with **worked examples** showing you how to answer questions. **Key points** you need to remember look like this:

■ **The distance around the edge of a shape is its perimeter.**

and are listed in a **summary** at the end of each unit.

## Investigations and information technology

Two units focus on particular skills you need for your course:

- **using and applying mathematics** (unit 18) – shows you some ways of investigating mathematical problems.

- **calculators and computers** (unit 19) – shows you some ways of using calculators and computers and will help with mental maths practice.

11

12

13

14

15

16

17

18

19

Heinemann Educational Publishers
Halley Court, Jordan Hill, Oxford, OX2 8EJ
a division of Reed Educational & Professional Publishing Ltd
Heinemann is a registered trademark of Reed Educational & Professional Publishing Ltd

OXFORD   MELBOURNE   AUCKLAND
JOHANNESBURG   BLANTYRE   GABARONE
IBADAN   PORTSMOUTH   NH (USA)   CHICAGO


© Heinemann Educational Publishers

First published 1999

ISBN 0 435 01760 8

02 01 00 99
10 9 8 7 6 5 4 3 2 1

Designed and typeset by TechSet Ltd, Gateshead, Tyne and Wear
Illustrated by Barry Atkinson, Barking Dog and TechSet
Cover design by Miller, Craig and Cocking
Printed and bound by Edelvives, Spain


**Acknowledgements**
The authors and publishers would like to thank the following for permission to use photographs:
P1:Robert Harding Picture Library; Science Photo Library/Prof.K.Seddon & Dr.T.Evans, Queen s University, Belfast; Pet Rescue magazine, John Brown Publishing/Channel 4. P15: Corbis. P46: China Span/Keren Su. P55: Holt Studios/Nigel Cattlin. P58 and 60: Robert Harding Picture Library. P61, 62 and 63: Action-Plus/Glyn Kirk; Peter Blakeman; Neil Tingle. P81: Science & Society Picture Library. P91: Action-Plus/Neil Tingle. P134: J. Allan Cash Ltd.; Action-Plus/Richard Francis. P147: Aerofilms. P164: J.Allan Cash Ltd. P178: Action-Plus/Glyn Kirk. P184: Direct Holidays; Robert Harding Picture Library; J.Allan Cash Ltd. P232: J.Allan Cash Ltd. P245: Robert Harding Picture Library. P251: Trevor Hill. P274: Action-Plus/Glyn Kirk.

Cover photo "Synchronicity" by Daniel Culloch © '87, Design Synergy, U.S.A., Tel: 505-986-1215, URL: http://www.dolphin-synergy.com

**Publishing team**                                        **Author team**
**Editorial**          **Design**                  Gareth Cole          Christine Medlow
Philip Ellaway         Phil Richards               Ray Fraser           Graham Newman
Sarah Caton            Colette Jacquelin           Barry Grantham       Sheila Nolan
Nigel Green            Mags Robertson              Karen Hughes         Keith Pledger
Anne Russell                                       Peter Jolly          Ian Roper
                                                   David Kent           John Sylvester
                       **Production**
                       David Lawrence
                       Jo Morgan

Tel:01865 888058  email:info.he@heinemann.co.uk

# Contents

# 6 Decimals

# 7 Measuring

# 8 Fractions

# 14   Angles

# 15   Handling data

# 16   Percentages

# 17  Averages

# 18  Using and applying mathematics

# 19  Calculators and computers

# Index

# 1 Shapes

## 1.1 Why do we study shapes?

The world is full of interesting shapes.

Engineers use shapes to make their structures strong . . .

Designers use shapes to make the page more interesting . . .

Scientists use shapes to help them understand molecular structure . . .

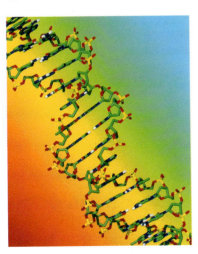

Mathematicians help us understand what is special about different shapes.

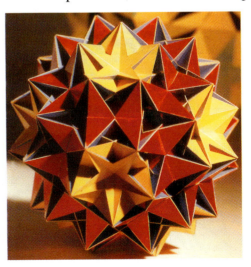

This unit introduces some shapes and shows you how to describe them.

## 1.2 Naming shapes

You name shapes like these by the number of sides they have:

| ■ Shape | Name | Hint |
|---|---|---|
| △ | Triangle: 3 sides | **Tri**cycles have 3 wheels. **Tri**plets are 3 babies. |
| ⬙ | Quadrilateral: 4 sides | **Quad** bikes have 4 wheels. **Quad**s are 4 babies. |
| ⬠ | Pentagon: 5 sides | A **penta**thlon has 5 athletic events. |
| ⬡ | Hexagon: 6 sides | Six and hexagon both use the letter **x**. |
| ⬢ | Heptagon: 7 sides | A **hepta**thlon has 7 athletic events. |
| ⯃ | Octagon: 8 sides | An **oct**opus has 8 legs. |

Notice that ⬡ and ⟫ are both hexagons.

### Exercise 1A

1   For each shape:
   - write down the number of sides
   - name the shape.

   The first shape has 3 sides. It is a triangle.

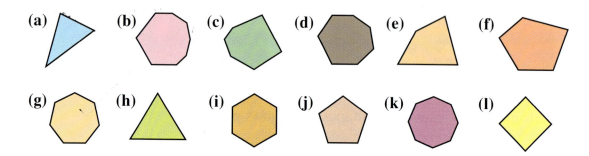

(a) (b) (c) (d) (e) (f) (g) (h) (i) (j) (k) (l)

**2**   On this tile:

(a)  how many triangles are there

(b)  how many quadrilaterals are there?

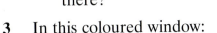

**3**   In this coloured window:

(a)  how many pentagons are there

(b)  how many hexagons are there

(c)  how many heptagons are there

(d)  how many octagons are there?

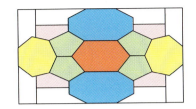

**4**   For each of these windows:

- list all the different shapes
- count how many of each shape there are.

**(a)** 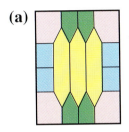   **(b)** 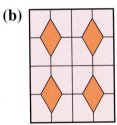   **(c)** 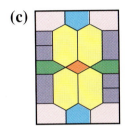   **(d)**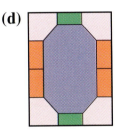

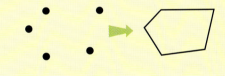

*How to sketch a shape*
To sketch a pentagon draw 5 dots like this: then join them up.

**5**   **(a)** Sketch a hexagon   **(b)** Sketch a heptagon   **(c)** Sketch an octagon
Hint: draw 6 dots

**6**   **Activity**   You need Activity sheet 1. Cut out the triangles and pentagons.

You can use a triangle and a pentagon to make a hexagon:

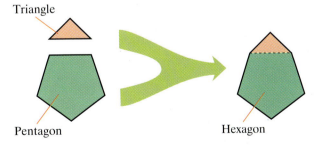

Triangle

Pentagon

Hexagon

**(a)** Use a triangle and a pentagon to make:

- two more hexagons
- two quadrilaterals

**(b)** Use two triangles and a pentagon to make:

- a heptagon (7 sides)
- a triangle
- a different sized pentagon

## 1.3 Mirror symmetry

This shape has symmetry:

This is a **line of symmetry**.

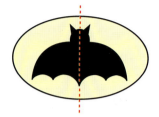

If you folded on the line of symmetry, one half would fit over the other exactly.

You can use a mirror to find the line of symmetry.

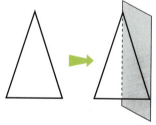

This shape has symmetry

The mirror image fits exactly

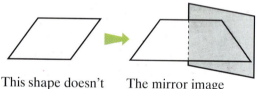

This shape doesn't have symmetry

The mirror image does not fit

■ **A shape has symmetry if you can fold it so that one side fits exactly on to the other.**
**The fold line is the line of symmetry.**
**A line of symmetry is also called a mirror line.**

### Example 1

How many lines of symmetry does this shape have?

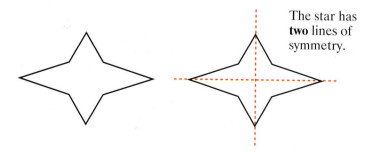

The star has **two** lines of symmetry.

## Exercise 1B

**1**  How many lines of symmetry does each shape have?

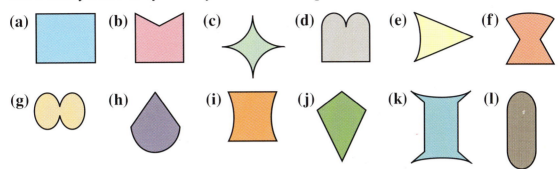

(a)  (b)  (c)  (d)  (e)  (f)

(g)  (h)  (i)  (j)  (k)  (l)

**2**  Copy these letters. Draw any lines of symmetry.
The first one has been done for you.

## A B C D E F H I W X N M O S

**3**  How many lines of symmetry do these words have?

## BOB   DAD   WOW   OXO   SOS

**4**  What is the longest word you can find that has a line of symmetry? (Hint: you may need to use your dictionary.)

**5**  You need Activity sheet 2.
Draw all the lines of symmetry on each shape.

## 1.4 Symmetry and regular shapes

These shapes are regular:

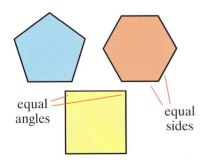

In each shape:
- the sides are equal lengths
- the angles are equal

These shapes are not regular:

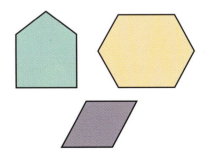

In each shape the sides and angles are **not** equal.

■  **A regular shape has equal sides and equal angles.**

**Example 2**

How many lines of symmetry does
this regular hexagon have?

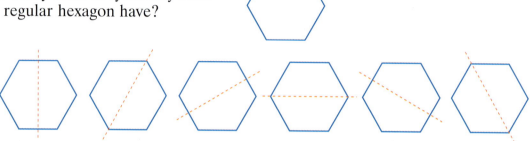

There are 6 lines of symmetry.

■   **A regular shape has the same number of lines of
    symmetry as sides.**

## Exercise 1C

For each shape:

● Is it regular or not regular?
● How many lines of symmetry has it got?

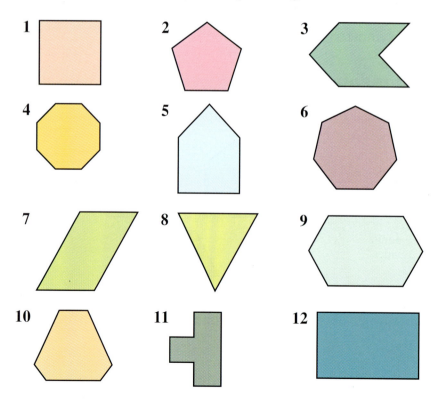

**Hint:** trace the
shapes into
your book first.

**13**  Copy and complete the sentences.
The first one has been done for you.

(a)  A regular quadrilateral has <u>4</u> equal sides and <u>4</u>
equal angles.
It has 4 lines of symmetry.

(b)  A regular hexagon has _____ equal sides and _____
equal angles.
It has 6 lines of symmetry.

(c)  A regular pentagon has _____ equal sides and _____
equal angles.
It has _____ lines of symmetry.

(d)  A regular triangle has _____ equal sides and _____
equal angles.
It has _____ lines of symmetry.

(e)  A regular octagon has _____ equal sides and _____
equal angles.
It has _____ lines of symmetry.

(f)  A regular heptagon has _____ equal sides and _____
equal angles.
It has _____ lines of symmetry.

## 1.5  Reflecting shapes

You can reflect this shape in a mirror ... to make another shape:

## Exercise 1D

**Activity**   You need a mirror. Use it to reflect the shapes below.

What shapes do you make?

Choose your answers from this box.

| | | | |
|---|---|---|---|
| Triangle | Hexagon | Regular quadrilateral | Regular triangle |
| Pentagon | Octagon | Regular pentagon | Regular hexagon |
| Heptagon | Quadrilateral | Regular heptagon | Regular octagon |

The first shape is a **quadrilateral**.

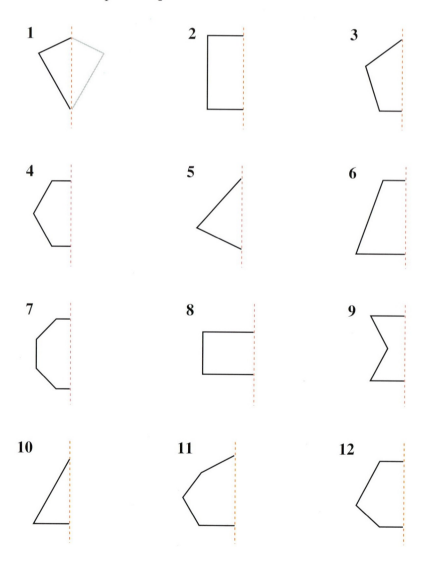

# 1.6 Symmetry and special triangles

Special triangles have special names:

**Equilateral**
All sides are equal.

**Isosceles**
Two sides are equal.

**Scalene**
No sides are equal.

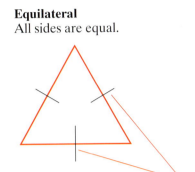
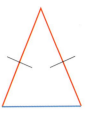
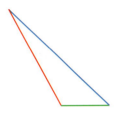

You mark equal sides with a dash.

and special symmetries:

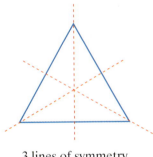
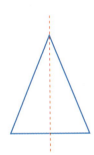
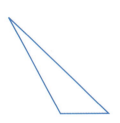

3 lines of symmetry        1 line of symmetry        no lines of symmetry

## Exercise 1E

For each triangle write down:

- how many sides are equal
- the name of the triangle
- how many lines of symmetry it has.

**1** 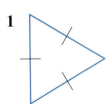   **2**    **3**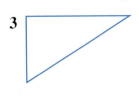

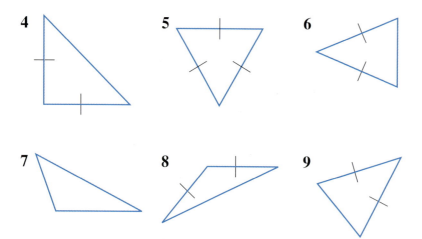

# 1.7 Symmetry in quadrilaterals

Sides marked with
the same number of
dashes are equal.

Sides marked with
the same number of
arrows are parallel.

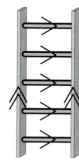

On this ladder:
the rungs are parallel
the sides are parallel

Special quadrilaterals have special names:

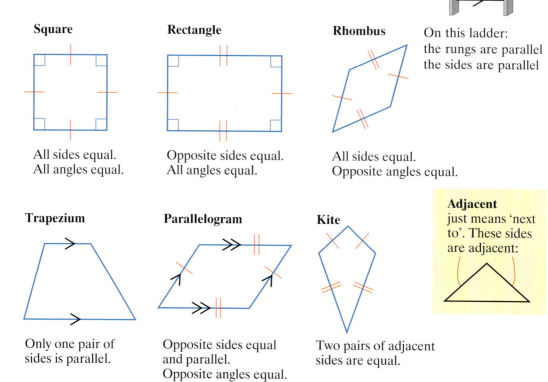

**Square**

All sides equal.
All angles equal.

**Rectangle**

Opposite sides equal.
All angles equal.

**Rhombus**

All sides equal.
Opposite angles equal.

**Trapezium**

Only one pair of
sides is parallel.

**Parallelogram**

Opposite sides equal
and parallel.
Opposite angles equal.

**Kite**

Two pairs of adjacent
sides are equal.

**Adjacent**
just means 'next
to'. These sides
are adjacent:

## Exercise 1F

For each shape write down:

- the name of the shape (give the reasons for your answer)
- how many lines of symmetry it has.

The first shape is a parallelogram.
Reason: Opposite sides are equal and parallel.
No lines of symmetry.

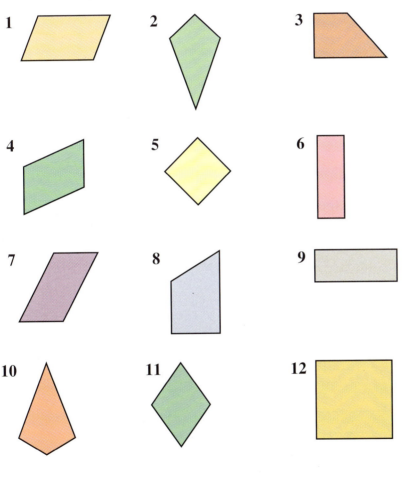

13  Copy and complete these sentences:
- **(a)** A quadrilateral has _____ sides.
- **(b)** A square has _____ lines of symmetry.
- **(c)** A kite has _____ line of symmetry.
- **(d)** A rhombus has _____ lines of symmetry.
- **(e)** A rectangle has _____ lines of symmetry.
- **(f)** A parallelogram has _____ lines of symmetry.

**14 Activity**   Use two equilateral triangles.

- How many different shapes can you make with them?
- Write down the name of any shape you have made.

You can trace this equilateral triangle.

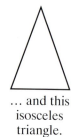

… and this isosceles triangle.

**15 Activity**   Repeat question **14** using:

**(a)** 3 equilateral triangles   **(b)** 4 equilateral triangles
**(c)** 2 isosceles triangles   **(d)** 3 isosceles triangles
**(e)** 4 isosceles triangles

Make sure that:

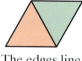

The edges line up like this …

… not like this!

No overlapping allowed.

## 1.8 Solid shapes

Here are four types of solid shapes.
You need to be able to recognise them.

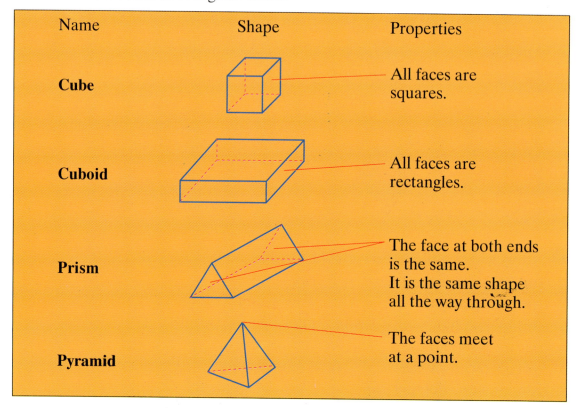

| Name | Shape | Properties |
|------|-------|------------|
| Cube | | All faces are squares. |
| Cuboid | | All faces are rectangles. |
| Prism | | The face at both ends is the same. It is the same shape all the way through. |
| Pyramid | | The faces meet at a point. |

## Exercise 1G

Which of these shapes are:
(**a**) cubes    (**b**) cuboids    (**c**) prisms    (**d**) pyramids?

1     2     3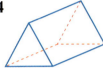

4     5     6

7 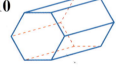    8     9

10 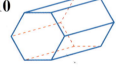    11     12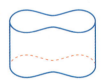

13 For each of these prisms, write down the shape of the end face.

This is the end face

(**a**)     (**b**) 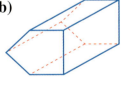    (**c**)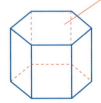

14 For each pyramid, write down the shape of the base.

(**a**)     (**b**)     (**c**)

# 1.9 Prisms and pyramids

## Naming prisms

A prism is the same shape all the way through.

You can cut any prism in two like this:

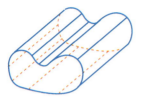  

The middle of a prism looks exactly the same as the end face.
It has a **constant cross section**.

You name a prism by the shape of its cross section.

Triangular prism          Hexagonal prism          Pentagonal prism

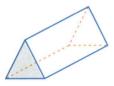          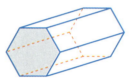          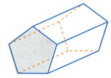

The cross section is a triangle     The cross section is a hexagon     The cross section is a pentagon

## Naming pyramids

You name a pyramid by the shape of its base.

Triangular based pyramid     Hexagonal based pyramid     Square based pyramid

The base is a triangle          The base is a hexagon          The base is a square

### Exercise 1H

Write down the name of each shape:

**1**      **2** 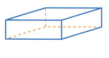     **3**      **4**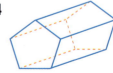

5 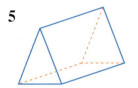   6 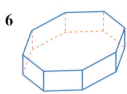   7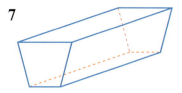

## 1.10  Plane symmetry

Some solid shapes have symmetry too.

■   **A plane of symmetry cuts a solid shape into two parts
     that are mirror images of each other.**

This building has plane symmetry.      This car has plane symmetry.      This wedge has plane symmetry.

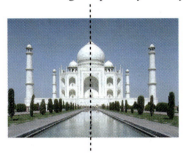      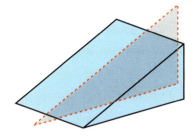

This is the plane of symmetry.

## 1.11  Plane spotting

A solid shape can have many planes of symmetry.

### Example 3

How many planes of symmetry
does this shape have?

It has 3 planes of symmetry.

**Example 4**

How many planes of symmetry does this prism have?

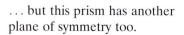

Every prism has this          ... but this prism has another
plane of symmetry......       plane of symmetry too.

This prism has two planes of symmetry

## Pyramids

If the base has symmetry the pyramid may have plane
symmetry.
It will only have plane symmetry if the top of the pyramid is
above a line of symmetry on the base.

**Example 5**

How many planes of symmetry does
this square based pyramid have?

The top of the pyramid is over
one corner of the square.

The square has
4 lines of
symmetry:

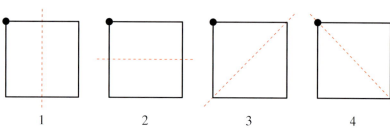

      1          2          3          4

Only one line of symmetry passes through the corner.
So the pyramid has 1 plane of symmetry.

## Exercise 1I

1   For each shape, write down the number of planes of
    symmetry it has.

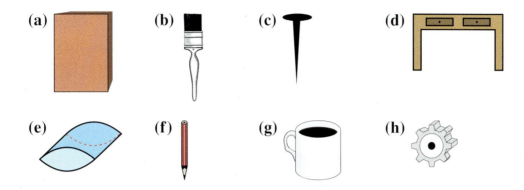

(a)   (b)   (c)   (d)

(e)   (f)   (g)   (h)

2   For each shape, write down:
    - the name of the shape
    - how many planes of symmetry it has.

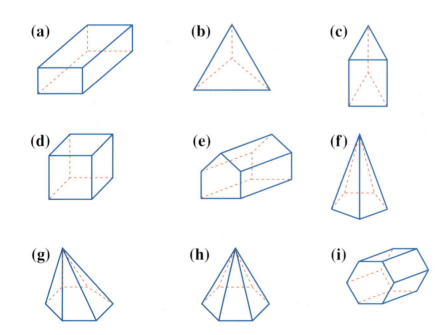

(a)   (b)   (c)

(d)   (e)   (f)

(g)   (h)   (i)

3   How many planes of symmetry does each shape have in
    Exercise **1H** (on pages 14 and 15)?

## Summary of key points

| 1 | Shape | Name | Hint |
|---|---|---|---|

Triangle: 3 sides — **Tri**cycles have 3 wheels. **Tri**plets are 3 babies.

Quadrilateral: 4 sides — **Quad** bikes have 4 wheels. **Quads** are 4 babies.

Pentagon: 5 sides — A **penta**thlon has 5 athletic events.

Hexagon: 6 sides — Si**x** and he**x**agon both use the letter **x**.

Heptagon: 7 sides — A **hepta**thlon has 7 athletic events.

Octagon: 8 sides — An **oct**opus has 8 legs.

**2**  A shape has symmetry if you can fold it so that one side fits exactly on to the other. The fold line is the line of symmetry. The line of symmetry is also called the mirror line.

**3**  A regular shape has equal sides and equal angles.

**4**  A regular shape has the same number of lines of symmetry as sides.

**5**  A plane of symmetry cuts a solid shape into two parts that are mirror images of each other.

# 2 Understanding numbers

## 2.1 Digits and place value

Our number system was invented in India over 1400 years ago...

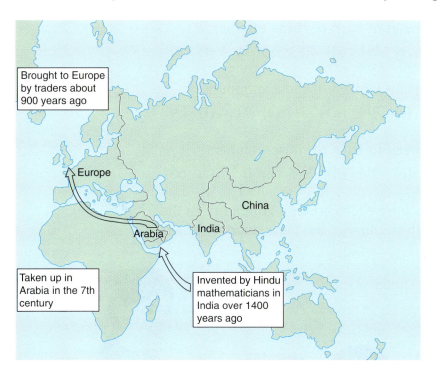

Brought to Europe by traders about 900 years ago

Europe

China

India

Arabia

Taken up in Arabia in the 7th century

Invented by Hindu mathematicians in India over 1400 years ago

You can use it to make large and small numbers using just ten **digits**:

$$0 \quad 1 \quad 2 \quad 3 \quad 4 \quad 5 \quad 6 \quad 7 \quad 8 \quad 9$$

■ **The value of a digit depends on its place in a number.**
You can see this in a place value diagram:

| The digit 4 means ... | Hundreds | Tens | Units | |
|---|---|---|---|---|
| 4 hundreds | 4 | 7 | 9 | Four hundred and seventy nine |
| 4 tens | 2 | 4 | 3 | Two hundred and forty three |
| 4 units | 7 | 0 | 4 | Seven hundred and four |

■ **82 is a two-digit number because it has two digits**
**704 is a three-digit number because it has three digits**

704 is also called a three-figure number.

## Exercise 2A

**1** What does the 2 mean in each of these numbers?
   **(a)** 723 **(b)** 462 **(c)** 291 **(d)** 42 **(e)** 29 **(f)** 206

**2** What does the 7 mean in each of these numbers?
   **(a)** 47 **(b)** 807 **(c)** 79 **(d)** 751 **(e)** 71 **(f)** 597

**3** What does the 0 mean in each of these numbers?
   **(a)** 503 **(b)** 280 **(c)** 204 **(d)** 90 **(e)** 0 **(f)** 601

**4** **(a)** These students have each chosen a number from the
      blackboard. Which number has each student chosen?

My number has 6 tens

My number has 2 hundreds and 5 units

Lauren

Nadia

My number has 8 units

My number has no hundreds and no tens

Ahmed

Wayne

**WHAT'S MY NUMBER?**

251    564
   285
4        382
     58
   46
        406

   **(b)** Choose a number from the blackboard and
      describe it.

**5** This is a machine for sorting numbers:

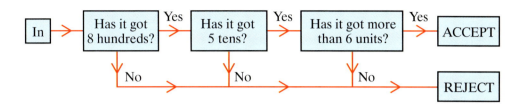

Which of these numbers are accepted and which are rejected?

**(a)** Eight hundred and fifty nine

**(b)** Five hundred and eighty nine

**(c)** Eight hundred and fifty seven

**(d)** Eight hundred and fifty five

**(e)** Eight hundred and fifty six

**(f)** Seven hundred and fifty eight

**6** This is another machine for sorting numbers:

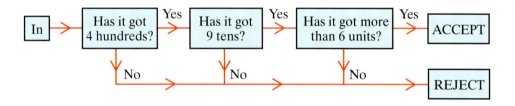

Which numbers will it accept?

**7** Design a number machine to accept only these three-digit numbers

**(a)** 648, 649  **(b)** 390, 391, 392  **(c)** 867, 877, 887, 897

**(d)** 873, 973  **(e)** 721, 821, 921  **(f)** 302, 312, 322, 332

**8** Design a number machine to accept these three-digit numbers only: 253, 254, 255.

Hint: you will need to ask two questions about the units.

## 2.2 Reading large numbers

Did you know...

You'll spend over 14 000 hours in school before you leave ...

There are about 690 000 students the same age as you in the UK ...

You'll eat over 10 000 tonnes of food in your lifetime ...

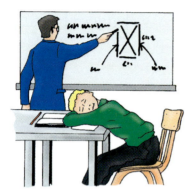

A place value diagram can help you read large numbers:

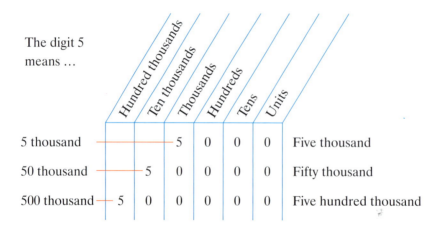

| The digit 5 means ... | Hundred thousands | Ten thousands | Thousands | Hundreds | Tens | Units | |
|---|---|---|---|---|---|---|---|
| 5 thousand | | | 5 | 0 | 0 | 0 | Five thousand |
| 50 thousand | | 5 | 0 | 0 | 0 | 0 | Fifty thousand |
| 500 thousand | 5 | 0 | 0 | 0 | 0 | 0 | Five hundred thousand |

You read and write large numbers like this:

67 382  Sixty seven thousand, three hundred and eighty two
324 167  Three hundred and twenty four thousand, one hundred and sixty seven

A space like this shows you where the thousands end.

### Example 1

How many thousands are there in each of these numbers?

(a) 28 394        (b) 407 302        (c) 5 293

(a) 28 thousands    (b) 407 thousands  (c) 5 thousands

## Exercise 2B

**1** How many thousands are there in each of these numbers?
  **(a)** 7 483    **(b)** 73 803    **(c)** 39 870    **(d)** 836 339
  **(e)** 8 401    **(f)** 923 458    **(g)** 873 994    **(h)** 47 824

**2** How many thousands are there in each of these numbers?
  **(a)** 5 089    **(b)** 50 398    **(c)** 407 338    **(d)** 490 704
  **(e)** 120 067    **(f)** 196 383    **(g)** 587 934    **(h)** 196 038

**3** What does the 6 mean in each of these numbers?
  **(a)** 26 277    **(b)** 365 789    **(c)** 648 925    **(d)** 960 382
  **(e)** 629 487    **(f)** 196 383    **(g)** 69 421    **(h)** 196 038

**4** Write these numbers using digits.
  **(a)** Five thousand two hundred and forty six.
  **(b)** Forty seven thousand three hundred and ninety six.
  **(c)** Three hundred and sixty four thousand nine hundred and fifty six.
  **(d)** Two hundred and five thousand nine hundred and eighty one.
  **(e)** Nine hundred thousand two hundred and fifteen.
  **(f)** Twenty six thousand and thirty eight.

**5** This is a number machine for sorting numbers with thousands:

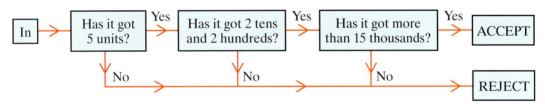

Which of these numbers are accepted and which are rejected by the machine?
  **(a)** 14 225    **(b)** 31 225    **(c)** 140 225    **(d)** 25 252
  **(e)** 280 255    **(f)** 225 525    **(g)** 789 225    **(h)** 15 225

**6** Design a number machine to accept these numbers only:
  **(a)** 21 507, 21 508, 21 509
  **(b)** 47 395, 48 395, 49 395
  **(c)** 899 423, 898 423, 897 423

Hint: you will need to ask two questions about the thousands.

## 2.3 Order, order!

In a lottery six balls are picked.

Then they are sorted in order of size, smallest first.

You can use a number line to help sort numbers into size order.

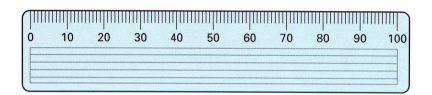

A millimetre ruler makes a good number line.

### Example 2

Put the numbers 24, 97, 47, 8, 66 in order of size.
Start with the smallest number.

Find the position of each number on a number line.

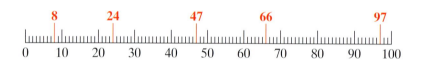

So the order is: 8, 24, 47, 66, 97.

### Exercise 2C

Put these numbers in size order. Start with the smallest.

**1** 81, 25, 4, 43     **2** 48, 96, 17, 33     **3** 94, 93, 36, 54

**4** 24, 38, 56, 15     **5** 50, 0, 49, 100     **6** 26, 14, 11, 84

**7** 98, 51, 69, 42     **8** 41, 83, 60, 7     **9** 18, 26, 54, 76

**10** 87, 54, 38, 11     **11** 79, 3, 99, 7     **12** 46, 20, 63, 77

**13** **Activity**   You need ten cards numbered:
0, 1, 2, 3, 4, 5, 6, 7, 8, 9.

Put them in a bag or a box and pick out two cards.

Can you make a number less than 50 with your two cards?

Can you make a number greater than fifty with your two cards?

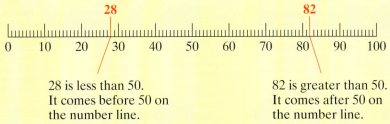

28 is less than 50.
It comes before 50 on the number line.

82 is greater than 50.
It comes after 50 on the number line.

Write down your results then put the two cards back in the bag.

Repeat the experiment until you have done it ten times.

(a)  Which pairs of cards can only be used to make numbers less than 50?

(b)  Which pairs of cards can only be used to make numbers greater than 50?

(c)  Which pairs of cards can be used to make one number less than 50 and one number greater than 50?

(d)  Are there any other possibilities?

**14** **Activity**   You need ten cards numbered:
0, 1, 2, 3, 4, 5, 6, 7, 8, 9.

Pick out three cards from the bag.

Make as many different two-digit numbers as you can with the three cards.

Write them down in order of size, smallest first.

Put the three cards back in the bag.

Repeat the experiment until you have done it five times.

**(a)** Name three cards that will only make numbers bigger than 50.

**(b)** Name three cards that will only make numbers smaller than 50.

**(c)** Name three cards that will only make numbers between 40 and 90.

## 2.4  Ordering large numbers

To sort large numbers you'd need a huge number line...

Here is another way to put large numbers in order.

**Example 3**

Put these numbers in order of size, starting with the smallest:

   392   365   589   121   633   583

First sort them using the **hundreds** digits:

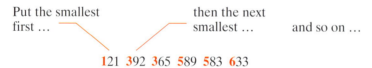

Put the smallest first ...          then the next smallest ...          and so on ...

121 392 365 589 583 633

392 and 365 both have 3 hundreds.
Sort them using the **tens** digits.

121 392 365 589 583 633

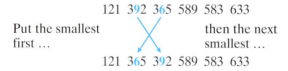

Put the smallest first ...          then the next smallest ...

121 365 392 589 583 633

589 and 583 both have 5 hundreds and 8 tens.
Sort them using the **units** digits.

121 392 365 589 583 633

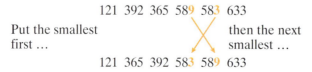

Put the smallest first ...          then the next smallest ...

121 365 392 583 589 633

Now the numbers are in size order: 121  365  392  583  589  633.

## Exercise 2D

Put each set of numbers in order of size, starting with the smallest.

**1** 533, 278, 514, 288, 233

**2** 876, 428, 407, 858, 849

> 65 has 0 hundreds

**3** 183, 938, 147, 958, 941

**4** 94, 438, 263, 488, 65

**5** 91, 684, 629, 392, 381

**6** 547, 36, 295, 216, 18

**7** 257, 838, 469, 472, 829, 437, 238

**8** 548, 485, 763, 492, 576, 559, 782

**9** **Activity** You need ten cards numbered: 0, 1, 2, 3, 4, 5, 6, 7, 8, 9.

Put them in a bag or box and pick out three cards.
Arrange the cards to make the largest three-digit number possible.
Arrange the three cards to make the smallest three-digit number possible.

Write down your results then put the three cards back into the bag.
Repeat the experiment until you have done it ten times.

(a) Write a rule to explain how to find the largest three-digit number.

(b) Write a rule to explain how to find the smallest three-digit number.

**10** Write down the smallest three-digit number and the largest 3-digit number that can be made from each set of cards.

(a) 5 2 9

(b) 7 8 3

(c) 2 1 7

(d) 4 9 7

(e) 4 2 9

(f) 1 9 3

(g) 8 4 1

(h) 6 7 4

(i) 2 4 3

(j) 5 8 7

(k) 7 3 7

(l) 4 8 0

> Remember: you don't write 0 at the front of a number.

**11** Write down the second largest three-digit number that can be made with each set of cards.

(a) [4][3][9]   (b) [2][9][6]   (c) [3][4][0]

(d) [3][1][6]   (e) [9][8][7]   (f) [3][4][5]

(g) [7][3][4]   (h) [0][8][1]   (i) [4][2][7]

**12** Write down the second smallest three-digit number that can be made with each set of cards.

(a) [5][2][9]   (b) [4][8][3]   (c) [2][5][1]

(d) [4][1][8]   (e) [6][7][8]   (f) [3][7][6]

(g) [8][7][6]   (h) [0][9][2]   (i) [3][5][7]

## 2.5 Mental maths

The next exercise will help you practise adding and subtracting small numbers in your head.

If you can do these you will be able to add and subtract larger numbers more easily.

 This sign next to an exercise means don't use your calculator!

### Exercise 2E

You can use this number line to help you answer the questions:

| 0 | 1 | 2 | 3 | 4 | 5 | 6 | 7 | 8 | 9 | 10 | 11 | 12 | 13 | 14 | 15 | 16 | 17 | 18 | 19 | 20 |

**1** Find two numbers next to each other which:

(a) add up to 7   (b) add up to 5   (c) add up to 11

(d) total 9   (e) total 15   (f) add up to 19

**2** Find three numbers next to each other which:

(a) add up to 12   (b) total 6   (c) add up to 3

(d) total 15   (e) add up to 9   (f) total 18

**3** Find as many pairs of numbers as you can which have a sum of:

(a) 9   (b) 12   (c) 10   (d) 15   (e) 18   (f) 20

**4** Find as many pairs as you can which have a difference of:

(a) 5   (b) 8   (c) 16   (d) 20   (e) 1   (f) 10

Remember: sum is another word for the total.

The numbers do not have to be next to each other. For example 19 and 1 make 20.

**5** Find as many different ways as you can to fill the square and triangular boxes.

(a) $\square + \triangle = 11$      (b) $2 + \square = \triangle$

(c) $\square - \triangle = 4$      (d) $12 - \square = \triangle$

(e) $\square - 5 = \triangle$      (f) $\square + 7 = \triangle$

(g) $\square + 2 = \triangle + 3$      (h) $20 - \square = 10 + \triangle$

For example:

$\square + \triangle = 11$

$\boxed{4} + \triangle_{7} = 11$

$\boxed{9} + \triangle_{2} = 11$

**6** Can you make each number from 8 to 20 by adding only threes and fives?

For example:

$11 = 3 + 3 + 5$

**7** What numbers can you make by adding twos and threes?

**8** Copy or trace this diagram into your book:

Write the numbers

1, 2, 3, 4, 5, 6, 7, 8, 9

in the circles so that each line of numbers adds up to 15.

Make up your own puzzle like this.

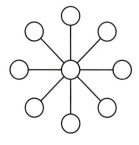

**9** This is called an arithmogon.
On each side of the triangle the total of the numbers in the circles is shown in the square.

Copy and complete these arithmogons.

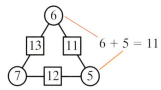

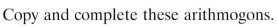

(a) 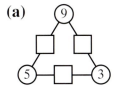      (b) 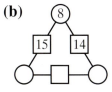      (c)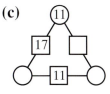

(d) 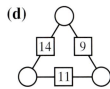      (e) 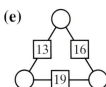      (f)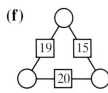

## 2.6 Mental maths with tens

Mental maths is easier if you can add and subtract 10 quickly.

■ **When you add 10 the units digit stays the same:**

$$8 + 10 = 18 \qquad \text{or} \qquad \begin{array}{r} 10 \\ 8 + \\ \hline 18 \end{array}$$

■ **When you subtract 10 from a larger number the units digit stays the same:**

$$37 - 10 = 27 \qquad \text{or} \qquad \begin{array}{r} 37 \\ 10 - \\ \hline 27 \end{array}$$

### Exercise 2F

1   **Activity**   You need a calculator to do this question.

Enter 9 on your calculator.
Add 10 and keep on adding 10.

**(a)** What do you notice about the way the answers change?

**(b)** Does it make any difference if you start by entering 19?

Enter 9 on your calculator.
Add 20 and keep adding 20.

**(c)** What do you notice about the way the answers change?

**(d)** Does it make any difference if you start by entering 19?

Enter 9 on your calculator.
Add 30 and keep on adding 30.

**(e)** What do you notice about the way the answers change?

**(f)** Does it make any difference if you start by entering 19?

Do the rest of this exercise mentally.
Do not use a calculator.

**2**  **(a)** $26 + 10$      **(b)** $45 + 10$      **(c)** $32 - 10$
    **(d)** $54 - 10$      **(e)** $87 + 10$      **(f)** $94 - 10$
    **(g)** $24 + 20$      **(h)** $47 + 20$      **(i)** $54 + 20$
    **(j)** $35 - 20$      **(k)** $82 - 20$      **(l)** $77 - 20$
    **(m)** $16 + 30$      **(n)** $32 + 30$      **(o)** $74 - 30$
    **(p)** $46 - 30$      **(q)** $54 + 30$      **(r)** $94 - 30$

**3**  **(a)** $22 + 40$      **(b)** $34 + 50$      **(c)** $29 + 70$
    **(d)** $74 - 40$      **(e)** $86 - 50$      **(f)** $98 - 70$
    **(g)** $15 + 80$      **(h)** $68 - 50$      **(i)** $23 + 60$
    **(j)** $51 + 40$      **(k)** $79 - 50$      **(l)** $88 - 60$

**4**  **(a)** $14 + 10 + 20$   **(b)** $47 + 10 + 20$   **(c)** $33 + 30 + 20$
    **(d)** $42 + 30 + 10$   **(e)** $15 + 30 + 40$   **(f)** $27 + 40 + 20$
    **(g)** $18 + 40 + 30$   **(h)** $39 + 30 + 30$

**5**  **(a)** $95 - 10 - 20$        **(b)** $89 - 10 - 20$
    **(c)** $67 - 30 - 20$        **(d)** $76 - 30 - 10$
    **(e)** $56 - 20 - 30$        **(f)** $87 - 40 - 30$
    **(g)** $99 - 40 - 40$        **(h)** $91 - 50 - 40$

**6**  **(a)** $23 + 40 - 10$        **(b)** $35 + 60 - 20$
    **(c)** $64 - 30 + 20$        **(d)** $48 + 50 - 30$
    **(e)** $62 - 20 + 30$        **(f)** $41 + 40 - 60$
    **(g)** $64 - 40 + 10$        **(h)** $67 - 50 + 80$

**7**  Pick a number from each cloud and add
them together.

How many different answers can you
make by doing this?

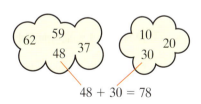

**8**  Pick a number from each cloud.

Add the first two numbers then
subtract the third number.

How many different numbers can
you make by doing this?

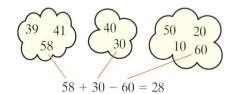

## 2.7 Mental maths methods

Here are some easy ways to do mental calculations by adding or subtracting 10:

### Two ways to add 9 and 12

$9 + 12 =$

12 is 10 + 2

$9 + 10 + 2$

$19 \quad + 2 = 21$

So $9 + 12 = 21$

$12 + 9 =$

9 is 10 − 1

$12 + 10 - 1$

$22 \quad - 1 = 21$

So $9 + 12 = 21$

### Two ways to subtract 11 from 19

$19 - 11$

11 is 10 + 1

To subtract 11, first subtract 10, then subtract 1.

$19 - 10 - 1 = 8$

So $19 - 11 = 8$

$19 - 11$

11 is 10 + 1

To subtract 11, first subtract 1, then subtract 10.

$19 - 1 - 10 = 8$

So $19 - 11 = 8$

To remember these methods just remember two examples:

■  **To add 9, first add 10, then subtract 1**

■  **To subtract 11, first subtract 10, then subtract 1**

### Exercise 2G

Work these out mentally:

| | | | |
|---|---|---|---|
| **1** $17 + 9$ | **2** $25 - 11$ | **3** $16 + 8$ | **4** $19 - 9$ |
| **5** $22 + 9$ | **6** $32 - 11$ | **7** $29 - 12$ | **8** $43 + 8$ |

**9** $51 - 9$     **10** $49 + 8$     **11** $27 + 9$     **12** $40 - 11$

**13** $73 - 9$     **14** $26 + 8$     **15** $43 - 8$     **16** $17 - 8$

Copy and complete these sentences:

**17** To add 8 you add 10 then take away ___ .

**18** To take away 8 you take away ___ then add ___ .

**19** To subtract 9 you subtract ___ then add ___ .

**20** To subtract 12 you subtract ___ then subtract ___ .

## 2.8 Mental maths: adding two-digit numbers

■ **You can make adding easier by breaking up numbers.**

Here are two ways to add 31 and 27:

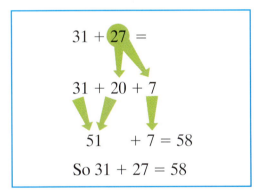
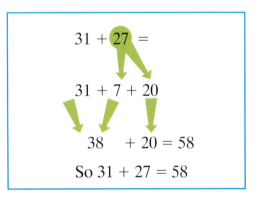

**Exercise 2H**

You should do this exercise mentally.
Do not use a calculator.

**1**   **(a)** $34 + 23$   **(b)** $25 + 23$   **(c)** $37 + 21$   **(d)** $31 + 25$
    **(e)** $46 + 33$   **(f)** $25 + 72$   **(g)** $32 + 55$   **(h)** $76 + 21$
    **(i)** $37 + 12$   **(j)** $24 + 73$   **(k)** $67 + 22$   **(l)** $26 + 51$

> Hint: it might be easier to think of this as $72 + 25$.

**2**   **(a)** $38 + 24$   **(b)** $49 + 25$   **(c)** $48 + 36$   **(d)** $68 + 23$
    **(e)** $37 + 55$   **(f)** $28 + 43$   **(g)** $42 + 29$   **(h)** $37 + 23$
    **(i)** $54 + 36$   **(j)** $29 + 53$   **(k)** $44 + 28$   **(l)** $36 + 36$

**3   Activity**   You need ten cards numbered:
0, 1, 2, 3, 4, 5, 6, 7, 8, 9.
Put them in a bag or box and pick out four cards.
Arrange the four cards to make two two-digit numbers.

Add them together.

$\boxed{5}\,\boxed{7}\;+\;\boxed{3}\,\boxed{2}\;=\;89$

Rearrange the cards to make two more
two-digit numbers and add them together.

$\boxed{3}\,\boxed{7}\;+\;\boxed{2}\,\boxed{5}\;=\;62$

(a)   How many different pairs of two-digit
numbers can you make?

(b)   How many different totals do you get?

(c)   Which arrangement gives the biggest total?

(d)   Which arrangement gives the smallest total?

> Hint: try to find a
> system for writing
> down all the pairs of
> 2-digit numbers

**4**   Put the cards back in the bag and repeat question **3**.

**5   Activity**   You need a 100 square.
Draw a rectangle on a 100 number square.
Add the numbers in opposite corners of the
rectangle like this:
Do this for other rectangles.
What do you notice?
Explain any pattern you notice.

$12 + 35$

| 1 | 2 | 3 | 4 | 5 | 6 | 7 | 8 | 9 | 10 |
|---|---|---|---|---|---|---|---|---|----|
| 11 | 12 | 13 | 14 | 15 | 16 | 17 | 18 | 19 | 20 |
| 21 | 22 | 23 | 24 | 25 | 26 | 27 | 28 | 29 | 30 |
| 31 | 32 | 33 | 34 | 35 | 36 | 37 | 38 | 39 | 40 |
| 41 | 42 | 43 | 44 | 45 | 46 | 47 | 48 | 49 | 50 |

$32 + 15$

## 2.9 Mental maths: subtracting two-digit numbers

■   **You can make subtracting easier by breaking up
numbers.**

Here are two ways to subtract 28 from 65:

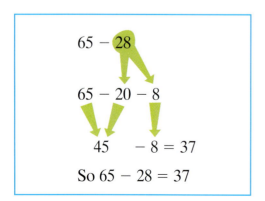

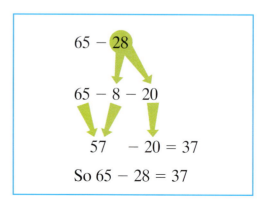

## Exercise 2I

Do this exercise mentally. Do not use a calculator.

**1**  **(a)** 34 – 13  **(b)** 45 – 12  **(c)** 37 – 14  **(d)** 68 – 24
    **(e)** 53 – 21  **(f)** 78 – 25  **(g)** 64 – 31  **(h)** 86 – 42
    **(i)** 96 – 52  **(j)** 89 – 63  **(k)** 48 – 31  **(l)** 93 – 71

**2**  **(a)** 34 – 15  **(b)** 43 – 24  **(c)** 36 – 17  **(d)** 54 – 26
    **(e)** 44 – 18  **(f)** 67 – 39  **(g)** 56 – 28  **(h)** 63 – 35
    **(i)** 84 – 57  **(j)** 93 – 47  **(k)** 75 – 27  **(l)** 88 – 59

**3**  These pupils have each chosen a pair of two-digit numbers from the whiteboard.

Lauren: The difference between my pair is 9

Nadia: The difference for my pair is 36

Ahmed: The difference for my pair is 25

Wayne: The difference for my pair is 38

> Remember: the difference means the largest number take away the smallest number. The difference between 28 and 53 is 53 – 28 = 25

**WHAT'S MY PAIR OF NUMBERS?**

34          46
     74     38
25     56     63

Which pair of numbers has each pupil chosen?

**4**  **Activity**

Choose any four two-digit numbers and write them at the four corners of a square.

43 ———— 27

16 ———— 83

Work out the difference between the numbers on each edge of the square and write the difference at the middle of that edge.

43 — **16** — 27
**27**          **57**
16 — **68** — 84

Join the four new numbers to make a square.

Work out the difference between the numbers at the ends of each edge of the new square and write the difference at the middle of that edge

43 — 16 — 27
 **11** — **41**
27          57
 **41** — **11**
16 — 68 — 84

Join the four new numbers to make a square.

**(a)** Continue this process until it is obvious you should stop.

**(b)** Repeat **(a)** using another four two-digit numbers.

**(c)** Explain what is happening.

**(d)** Try choosing three two-digit numbers and writing them at the corners of a triangle.

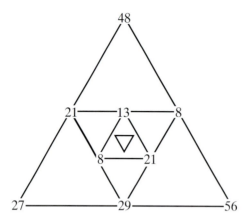

**5** Start with 100.

Move along the arrows from start to finish, subtracting the numbers shown on the arrows as you go.

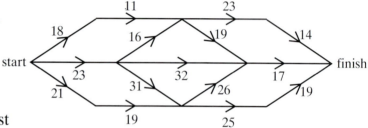

**(a)** What is the smallest number you can finish with?

**(b)** What is the largest number you can finish with?

## 2.10 Using mental maths to solve problems

You can use mental maths to solve everyday problems.

First decide whether to add or subtract to solve the problem.

These words usually mean you **add**:

> **total, sum, altogether, plus**

These words and phrases usually mean you **subtract**:

> **minus, take away, less**
> **How many more?**
> **How much change?**
> **What is the difference between . . . ?**

**Example 4**

Paul bought a bar of chocolate for 38p and a packet of
chewing gum for 45p.

How much change did he get from a £1 coin?

The total cost was $38 + 45 = 83p$

The change was    $£1 - 83p = 100p - 83p = 17p.$

## Exercise 2J

**1**   In a class of children there are
17 girls and 15 boys.

What is the total number of children
in the class?

> **Class 7B**
> Girls 17
> Boys 15
> Total . . .

**2**   Two classes of children went on a trip together.
There were 34 children from one class and 29 children
from the other class.
How many children went on the trip?

**3**   98 children from a school went on a half day visit.
47 children went in the morning.
How many went in the afternoon?

**4**   A water tank holds 72 litres when full.
There are 44 litres of water in the tank.
How many more litres of water can be
put into the tank?

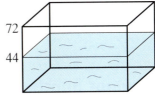

**5**   Zoe buys a drink for 48p and a bar of chocolate
for 36p.

(a)  What is the total cost?

(b)  What change should she get if she pays with a £1
coin?

**6**   An electricity pylon is 33 metres tall.
A church tower is 25 metres tall.
How much taller is the pylon
than the tower?

**7**   In a pond there are 28 mirror carp and 65 koi carp.

(a)   What is the total number of carp in the pond?

(b)   How many more koi carp than mirror carp are there?

**8**   In a class of 32 children, 18 have school dinner and the rest bring packed lunches.
How many children bring packed lunches?

> **Class 8C**
> School dinner    18
> Packed lunches ...
> Total                32

**9**   In a darts match Morag scored 54 and 18 with her first two darts. After her third dart she had scored a total of 96.
What did she score with her third dart?

**10**   A computer shop had software for sale at these prices.
Marco bought three items of software for a total cost of £90.
Find all the possible costs of the three items Marco bought.

£18   £40   £44

£28   £32   £6   £52

£20   £30

## 2.11  Adding numbers on paper

You can add large numbers together on paper.
Sometimes it's easier than adding them in your head.

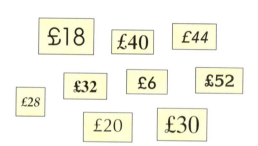

| Line up the units. Use headings to help you. | Add the units together. 4 + 5 = 9 | Now add the tens. 2 + 6 = 8 | Add the hundreds. 1 + 3 = 4 |
|---|---|---|---|
| H T U<br>  1 2 4<br>+3 6 5<br>——— | H T U<br>  1 2 4<br>+3 6 5<br>———<br>      9 | H T U<br>  1 2 4<br>+3 6 5<br>———<br>    8 9 | H T U<br>  1 2 4<br>+3 6 5<br>———<br>  4 8 9 |

## Example 5

Add 35 and 48.

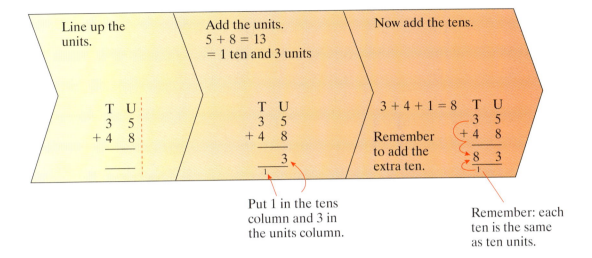

So 35 + 48 = 83

You can check your answer on a number line.

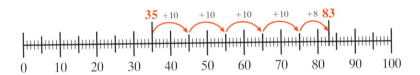

## Example 6

Add 28, 17 and 36.

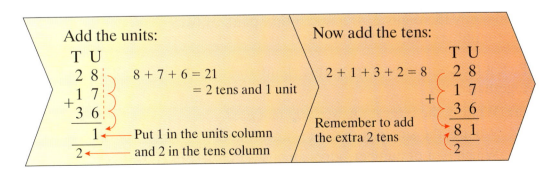

## Exercise 2K

**1**  (a) $38 + 25$   (b) $46 + 18$   (c) $52 + 36$   (d) $35 + 23$
      (e) $49 + 28$   (f) $33 + 28$   (g) $73 + 24$   (h) $64 + 29$
      (i) $43 + 27$   (j) $62 + 28$   (k) $46 + 46$   (l) $69 + 29$

**2**  (a) $54 + 23$   (b) $45 + 38$   (c) $56 + 39$   (d) $27 + 54$
      (e) $32 + 49$   (f) $43 + 27$   (g) $26 + 67$   (h) $38 + 48$
      (i) $38 + 38$   (j) $22 + 47$   (k) $37 + 27$   (l) $59 + 24$

**3**  (a) $35 + 26 + 23$   (b) $34 + 37 + 25$   (c) $27 + 34 + 28$
      (d) $37 + 29 + 28$   (e) $29 + 28 + 36$   (f) $46 + 28 + 16$
      (g) $39 + 25 + 28$   (h) $17 + 28 + 37$

**4**  (a) $85 + 54$   (b) $76 + 49$   (c) $64 + 83$   (d) $91 + 38$
      (e) $87 + 68$   (f) $55 + 79$   (g) $89 + 89$   (h) $67 + 75$
      (i) $73 + 67$   (j) $48 + 52$   (k) $86 + 95$   (l) $56 + 49$

**5**  (a) $46 + 43 + 34$   (b) $53 + 65 + 34$   (c) $36 + 81 + 57$
      (d) $48 + 37 + 39$   (e) $28 + 69 + 36$   (f) $73 + 80 + 84$
      (g) $89 + 86 + 78$   (h) $88 + 94 + 79$

**6**  (a) $259 + 134$   (b) $407 + 285$   (c) $658 + 183$
      (d) $758 + 681$   (e) $679 + 583$   (f) $398 + 843$
      (g) $564 + 487$   (h) $672 + 428$   (i) $837 + 163$
      (j) $987 + 689$

**7**  (a) $642 + 25$   (b) $368 + 24$   (c) $49 + 374$
      (d) $465 + 78$   (e) $67 + 206$   (f) $535 + 85$
      (g) $724 + 79$   (h) $563 + 37$   (i) $59 + 684$
      (j) $96 + 748$

> Remember to line up the units first.

**8**  You can use the digits 2, 3, 4 and 5 to make a pair of
      two-digit numbers that add up to 77.
      Using the same digits find other pairs of two-digit
      numbers that add up to 77.

$$\begin{array}{r} 45 \\ +32 \\ \hline 77 \end{array}$$

**9**  Using only the digits 3, 4, 5 and 6 find pairs of two-
      digit numbers that add up to 99.

**10**  Pick a pair of numbers from this cloud and add them
      together.

      (a) What is the largest answer you can get?
      (b) What is the smallest answer you can get?
      (c) Which pair of numbers gives an answer closest to 100?

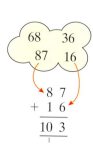

**11** Repeat question **10** for each of these clouds.

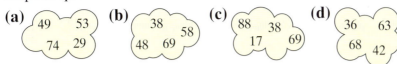

(a) 49 53 74 29  (b) 38 48 69 58  (c) 88 38 17 69  (d) 36 63 68 42

**12** Find the digits to fill each box, ☐, in these addition sums.

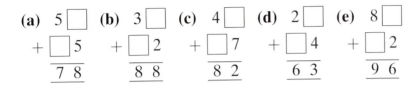

(a)
```
  5 ☐
+ ☐ 5
─────
  7 8
```
(b)
```
  3 ☐
+ ☐ 2
─────
  8 8
```
(c)
```
  4 ☐
+ ☐ 7
─────
  8 2
```
(d)
```
  2 ☐
+ ☐ 4
─────
  6 3
```
(e)
```
  8 ☐
+ ☐ 2
─────
  9 6
```

(f)
```
  2 1
  4 ☐
+ ☐ 7
─────
  9 6
```
(g)
```
  ☐ 7
  3 ☐
+ 1 8
─────
  8 1
```
(h)
```
  2 6
  1 ☐
+ ☐ 8
─────
  9 3
```
(i)
```
  3 ☐
  ☐ 7
+ 1 9
─────
  8 4
```
(j)
```
  1 ☐
  3 5
+ ☐ 4
─────
  9 5
```

(k)
```
  3 ☐
  ☐ 2
+ 6 3
─────
1 7 9
```
(l)
```
  ☐ 8
  6 3
+ 2 ☐
─────
1 3 7
```
(m)
```
  9 ☐
  7 2
+ ☐ 5
─────
2 5 3
```
(n)
```
  ☐ 9
  8 ☐
+ 3 5
─────
☐ 7 1
```
(o)
```
  8 6
  4 ☐
+ ☐ 8
─────
☐ 1 3
```

**13** Choose any three-digit number.
Reverse the digits.
Add the two numbers together.

```
  528
+ 825
─────
 1353
 1 1
```

Reverse the digits of the answer.
Add the two numbers.

```
  1353
+ 3531
─────
  4884
```

4884 is called a palindromic number.
A palindromic number stays the same when you reverse its digits.

Try this for each of these three-digit numbers.

(a) 427    (b) 635    (c) 834    (d) 264

(e) Try other three-digit numbers.

Do you always get a palindromic number eventually?

Keep reversing the digits and adding until you get a palindromic number.

## 2.12 Subtracting numbers on paper

You can subtract two numbers on paper like this:

| To find 289 − 153 first line up the units: | Subtract the units: 9 − 3 = 6 | Subtract the tens: 8 − 5 = 3 | Subtract the hundreds: 2 − 1 = 1 |
|---|---|---|---|
| H T U<br>2 8 9<br>− 1 5 3 | H T U<br>2 8 9<br>− 1 5 3<br>      6 | H T U<br>2 8 9<br>− 1 5 3<br>   3 6 | H T U<br>2 8 9<br>− 1 5 3<br>1 3 6 |

### Example 7

Find 172 − 58

| Line up the units. Be careful! Notice 2 is smaller than 8 | Change 70 into 6 tens and 10 units. | Now take away the tens: 6 − 5 = 1 | Finally take away the hundreds. Here there is nothing to take away 1 − 0 = 1 |
|---|---|---|---|
| H T U<br>1 7 2<br>−   5 8 | H T U   10 + 2 =<br>1 ⁶7̸ ¹2   12 units<br>−    5 8<br>     4<br><br>Take away the units: 12 − 8 = 4 | H T U<br>1 ⁶7̸ ¹2<br>−   5 8<br>   1 4 | H T U<br>1 ⁶7̸ ¹2<br>−   5 8<br>1 1 4 |

## Exercise 2L

**1**
(a) 85 − 23   (b) 54 − 31   (c) 67 − 46   (d) 38 − 23
(e) 96 − 21   (f) 47 − 37   (g) 59 − 54   (h) 78 − 48
(i) 96 − 14   (j) 77 − 25   (k) 48 − 36   (l) 59 − 23

**2**
(a) 64 − 27   (b) 43 − 29   (c) 56 − 27   (d) 36 − 19
(e) 80 − 47   (f) 61 − 28   (g) 53 − 45   (h) 90 − 38
(i) 57 − 38   (j) 70 − 28   (k) 48 − 19   (l) 91 − 25

**3**
(a) 687 − 543   (b) 496 − 132   (c) 584 − 230
(d) 769 − 345   (e) 947 − 207   (f) 856 − 653
(g) 478 − 278   (h) 574 − 532   (i) 769 − 719
(j) 685 − 681   (k) 357 − 351   (l) 113 − 101

**4** **(a)** 546 − 127  **(b)** 864 − 328  **(c)** 750 − 416

 **(d)** 457 − 208  **(e)** 675 − 467  **(f)** 947 − 362

 **(g)** 854 − 671  **(h)** 605 − 294  **(i)** 748 − 656

 **(j)** 537 − 492  **(k)** 537 − 238  **(l)** 852 − 357

 **(m)** 645 − 269  **(n)** 543 − 465  **(o)** 767 − 689

**5** **(a)** 684 − 23  **(b)** 567 − 32  **(c)** 483 − 53

 **(d)** 494 − 60  **(e)** 539 − 31  **(f)** 486 − 28

 **(g)** 563 − 37  **(h)** 743 − 38  **(i)** 646 − 62

 **(j)** 534 − 71  **(k)** 845 − 75  **(l)** 736 − 62

 **(m)** 428 − 59  **(n)** 942 − 78  **(o)** 356 − 89

**6** Pick a pair of numbers, one from each cloud, and find the difference.

 **(a)** Which pair gives the largest answer?

 **(b)** Which pair gives the smallest answer?

 **(c)** Which pair gives the answer closest to 400?

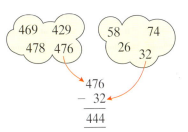

**7** Repeat question **6** for this pair of clouds.

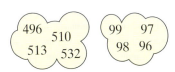

**8** Put the digits 4, 5, 6, 7 and 8 in the boxes of this take-away sum and work out the answer.

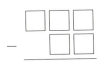

 **(a)** Which arrangement gives the biggest answer?

 **(b)** Which arrangement gives the smallest answer?

 **(c)** Which arrangement gives the answer closest to 500?

**9**   Take any two-digit number                                                  36
Reverse the digits to make another two-digit number.              63

Find the difference between the two numbers.

$$\begin{array}{r} 63 \\ -36 \\ \hline 27 \end{array}$$

Do the same for the answer,

$$\begin{array}{r} {}^{6}\!\!\not{7}{}^{1}2 \\ -27 \\ \hline 45 \end{array}$$

and again.

$$\begin{array}{r} {}^{4}\!\!\not{5}{}^{1}4 \\ -45 \\ \hline 9 \end{array}$$

Try this for other two-digit numbers.
Do you always get the answer 9 eventually?
Does the same happen for three-digit numbers?

## Summary of key points

**1**   The value of a digit depends on its place in a
number.
You can see this in a place value diagram:

The digit 4
means …

| | Hundreds | Tens | Units | |
|---|---|---|---|---|
| 4 hundreds | 4 | 7 | 9 | Four hundred and seventy nine |
| 4 tens | 2 | 4 | 3 | Two hundred and forty three |
| 4 units | 7 | 0 | 4 | Seven hundred and four |

**2**   82 is a two-digit number because it has two digits
704 is a three-digit number because it has three
digits

704 is also called a three-figure number.

**3**   When you add 10 the units digit stays the same:

$$8 + 10 = 18 \qquad \text{or} \qquad \begin{array}{r} 10 \\ 8 + \\ \hline 18 \end{array}$$

When you subtract 10 from a larger number the units digit stays the same:

$$37 - 10 = 27 \qquad \text{or} \qquad \begin{array}{r} 37 \\ 10 - \\ \hline 27 \end{array}$$

**4**   To add 9, first add 10, then subtract 1

   To subtract 11, first subtract 10, then subtract 1

**5**   You can make adding easier by breaking up numbers.

**6**   You can make subtracting easier by breaking up numbers.

# 3 Number patterns

People have been fascinated by number patterns for centuries.

You will explore some number patterns in this unit.

This altar in China has nine circles, each with a multiple of nine stones.
The ancient Chinese believed that using nine's brought them closer to Heaven.

## 3.1 Patterns from matchsticks

Here are the first four shapes in a matchstick pattern:

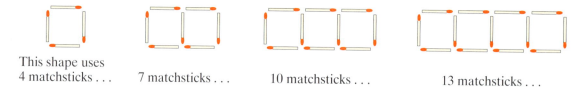

This shape uses 4 matchsticks . . .    7 matchsticks . . .    10 matchsticks . . .    13 matchsticks . . .

Using numbers the pattern is:

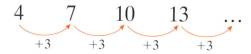

The rule to go from one shape to the next is 'add 3'.

---

**Exercise 3A**

---

Copy these matchstick patterns.
For each pattern:

- draw the next two shapes
- write down the pattern using numbers
- write down the rule to go from one shape to the next.

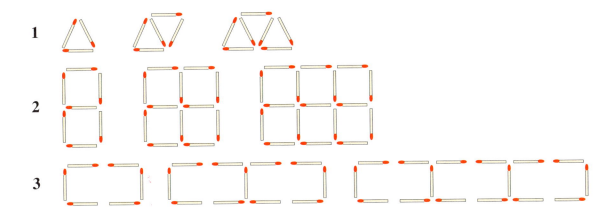

## 3.2 Dot patterns

Here are the first five shapes in a dot pattern:

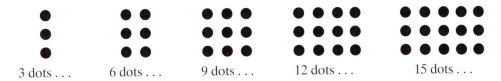

3 dots . . .     6 dots . . .     9 dots . . .     12 dots . . .     15 dots . . .

Using numbers the pattern is:

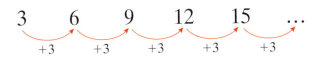

The rule to go from one shape to the next is '**add 3**'.

Exercise 3B

1   Copy the dot patterns below.
    For each pattern:

  • write down the pattern using numbers
  • write down the rule to go from one shape to the next.

**(a)** 
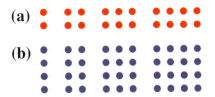

**(b)**

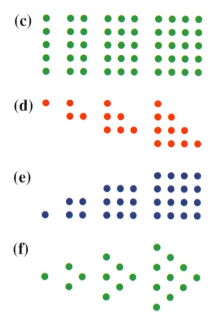

**2**  Draw dots to show these number patterns.
Write down what you notice about them.

(a)  2, 4, 6, 8, 10

(b)  0, 5, 10, 15, 20

(c)  2, 5, 8, 11, 14

(d)  3, 7, 11, 15, 19

(e)  1, 7, 13, 19, 25

## 3.3  Number machines

■  **You can use number machines to make number
patterns.**

Here is a number machine for multiplying by 3:

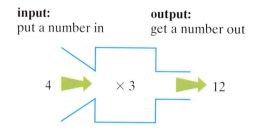

If you put a number pattern into a number machine, the
output numbers will make a pattern too.

## Example 1

**(a)** Input the number pattern 1, 2, 3, 4, 5, and 6 into this machine:

**(b)** List the output numbers.

**(c)** Describe the pattern.

**(a)**

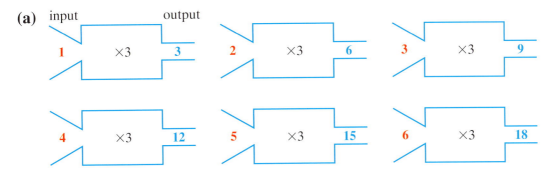

**or:**

Write your results in a table like this:

| ×3 | |
| input | output |
| 1 ×3 | 3 |
| 2 ×3 | 6 |
| 3 ×3 | 9 |
| 4 ×3 | 12 |
| 5 ×3 | 15 |
| 6 ×3 | 18 |

**(b)** The output numbers are 3, 6, 9, 12, 15 and 18.

**(c)** The pattern is: the output numbers go up in 3's.

Notice that you can see the pattern if you shade the output numbers on a 100 square. The pattern continues...

| 1 | 2 | 3 | 4 | 5 | 6 | 7 | 8 | 9 | 10 |
|---|---|---|---|---|---|---|---|---|---|
| 11 | 12 | 13 | 14 | 15 | 16 | 17 | 18 | 19 | 20 |
| 21 | 22 | 23 | 24 | 25 | 26 | 27 | 28 | 29 | 30 |
| 31 | 32 | 33 | 34 | 35 | 36 | 37 | 38 | 39 | 40 |
| 41 | 42 | 43 | 44 | 45 | 46 | 47 | 48 | 49 | 50 |
| 51 | 52 | 53 | 54 | 55 | 56 | 57 | 58 | 59 | 60 |
| 61 | 62 | 63 | 64 | 65 | 66 | 67 | 68 | 69 | 70 |
| 71 | 72 | 73 | 74 | 75 | 76 | 77 | 78 | 79 | 80 |
| 81 | 82 | 83 | 84 | 85 | 86 | 87 | 88 | 89 | 90 |
| 91 | 92 | 93 | 94 | 95 | 96 | 97 | 98 | 99 | 100 |

## Exercise 3C

For each question:

**(a)** Input the number pattern 1, 2, 3, 4, 5, 6.

**(b)** List the output numbers.

**(c)** Describe the pattern.

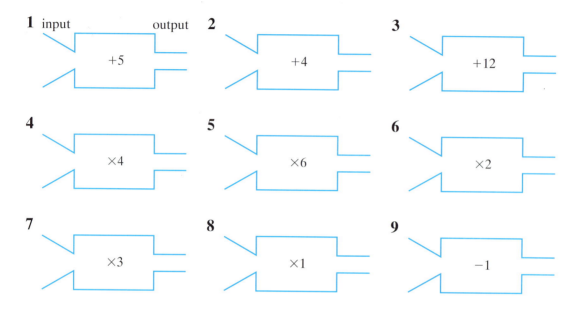

## 3.4 Sequences

Another name for a number pattern is a **sequence**.

■ **A sequence is a number pattern.**
The numbers are usually written in a row like this:

2, 4, 6, 8, 10, ...

The dots show the sequence goes on forever.

### Example 2

**(a)** Describe this sequence of numbers in words.

**(b)** Find the next two numbers in the sequence.

1, 4, 7, 10, 13, 16, ...

**(a)** The numbers go up in threes. So the sequence is:
Start at 1 and keep adding on 3.

**(b)** To find the next two numbers you add on three

$$16 + 3 = 19$$
$$19 + 3 = 22$$

The next two numbers are 19 and 22.

## Example 3

**(a)** Find the next number in the sequence:

12, 10, 8, 6, 4, ...

**(b)** Write down the rule for finding the next number.

**(a)** The numbers go down by 2 each time, so you subtract 2 to find the next number:

$$4 - 2 = 2.$$

The next number is 2.

**(b)** The rule is: subtract 2.

## Exercise 3D

For each sequence:

**(a)** Write down the next two numbers.

**(b)** Write down the rule for finding the next number.

**1**  1, 3, 5, 7, 9, ..., ...

**2**  0, 3, 6, 9, 12, ..., ...

**3**  0, 5, 10, 15, ..., ...

**4**  2, 5, 8, 11, 14, ..., ...

**5**  1, 2, 3, 4, 5, ..., ...

**6**  1, 4, 7, 10, 13, ..., ...

**7**  4, 8, 12, 16, 20, ..., ...

**8**  10, 20, 30, 40, ..., ...

**9**  3, 7, 11, 15, 19, ..., ...

**10**  2, 6, 10, 14, ..., ...

**11**  0, 7, 14, 21, 28, ..., ...

**12**  9, 18, 27, 36, ..., ...

**13**  20, 18, 16, 14, 12, ..., ...

**14**  18, 15, 12, 9, ..., ...

**15**  25, 10, 15, 10, ..., ...

**16**  19, 17, 15, 13, ..., ...

**17**  70, 60, 50, 40, ..., ...

**18**  20, 17, 14, 11, ..., ...

**19**  8, 7, 6, 5, 4, ..., ...

**20**  23, 19, 15, 11, ..., ...

**21**  16, 13, 10, 7, ..., ...

**22**  23, 21, 19, 17, ..., ...

**23**  80, 75, 70, 65, ..., ...

**24**  54, 45, 36, 27, ..., ...

**Example 4**

Find the missing numbers in these sequences:

**(a)** 32, 28, 24, __, __, 12, __
**(b)** 3, 6, 12, __, __, 96

**(a)**
The rule connecting the numbers is **subtract 4**.

**(b)**
The rule connecting the numbers is **multiply by 2**.

### Exercise 3E

Find the missing numbers in these sequences:

**1** 1, 3, 9, __, __, 243, __
**2** 64, 59, 54, __, __, 39, __
**3** 108, 96, 84, __, __, 48, __
**4** 7, 14, 21, __, __, 42, __, 56
**5** 0, 10, 20, __, __, 50, __
**6** 38, 34, 30, __, __, 18, __
**7** 1, 2, 4, __, __, 32
**8** 90, 80, 70, __, __, 40, __
**9** 3, 7, 11, __, __, 23, __, __

## 3.5 Two step number machines

This is a two step number machine.

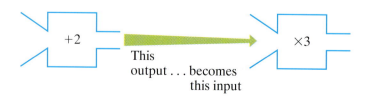

This output . . . becomes this input

## Example 5

For this two step number machine,
find the output if the input is 5.

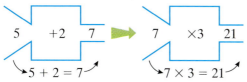

The output is 21.

You can also make patterns with two step machines.

## Example 6

(a) Input the number pattern 1, 2, 3, 4 and 5
    in this machine.

(b) Show your results in a table.

(c) Describe the pattern of output numbers.

(a)

input 1:    1    ×2    2    →    2    −1    1
            $1 \times 2 = 2$         $2 - 1 = 1$

input 2:    2    ×2    4    →    4    −1    3
            $2 \times 2 = 4$         $4 - 1 = 3$

input 3:    $3 \times 2 = 6$         $6 - 1 = 5$
input 4:    $4 \times 2 = 8$         $8 - 1 = 7$
input 5:    $5 \times 2 = 10$        $10 - 1 = 9$

(b)

×2 → −1

| input | output |
|-------|--------|
| 1 | 1 |
| 2 | 3 |
| 3 | 5 |
| 4 | 7 |
| 5 | 9 |

(c)  The pattern is: the output numbers go up in 2's.
     The output numbers are the odd numbers.

■  **In a two step number machine the output from the first
   machine becomes the input for the second machine.**

### Exercise 3F

Write down the output numbers for these two step machines.

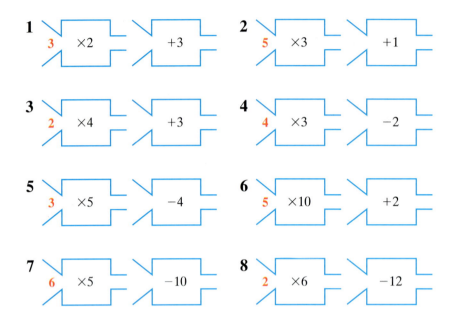

For questions **9** to **17**:

**(a)** Input the numbers 1, 2, 3, 4, 5, 6.

**(b)** Show your results in a table.

**(c)** Describe the pattern of output numbers.

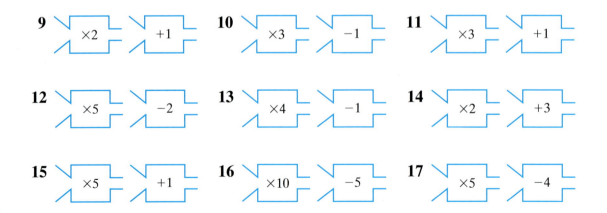

**18**  Use the numbers 2, 3, 5, 7, 11 in the two step machines in questions **9** to **14**. Show your results in a table.

## 3.6 Some special number patterns

Here are three number patterns you need to be able to recognize:

### Square numbers

This dot pattern shows some **square numbers**:

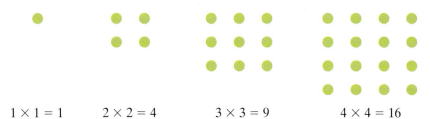

$$1 \times 1 = 1 \qquad 2 \times 2 = 4 \qquad 3 \times 3 = 9 \qquad 4 \times 4 = 16$$

You can see how to use your calculator for square numbers on page 286.

■ **A square number is the result of multiplying a number by itself.**

### Triangular numbers

This dot pattern shows some **triangular numbers**:

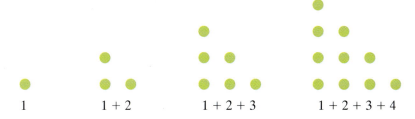

$$1 \qquad 1 + 2 \qquad 1 + 2 + 3 \qquad 1 + 2 + 3 + 4$$

### Fibonacci sequences

These numbers form a **Fibonacci sequence**:

1, 1, 2, 3, 5, 8, 13...

Here is how to make the sequence:

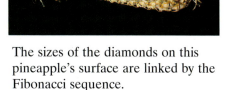

The sizes of the diamonds on this pineapple's surface are linked by the Fibonacci sequence.

These two numbers start the sequence.

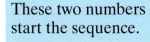

1  1  2  3  5  8  13  . . .       1  1  2  3  5  8  13  . . .

Add the first two numbers . . .

Add the next two numbers . . .          . . . and so on

## Exercise 3G

**1**  From this list of numbers:

9, 6, 8, 1, 3, 13, 2

write down:
  **(a)** the square numbers
  **(b)** the triangular numbers
  **(c)** the Fibonacci numbers

**2**  Write down:
  **(a)** the fourth square number
  **(b)** the fifth Fibonacci number
  **(c)** the sixth square number
  **(d)** the seventh triangular number
  **(e)** the eighth Fibonacci number

## Summary of key points

**1**  You can use number machines to make number patterns.

Here is a number machine for multiplying by 3:

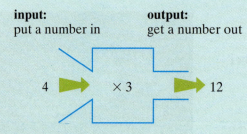

input:
put a number in

output:
get a number out

4  → ×3 → 12

**2**  A sequence is a number pattern.
The numbers are usually written in a row like this:

2, 4, 6, 8, 10, ...

The dots show the sequence goes on forever.

**3**  In a two step number machine the output from the
first machine becomes the input for the second
machine:

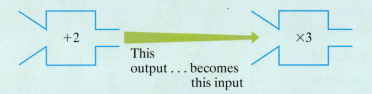

This
output . . . becomes
this input

**4**  A square number is the result of multiplying a
number by itself.
For example:

$1 \times 1 = 1$    $2 \times 2 = 4$    $3 \times 3 = 9$    $10 \times 10 = 100$

square numbers

**5**  Here is how to make a sequence of triangular
numbers:

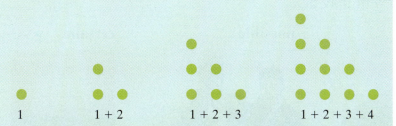

1            1 + 2            1 + 2 + 3            1 + 2 + 3 + 4

**6**  Here is how to make a Fibonacci sequence:

1    1    2    3    5    8    13    . . .

Add the first
two numbers . . .

1    1    2    3    5    8    13    . . .

Then add the
next two numbers . . .        . . . and so on.

# 4 Probability

Philip and Sarah are going to play tennis. Sarah spins her raquet to decide who will serve first.

It has a blue side and a red side.

Spinning the racquet is an **event**.

This event has two possible outcomes: blue and red.

In this unit you will learn how to measure the chance of different outcomes happening.

## 4.1 Certain, impossible or possible

The outcome of an event may be:

**impossible**

You will get 12 out of 10 in a Geography test.

**possible**

It will rain tomorrow.

**certain**

The sun will rise tomorrow.

**Example 1**

Write down whether these outcomes are: impossible, possible or certain

(a) A car will break down on the M25 tomorrow.
(b) A dog will have kittens.
(c) Tuesday will be the day after Monday next week.

**(a)** It is possible that a car will break down on the M25 tomorrow.

**(b)** It is impossible for a dog to have kittens.

**(c)** It is certain that Tuesday will be the day after Monday next week.

It is not certain or impossible.

## Exercise 4A

Write down whether these outcomes are:
certain, impossible or possible.

**1** The school netball team will win their next match.

**2** You will throw a 7 with a normal dice.

**3** A red car will pass the school this evening.

**4** You will have chips for tea tonight.

**5** Thursday will be the day after Wednesday next week.

**6** A plane will land at Manchester airport tomorrow.

**7** Your friend will go to the moon next summer.

**8** A cat will have puppies next year.

**9** You will have a birthday next year.

**10** You will receive a telephone call from a friend tonight.

## 4.2 Likely or unlikely?

Some outcomes are more likely to happen than others:

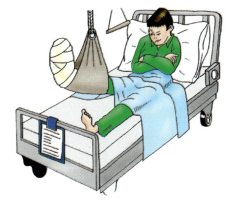

It is likely that you will eat breakfast tomorrow        It is unlikely that you will break a leg tomorrow

**Example 2**

Is this outcome likely or unlikely?
It will snow in Switzerland in January.
Give a reason for your answer.

It is likely to snow in Switzerland in January because Switzerland has very cold winters.

## Exercise 4B

Is each outcome likely or unlikely?
Give a reason for your answer.

1   You will break your leg next week.

2   You will see a famous film star in school next week.

3   You will watch Eastenders tonight.

4   Someone in your class will be absent next week.

5   It will rain in England in April.

6   When a card is taken from a normal pack it will be a number card.

7   Copy the table. Complete it by filling in 5 likely and 5 unlikely outcomes.

| Outcome | |
|---|---|
| Likely | Unlikely |
|  |  |
|  |  |
|  |  |
|  |  |
|  |  |

## 4.3 An even chance

At the start of a football match a
coin is tossed to decide which team
kicks off.

There are two possible outcomes:
heads or tails.

Both outcomes are equally likely.

Each outcome has an **even chance**
of happening.

■  **When an event has two equally likely outcomes, each
outcome has an even chance of happening.**

### Exercise 4C

Which of these outcomes have an even chance of happening?
Give a reason for each outcome you choose.

1  The next baby to be born will be female.

2  The next car to pass your school will be white.

3  You will have an accident on the way home.

4  The number on the top of an ordinary dice will be odd.

5  The top card in a well shuffled pack will be black.

## 4.4 How likely is it?

The outcomes of an event can have different chances of
happening. This table shows the different chances:

| Likelihood | Explanation |
|---|---|
| Impossible | There is no chance it will happen |
| Unlikely | It has a greater chance of not happening than happening |
| Even chance | It has the same chance of happening as not happening |
| Likely | It has a greater chance of happening than not happening |
| Certain | It will definitely happen |

## Example 3

Choose the likelihood which matches the outcome of each event:
impossible, unlikely, even chance, likely or certain.

Give a reason for your answers.

**(a)** The mountaineer will be hurt if he falls off the mountain.
**(b)** The number on the top face of an ordinary dice will be less than 7.
**(c)** Mr Smith will cut the grass on his lawn when it is snowing.
**(d)** The *Titanic* will float back up to the top of the ocean.
**(e)** The card at the top of a shuffled pack is a King.
**(f)** The card at the top of a shuffled pack is red.

**(a)** is likely. The mountain is hard and it will hurt if the mountaineer falls.
**(b)** is certain. The numbers on an ordinary dice are 1, 2, 3, 4, 5 and 6.
**(c)** is unlikely. Nobody with any sense cuts the grass when it is snowing.
**(d)** is impossible. The *Titanic* is made of metal and it will not rise.
**(e)** is unlikely. There are only 4 Kings in a pack of 52 cards.
**(f)** is an even chance. The top card will be either red or black.

## Exercise 4D

Choose the likelihood which matches the outcome of each event: impossible, unlikely, an even chance, likely or certain.

Give a reason for your answers.

1 It will rain in London at some time during April.

2 The winner of next year's mens finals at Wimbledon will be aged over 30 years.

3 Next year's FA Cup Final will be won by a team from the third division.

**4** The next baby to be born will be male.

**5** There will be more hours of light during the night than during the day.

**6** The record at number 1 in the charts this week will be in the top 10 next week.

**7** The Division 1 title will be won by a team from Division 2.

**8** Elvis Presley is still alive.

**9** You will be involved in a road accident on your way home today.

**10** Someone will be involved in a road accident today.

## 4.5 The likelihood scale

You can mark the chance of an outcome happening on a likelihood scale:

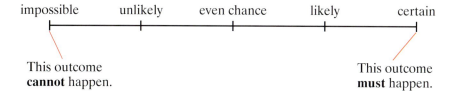

impossible     unlikely     even chance     likely     certain

This outcome **cannot** happen.

This outcome **must** happen.

**Example 4**

Draw a likelihood scale.
Put each of these outcomes in a suitable place on your scale:

**(a)** It will rain in Ireland next year.
**(b)** The next baby to be born will be male.
**(c)** Your dog will live forever.
**(d)** The next car to pass your school will be P registered.

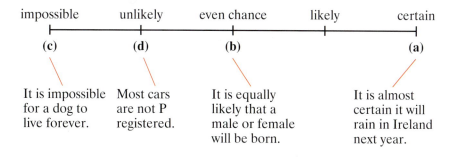

impossible     unlikely     even chance     likely     certain

(c)          (d)          (b)                      (a)

It is impossible for a dog to live forever.

Most cars are not P registered.

It is equally likely that a male or female will be born.

It is almost certain it will rain in Ireland next year.

■ **A likelihood scale runs from impossible to certain, with an 'even chance' in the middle.**

Draw a likelihood scale.
Mark an estimate of each of these outcomes on your scale.

**(a)** Sumreen's Budgie will live for ever.

**(b)** A car travelling on a motorway will be doing 25 miles per hour.

**(c)** The number on the top face of an ordinary dice will be even.

**(d)** The day after Christmas Day will be Boxing Day.

**(e)** It will rain in Manchester during at least one day in March next year.

## 4.6 Probability

■ **Probability uses numbers to measure the chance of an outcome happening.**

Probability was developed in the 17th Century when Mathematicians tried to work out the likelihood of success and failure in games of chance such as playing with cards or dice.

## The probability scale

You can mark the probability of an outcome happening on a probability scale:

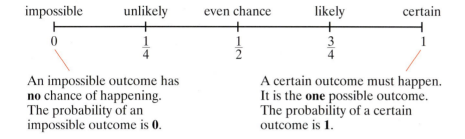

An impossible outcome has **no** chance of happening. The probability of an impossible outcome is **0**.

A certain outcome must happen. It is the **one** possible outcome. The probability of a certain outcome is **1**.

■ **All probabilities have a value from 0 to 1.**

### Example 5

Mark each of these outcomes on a probability scale.
Give reasons for your answers.

**(a)** It will rain in Scotland on at least one day next year.
**(b)** The next object you see flying in the sky will be a pink elephant.
**(c)** The card on the top of a well shuffled pack will be red.
**(d)** It will be warm in London next July.
**(e)** The winner of next year's mens final at Wimbledon will be aged over 30.

**(a)** is certain, it is bound to rain at some time.
**(b)** is impossible.
**(c)** is an even chance, the card will be either red or black and both are equally likely.
**(d)** is likely.
**(e)** is unlikely, the winner is usually in his twenties.

So on the probability scale the answers look like this:

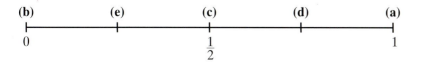

## Exercise 4F

**1** Draw a probability scale.
Mark each of these outcomes on your scale.
Give reasons for your answers.

**(a)** The school bus will break down tomorrow.

**(b)** The next baby to be born will be a girl.

**(c)** An ice cube will melt when it is left outside on a hot day.

**(d)** A heavy stone will float when it is dropped in the sea.

**(e)** The winner of the women's Olympic 100 metres final will be aged under 35 years.


**2** An ordinary pack of 52 cards is well shuffled.
The top card is then turned over.
Draw a probability scale and mark on it each of these outcomes:

Give reasons for your answers

**(a)** The top card will be black.

**(b)** The top card will not be a picture card.

**(c)** The top card will be a King.

**(d)** The top card will be the Queen of Hearts.

**(e)** The top card will be blank.

**(f)** The top card will be either a number card or a picture card.


**3** Look at this probability scale:

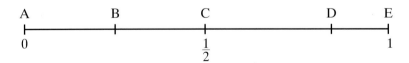

Outcomes A, B, C, D and E have been marked on the scale.
Give at least two possible outcomes for each of these probabilities.

## Summary of key points

1   When an event has two equally likely outcomes each outcome has an even chance of happening. For example, when you toss a coin, heads and tails are equally likely. They have an even chance of happening.

2   A likelihood scale runs from impossible to certain, with an 'even chance' in the middle.

3   Probability uses numbers to measure the chance of an outcome happening.

4   All probabilities have a value from 0 to 1.

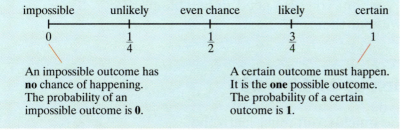

impossible       unlikely       even chance       likely       certain

$0$       $\frac{1}{4}$       $\frac{1}{2}$       $\frac{3}{4}$       $1$

An impossible outcome has **no** chance of happening. The probability of an impossible outcome is **0**.

A certain outcome must happen. It is the **one** possible outcome. The probability of a certain outcome is **1**.

# 5 Multiplication and division

Four hundred years ago most people did not need to multiply and divide.

Today most people do need to multiply and divide.

Calculators can help you, but you also need to be able to multiply and divide without them.

## 5.1 Multiplication up to 10 × 10

To multiply and divide **quickly** you must learn the multiplication tables up to $10 \times 10$.

Learning them takes time and practice. Exercise **5A** contains activities to help you practise.

### Exercise 5A

1   **Activity**   You need a set of cards numbered 1 to 10, a watch which shows seconds and a copy of the multiplication table you wish to practise, for example the 6 times multiplication table.

- Shuffle the cards and then turn one over. For each card that is turned over write down its number and multiply it by 6.
- Time how long it takes you to do all ten cards and then check your answers.
- Do this several times.

If you can beat 30 seconds you are doing well.

**2** **Activity** You need a set of cards numbered 1 to 10.

- Shuffle the cards.
- Turn over the top two cards and multiply the numbers together.
- Turn over the next two cards and multiply the numbers together.
- Continue until you have used all ten cards.
- Add together your five answers to get a total.

Do this several times then try to answer the following questions.

**(a)** What is the smallest total you could make?

**(b)** What is the largest total you could make?

$3 \times 7 = 21$
$8 \times 2 = 16$
$10 \times 5 = 50$
$6 \times 1 = 6$
$4 \times 9 = 36$

Total  129

**3** **Activity** This is a game for two players. You need a dice.

**Player 1**
Roll the dice twice. Multiply the two numbers together.

**Player 2**
Roll the dice three times. Multiply two of the three numbers together to try to beat Player 1's total.

The player with the higher total gets a point.

Do this five times then change places. The player with the highest number of points, after all ten go's, wins.

You can use your calculator to practise your times tables. Page 289 shows you how.

## 5.2 Multiples

This is the 3 times multiplication table:

$1 \times 3 = 3$
$2 \times 3 = 6$
$3 \times 3 = 9$
$4 \times 3 = 12$
$5 \times 3 = 15$

These are the multiples of 3

$28 \times 3 = 84$
$29 \times 3 = 87$

$28 \times 3 = 84$ so 84 is a multiple of 3

The answers 3, 6, 9, 12, 15, 18, ... are called the **multiples** of 3.

You only need to learn the 3 times multiplication table up to $10 \times 3$ but it actually goes on for ever!

That means the multiples of 3 also go on for ever.

Remember:
Multiples of 2 are called even numbers:
2, 4, 6, 8, 10, ...
The numbers
1, 3, 5, 7, ...
are odd

■ **The multiples of 3 are the answers in the 3 times multiplication table.**
You can find the multiples of 3 by multiplying 3 by 1, 2, 3, 4, 5, ...

If you colour the multiples of 3 on a number line you colour every third number.

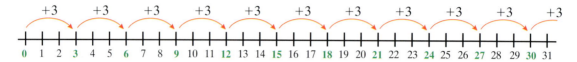

### Example 1

What are the multiples of 6 between 50 and 80?

54 is a multiple of 6 because $9 \times 6 = 54$
60 is a multiple of 6 because $6 \times 10 = 60$

Continue to count on in sixes on the number line.

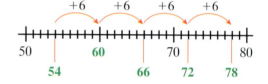

The multiples of 6 between 50 and 80 are 54, 60, 66, 72 and 78.

### Example 2

Is 79 a multiple of 4?

$79 \div 4 = 19$ remainder 3, so 79 is not a multiple of 4.

$$\begin{array}{r} 1\ 9 \text{ remainder 3} \\ 4\overline{)7\ 9} \\ \underline{4} \\ 3\ 9 \end{array}$$

## Exercise 5B

1   Which of these numbers is a multiple of 4?
   (a) 15        (b) 16        (c) 32        (d) 31
   (e) 24        (f) 36        (g) 43        (h) 48
   (i) 47        (j) 39        (k) 27        (l) 44

2   Which of these statements is true?
   (a) 45 is a multiple of 5      (b) 56 is a multiple of 8
   (c) 46 is a multiple of 6      (d) 63 is a multiple of 9
   (e) 48 is a multiple of 8      (f) 54 is a multiple of 6
   (g) 38 is a multiple of 8      (h) 26 is a multiple of 7
   (i) 38 is a multiple of 4      (j) 42 is a multiple of 7
   (k) 35 is a multiple of 9      (l) 67 is a multiple of 8

**3**  What are the multiples of 6 between 60 and 90?

**4**  What are the multiples of 7 between 80 and 110?

**5**  What are the first three multiples of 8 after 100?

**6**  For each statement write true or false.
    **(a)** 72 is a multiple of 3    **(b)** 138 is a multiple of 5
    **(c)** 245 is a multiple of 7    **(d)** 236 is a multiple of 6
    **(e)** 196 is a multiple of 8    **(f)** 332 is a multiple of 4
    **(g)** 623 is a multiple of 9    **(h)** 392 is a multiple of 7
    **(i)** 746 is a multiple of 6    **(j)** 882 is a multiple of 9
    **(k)** 837 is a multiple of 3    **(l)** 414 is a multiple of 7

**7**  Which is the first number that is a multiple of both:
    **(a)** 2 and 3    **(b)** 3 and 4    **(c)** 4 and 6
    **(d)** 6 and 8    **(e)** 6 and 9    **(f)** 3, 4 and 5?

**8**  What is the largest multiple of both 4 and 7 which is less than 100?

## 5.3 Factors

■ **The factors of a number are the numbers that divide into it exactly.**
For example, 1, 2, 3 and 6 are the factors of 6.
A factor is always a whole number.

You can think of factors in several other ways:

**1**  In the multiplication tables, 6 appears as an answer in the tables for 1, 2, 3 and 6. It does not appear as an answer in any other tables.

The numbers 1, 2, 3 and 6 are called the factors of 6.

```
1 × 1 = 1    1 × 2 = 2    1 × 3 = 3    1 × 6 = 6
2 × 1 = 2    2 × 2 = 4    2 × 3 = 6
3 × 1 = 3    3 × 2 = 6
4 × 1 = 4
5 × 1 = 5
6 × 1 = 6
```

**2**  The number 6 is a multiple of 1, 2, 3 and 6.
The numbers 1, 2, 3 and 6 are called the factors of 6.

**3** If you take 6 square tiles and put them together to form a rectangle, you can do it in two ways.

$$2 \times 3 = 6 \qquad \text{and} \qquad 1 \times 6 = 6$$

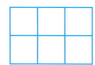

The numbers 1, 2, 3 and 6 are called the factors of 6.

## Example 3

What are the factors of 12?

Think of pairs of whole numbers which multiply together to give 12.

The factors of 12 are 1, 2, 3, 4, 6 and 12.

$1 \times 12 = 12$
$2 \times 6 = 12$
$3 \times 4 = 12$

The factors of 12

## Example 4

Show that 3 is a factor of 48.

$$\begin{array}{r} 1\,6 \\ 3\overline{)4\,8} \\ 3 \\ \hline 18 \end{array}$$    3 divides into 48 exactly

so 3 is a factor of 48.

## Exercise 5C

**1** What are the factors of

(a) 10  (b) 18  (c) 7  (d) 20  (e) 16  (f) 48
(g) 24  (h) 36  (i) 72  (j) 100  (k) 84  (l) 96?

Hint:  Try $1\overline{)48}$

$2\overline{)48}$

$3\overline{)48}$

until you need
go no further

**2** Which of these are true and which are false?

(a) 7 is a factor of 196    (b) 9 is a factor of 216
(c) 8 is a factor of 366    (d) 6 is a factor of 438
(e) 7 is a factor of 347    (f) 4 is a factor of 356
(g) 8 is a factor of 746    (h) 9 is a factor of 576
(i) 3 is a factor of 492

**3**  **(a)**  Which number less than 30 has the greatest number of factors?

   **(b)**  What are its factors?

**4**  Which number less than 90 has the greatest number of factors and what are its factors? Hint: it is a multiple of the answer to question **3(a)**.

## 5.4 Square numbers

You can arrange 9 square tiles to make a $3 \times 3$ square.
9 is called a **square number.**

$3 \times 3 = 9$

9 is a square number.

You can't arrange 8 tiles to make a square so 8 is *not* a square number.

$2 \times 4 = 8$

$1 \times 8 = 8$

■  **When you multiply a whole number by itself you get a square number.**

  $1 \times 1 = 1,$   $2 \times 2 = 4,$   $4 \times 4 = 16,$   $5 \times 5 = 25\ldots$

  **1, 4, 9, 16, 25 ... are square numbers.**

### Exercise 5D

**1**  Find all the square numbers up to 100.

**2**  **(a)**  When you add together consecutive odd numbers, starting at one, you get the square numbers. Explain why.

  **Hint**: this picture may help.

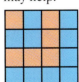

$$1 = 1$$
$$1 + 3 = 4$$
$$1 + 3 + 5 = 9$$
$$1 + 3 + 5 + 7 = 16$$

Use this fact to help you answer the following questions. Do not just add the numbers up.

  **(b)**  $1 + 3 + 5 + 7 \ldots + 97 + 99 = ?$
  **(c)**  $1 + 3 + 5 + 7 \ldots + 47 + 49 = ?$
  **(d)**  $51 + 53 + 55 \ldots + 97 + 99 = ?$
  **(e)**  $27 + 29 + 31 \ldots + 47 + 49 = ?$
  **(f)**  $17 + 19 + 21 \ldots + 97 + 99 = ?$
  **(g)**  $2 + 6 + 10 + 14 \ldots + 94 + 98 = ?$

**consecutive** means one after another without gaps.

1 3 5 ...

are consecutive odd numbers.

## 5.5 Prime numbers

■ **A prime number is a whole number greater than 1 with only two factors: itself and 1.**

2, 3, 5, 7, 11, 13, 17, 19, 23, ...
are prime numbers.

1, 4, 6, 8, 9, 10, 12, 14, 15, 16, 18, 20, 21, 22, ...
are not prime numbers.

There is no pattern to the prime numbers and they go on for ever.

2 is the only even prime number.

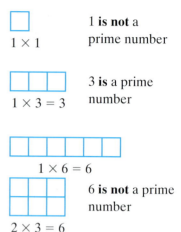

1 × 1     1 **is not** a prime number

1 × 3 = 3     3 **is** a prime number

1 × 6 = 6

2 × 3 = 6     6 **is not** a prime number

### Exercise 5E

1  **Activity**  You need a 100 square for part **(a)**.
You may need a 400 square for part **(b)**.

One way to find prime numbers is to use the sieve of Eratosthenes.

- On your 100 square cross out 1 because it is not a prime number.
- Circle 2 then cross out all other multiples of 2. The next number that is not crossed out is 3.
- Circle 3 then cross out all other multiples of 3.
  The next number that is not crossed out is 5.
- Circle 5 then cross out all other multiples of 5. Continue like this until you cannot circle any more numbers.
  The circled numbers are the prime numbers less than 100.

> Eratosthenes was a Greek mathematician who lived in the third century BC. He was a librarian in Alexandria in Egypt.

**(a)** Why don't you have to cross off any numbers after you have done the multiples of 7?

**(b)** Which multiples will you have to check to find all the prime numbers less than 400?

**(c)** Which numbers will you have to check to find all the prime numbers less than 1000?

**2**   Can all the square numbers up to 100 be written as the sum of two prime numbers?
For example, 36 can because $17 + 19 = 36$.

**3**   Here are the rules for growing magic number seeds:
- the stalk splits if you can find factors like $5 \times 6$
- a leaf grows if the only factors you can find are 1 and the number itself

Plant the number 30 seed …

… the stalk splits into 5 and 6 because $5 \times 6 = 30$

… the 6 stalk splits into 2 and 3 because $2 \times 3 = 6$

… the 5 stalk grows a leaf

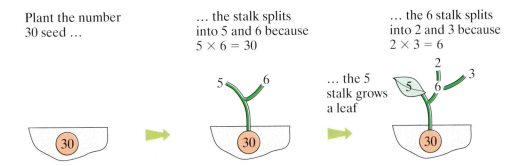

**(a)** Draw the plants that can grow from a number 12 seed.

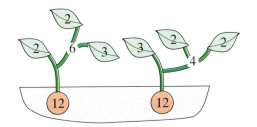

More than one plant can grow from a number 12 seed because $2 \times 6 = 12$ and $3 \times 4 = 12$

**(b)** Draw the plants that can grow from a number 15 seed.
**(c)** Which number seeds will not grow?
**(d)** Which number seeds less than 50 can grow most plants?
**(e)** Which number seeds less than 50 grow the tallest?

## 5.6 Multiplying by 10, 100 and 1000

All multiples of 10 have zero units. For example:

10  20  30  40  50  60  70  80  90  100  110  120  130

30 has zero units          120 has zero units

■ **To multiply a whole number by 10 move each digit one column to the left and put 0 in the units column.**

For example:   $24 \times 10 = 240$

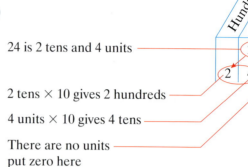

24 is 2 tens and 4 units ────

2 tens × 10 gives 2 hundreds ────

4 units × 10 gives 4 tens ────

There are no units put zero here ────

There is also a quick way to multiply by 100:

$$100 = 10 \times 10$$
$$\text{So } 24 \times 100 = 24 \times 10 \times 10$$
$$\text{So } 24 \times 100 = 2400$$

$100 = 10 \times 10$ so you can multiply by 10 and then by 10 again.

■ **To multiply a whole number by 100 move each digit two columns to the left, then put 0 in the tens and units columns.**

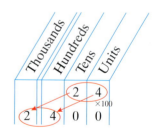

■ **To multiply a whole number by 1000 move each digit three columns to the left, then put 0 in the hundreds, tens and units columns**

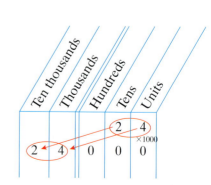

# Exercise 5F

**1**  **(a)** $23 \times 10$   **(b)** $76 \times 10$   **(c)** $48 \times 100$
   **(d)** $10 \times 97$   **(e)** $10 \times 53$   **(f)** $100 \times 72$
   **(g)** $143 \times 10$   **(h)** $7 \times 1000$   **(i)** $17 \times 1000$
   **(j)** $1000 \times 91$   **(k)** $1000 \times 128$   **(l)** $4217 \times 1000$

> Remember $100 \times 72$ is the same as $72 \times 100$.

**2**  **(a)** $4 \times 10 \times 100$   **(b)** $10 \times 7 \times 100$
   **(c)** $10 \times 80 \times 10$   **(d)** $100 \times 6 \times 10$
   **(e)** $10 \times 37 \times 10$   **(f)** $10 \times 10 \times 21$
   **(g)** $20 \times 100$   **(h)** $10 \times 300$

**3**  Which of these numbers are multiples of 10?
   **(a)** 270   **(b)** 138   **(c)** 760   **(d)** 1000
   **(e)** 408   **(f)** 1470   **(g)** 580   **(h)** 706
   **(i)** 90   **(j)** 6800   **(k)** 1003   **(l)** 2090

**4**  Which of these numbers are multiples of 100?
   **(a)** 2460   **(b)** 3200   **(c)** 7040   **(d)** 9000
   **(e)** 95 000   **(f)** 8000   **(g)** 250   **(h)** 4000
   **(i)** 9002   **(j)** 1000   **(k)** 4300   **(l)** 1001

**5**  Which of these numbers are multiples of 1000?
   **(a)** 1760   **(b)** 9010   **(c)** 4100   **(d)** 6000
   **(e)** 95 000   **(f)** 1650   **(g)** 11 000   **(h)** 10 000
   **(i)** 10 010   **(j)** 2000   **(k)** 22 000   **(l)** 17 000

## 5.7 Dividing by 10, 100 and 1000

■  **To divide a whole number by 10 move each digit one column to the right.**

For example,
   $140 \div 10 = 14$

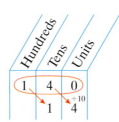

■ **To divide a whole number by 100 move each digit two columns to the right.**

For example,

$$2600 \div 100 = 26$$

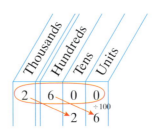

■ **To divide a whole number by 1000 move each digit three columns to the right.**

For example,

$$39\,000 \div 1000 = 39$$

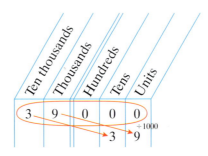

## Exercise 5G

**1**  (a)  $570 \div 10$      (b)  $890 \div 10$      (c)  $2040 \div 10$
      (d)  $300 \div 10$      (e)  $4000 \div 10$      (f)  $2300 \div 10$

**2**  (a)  $4700 \div 100$    (b)  $3900 \div 100$    (c)  $4200 \div 100$
      (d)  $7000 \div 100$    (e)  $100 \div 100$     (f)  $4300 \div 100$

**3**  (a)  $4000 \div 1000$           (b)  $17\,000 \div 1000$
      (c)  $171\,000 \div 1000$        (d)  $90\,000 \div 1000$
      (e)  $237\,000 \div 1000$        (f)  $66\,000 \div 1000$

**4**  (a)  $29 \times 100 \div 10$        (b)  $46 \times 100 \div 10$
      (c)  $380 \div 10 \times 100$       (d)  $780 \div 10 \times 100$
      (e)  $960 \times 10 \div 100$       (f)  $120 \times 10 \div 100$

## 5.8 Multiplying by multiples of 10, 100 and 1000

What is 23 × 40?

40 is a multiple of 10.

Think of 40 as 4 × 10.

Multiply 23 by 4.                    $23 \times 4 = 92$

Then multiply your answer by 10.     $92 \times 10 = 920$

$34 \times 40 = 920$

> On paper you could write this as:
>
> $$\begin{array}{r} 23 \\ \times\ \ 4 \\ \hline 92 \\ \hline {}_1 \end{array}$$

■  **To multiply by 40, first multiply by 4 then multiply your answer by 10.**

**To multiply by 400, first multiply by 4 then multiply your answer by 100.**

**To multiply by 4000, first multiply by 4 then multiply your answer by 1000.**

> To multiply by 200 think of 200 as $2 \times 100$

### Exercise 5H

1  (a) $32 \times 20$  (b) $21 \times 30$  (c) $43 \times 40$  (d) $63 \times 60$
   (e) $28 \times 50$  (f) $30 \times 37$  (g) $70 \times 18$  (h) $50 \times 81$
   (i) $40 \times 93$  (j) $60 \times 75$

2  (a) $18 \times 200$     (b) $4 \times 400$     (c) $31 \times 300$
   (d) $7 \times 600$      (e) $22 \times 300$    (f) $21 \times 400$

3  (a) $32 \times 80$      (b) $9 \times 500$     (c) $70 \times 75$
   (d) $900 \times 3$      (e) $5 \times 700$     (f) $90 \times 400$

4  (a) $4 \times 9000$     (b) $18 \times 2000$   (c) $6000 \times 14$
   (d) $8000 \times 12$    (e) $5000 \times 17$   (f) $110 \times 3000$

## 5.9 Multiplication and division problems up to 10 × 10

There are many problems for which you need to multiply or divide to find the answer.

Dividing often produces a remainder and you will need to decide what is a sensible answer.

### Example 5

A henkeeper has 50 eggs to put
into boxes.
Each box will hold 6 eggs.
How many boxes can she fill?

$$50 \div 6 = 8 \text{ remainder } 2$$

The henkeeper can fill 8 boxes.
She has 2 eggs left over.

### Example 6

A group of 23 people are going to a restaurant by taxi.
Each taxi can take 4 people.
How many taxis do they need?

$$23 \div 4 = 5 \text{ remainder } 3$$

If they order 5 taxis there will not be room for 3 people so
they must order 6 taxis.

### Exercise 5I

In this exercise you must decide whether to multiply or
divide. If you divide and there is a remainder you will need
to decide what is a sensible answer.

1   Sandrine bought 3 packs of fruit juice.
    Each pack cost £4 and contained 9 cartons of fruit
    juice.

    **(a)** How many cartons of fruit juice did she buy?

    **(b)** How much did she pay in total?

2   Laurent is organising the food
    for a party.

    He must buy enough sausages
    and bread rolls to make 31 hot
    dogs.

    He buys 4 packs of 8 sausages
    and 5 packs of 6 bread rolls.

    Has he bought enough?

3 Mr Farmer runs a country dance club.
He can put the dancers into groups of 6 or into groups
of 8.
One day he has 30 dancers present.
Should he put them into groups of 6 or 8?

4 A fruit grower has 35 apples to put into packets.
Each packet holds 4 apples.
How many packets can he fill?

5 A group of 28 Guides are going
camping.
Each tent holds 6 people.
How many tents do they need to
take?

6 Minakshi wants to post 68 Christmas cards.
How many books of 10 stamps must she buy?

7 A baker is packing doughnuts in boxes.
She can put them in boxes of 5 or in boxes of 8.
She fills 10 boxes of 5 and 4 boxes of 8 and has 1
doughnut left over.
How could she have packed them to have no
doughnuts left over?

## 5.10 Multiplying or dividing a 3 digit number by a 1 digit number

Today you have calculators to help you with harder
problems.

But you still must be able to do multiplications and
divisions using only pencil and paper.

The first pocket calculators
appeared in shops in the
early 1970s. They were very
expensive, about £70.

## Example 7

A shop ordered 7 boxes of pencils.
Each box contained 144 pencils.
How many pencils did the shop order?

$$
\begin{array}{r}
1\,4\,4 \\
\times \quad 7 \\
\hline
1\,0\,0\,8 \\
{\scriptstyle 3\ 2}
\end{array}
$$

$144 \times 7 = 1008$ pencils

## Example 8

A fruit grower is packing apples.
Each pack holds 4 apples and he has 650 apples.
How many packs can he fill?

$$
\begin{array}{r}
1\,6\,2 \\
4{\overline{\smash{)}\,6\,5\,0}} \\
-4\phantom{\,5\,0} \\
\hline
2\,5\phantom{\,0} \\
-2\,4\phantom{\,0} \\
\hline
1\,0 \\
-\ 8 \\
\hline
2\ \text{(remainder)}
\end{array}
$$

$650 \div 4 = 162$ remainder 2

He can fill 162 packs.

## Exercise 5J

**1**  A girl gets £7 pocket money a week.
How much does she get in a year?

> 1 year is 52 weeks and 1 day
> 1 year is 365 days

**2**  A violinist practises for 4 hours every day.
How many hours does he practise in a year?

**3**  Eight people shared a lottery win of £376.
How much did they each get?

**4**  160 people are invited to a wedding reception.
They are each given a glass of champagne for a toast.
Each bottle of champagne filled 6 glasses.
How many bottles of champagne were needed?

**5**  Vasbert ran 7 laps of a running track.
Each lap of the track was 440 metres.
How many metres did he run in total?

**6**  A racing cyclist does 300 miles of training a week.
He does the same number of miles each day.
How many miles does he cycle each day?

**7**  Gayle made 9 photocopies of a 24 page booklet.
Each photocopy cost 4p to make.
What was the total cost?

**8** In a tombola the tickets which are multiples of 6 win a prize.
Which of the tickets shown would win prizes?

94   504   364   824   744   924

**9** **Investigation** Choose any three different digits.
Arrange them as a 2 digit number multiplied by a 1 digit number and do the multiplication.
Try other arrangements of the same digits.

(a) How many different arrangements are there?

(b) Which arrangement gives the largest answer?

(c) Which arrangement gives the smallest answer?

(d) Try other sets of digits.

(e) Can you spot any rules to help you answer parts
(b) and (c)?

7, 4, 6

$67 \times 4 = 268$

$76 \times 4 =$     $46 \times 7 =$

## 5.11 Multiplying a 3 digit number by a 2 digit number

This section shows you how to do multiplications such as
$473 \times 64$

Think of 64 as $60 + 4$

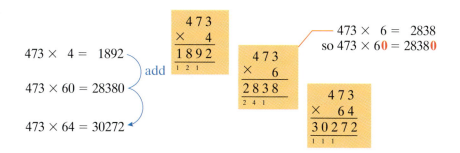

$473 \times 4 = 1892$

$473 \times 60 = 28380$

$473 \times 64 = 30272$

$$\begin{array}{r} 4\,7\,3 \\ \times \quad 4 \\ \hline 1\,8\,9\,2 \\ {}^{1\ 2\ 1} \end{array}$$

add

$$\begin{array}{r} 4\,7\,3 \\ \times \quad 6 \\ \hline 2\,8\,3\,8 \\ {}^{2\ 4\ 1} \end{array}$$

$473 \times 6 = 2838$
so $473 \times 60 = 28380$

$$\begin{array}{r} 4\,7\,3 \\ \times \quad 6\,4 \\ \hline 3\,0\,2\,7\,2 \\ {}^{1\ 1\ 1} \end{array}$$

You can set out $473 \times 64$ like this:

$$\begin{array}{r} 4\ 7\ 3 \\ \times \quad 6\ 4 \\ \hline 1\ 8{,}9{,}2 \\ 2\ 8{,}3{,}8\ 0 \\ \hline 3\ 0\ 2\ 7\ 2 \\ {}_{1\ \ 1\ \ 1} \end{array}$$

$473 \times 4$

Put a 0 in the units column then multiply $473 \times 6$.
This is the same as $473 \times 60$.

Add 1892 and 28380 to get $473 \times 64$.

## Exercise 5K

**1** **(a)** $212 \times 31$     **(b)** $123 \times 23$     **(c)** $234 \times 32$
   **(d)** $436 \times 26$     **(e)** $364 \times 43$     **(f)** $275 \times 34$
   **(g)** $107 \times 27$     **(h)** $461 \times 42$     **(i)** $418 \times 64$
   **(j)** $602 \times 58$     **(k)** $540 \times 76$     **(l)** $183 \times 92$

**2** Choose any five digits, for example 2, 3, 6, 8, 9.
Write them as a 3 digit × 2 digit multiplication
and work out the answer.
Try other arrangements of your five digits.
Which arrangement gives the largest answer?
Which arrangement gives the smallest answer?

$$
\begin{array}{r}
6\,2\,8 \\
\times \quad 3\,9 \\
\hline
5\,6\,5\,2 \\
1\,8\,8\,4\,0 \\
\hline
2\,4\,4\,9\,2 \\
\end{array}
$$

## 5.12 Dividing a 3 digit number by a 2 digit number

This section shows you how to do divisions such as
$875 \div 24$.

First, here is a simpler example: $947 \div 4$

Divide the 9 hundreds by 4
$9 \div 4 = 2$ remainder 1

Divide the 14 tens by 4
$14 \div 4 = 3$ remainder 2

Divide the 27 units by 4
$27 \div 4 = 6$ remainder 3

You could also set it out like this:

Divide the 9 hundreds by 4
$9 \div 4 = 2$ remainder 1

Divide the 14 tens by 4
$14 \div 4 = 3$ remainder 2

Divide the 27 units by 4
$27 \div 4 = 6$ remainder 3

The second method looks complicated but it is a good way
to set out a division such as $875 \div 24$

You can set out $875 \div 24$ like this:

You cannot divide the 8 hundreds by 24.
Divide the 87 tens by 24.
$87 \div 24 = 3$ remainder 15

```
      3
24)8 7 5
  -7 2
    1 5
```

```
  2 4
×   3
  7 2
```

```
    3 6 rem. 11
24)8 7 5
  -7 2
    1 5 5
  -1 4 4
      1 1
```

```
  2 4
×   6
1 4 4
```

Divide the 155 units by 24.
$155 \div 24 = 6$ remainder 11

---

## Exercise 5L

1   (a) $346 \div 13$    (b) $367 \div 17$    (c) $294 \div 15$
    (d) $691 \div 14$    (e) $719 \div 19$    (f) $849 \div 18$
    (g) $699 \div 13$    (h) $842 \div 16$

2   (a) $879 \div 23$    (b) $963 \div 34$    (c) $854 \div 26$
    (d) $987 \div 42$    (e) $992 \div 47$    (f) $763 \div 21$
    (g) $792 \div 39$    (h) $948 \div 45$

3   (a) $847 \div 76$    (b) $993 \div 82$    (c) $974 \div 91$
    (d) $895 \div 63$    (e) $764 \div 58$    (f) $947 \div 71$
    (g) $863 \div 85$    (h) $683 \div 52$

## Exercise 5M

In these questions you will need to either multiply or divide
a 3 digit number by a 2 digit number. If you divide and
there is a remainder you will need to decide what is a
sensible answer.

1   Jack works in a supermarket. He earns £186 a week.
    How much does he earn in a 52 week year?

2   A group of 36 children went on a school journey for a
    week to the Isle of Wight. Each child paid £213.
    What was the total cost of the trip?

**3** A garage charges £24 an hour for labour. The garage charges Nigel £336 labour to replace the engine in his car. For how many hours of labour was he charged?

**4** A department store ordered 34 television sets at a cost of £357 each. What was the total cost of the television sets?

**5** Every year on sports day a school gives a can of cola to each pupil. There are 950 pupils in the school and the cola comes in packs of 24. How many packs does the school need to order?

**6** A car uses a gallon of petrol for every 58 miles it travels. How many gallons of petrol will the car use for a journey of 860 miles?

## 5.13 Powers of whole numbers

Large numbers such as 100, 1000 and 1 000 000 (1 million) can be written as powers of ten.

| | How you write it: | How you say it: |
|---|---|---|
| $10 = 10$ | $10^1$ | 10 to the power 1 |
| $100 = 10 \times 10$ | $10^2$ | 10 to the power 2 |
| $1\,000 = 10 \times 10 \times 10$ | $10^3$ | 10 to the power 3 |
| $10\,000 = 10 \times 10 \times 10 \times 10$ | $10^4$ | 10 to the power 4 |
| $100\,000 = 10 \times 10 \times 10 \times 10 \times 10$ | $10^5$ | 10 to the power 5 |
| $1\,000\,000 = 10 \times 10 \times 10 \times 10 \times 10 \times 10$ | $10^6$ | 10 to the power 6 |

Other numbers can also be written as powers; for example:

- **$3^5$ is '3 to the power 5'**
  **$3^5 = 3 \times 3 \times 3 \times 3 \times 3 = 243$**

A power is also called an **index**.

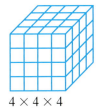

4 × 4

$4^2$ is also called 4 squared because it is the number of small tiles in a 4 × 4 square.

4 × 4 × 4

$4^3$ is also called 4 cubed because it is the number of small cubes in a 4 × 4 × 4 cube.

4 × 4 = 16

16 is a **square number**.

There is more about square numbers on page 73.

■ $4^2$ or '4 to the power 2' is also called '4 squared'.
$4^3$ or '4 to the power 3' is also called '4 cubed'.

**Example 9**

Write $5 \times 5 \times 5 \times 5$ as a power of 5.

$$5 \times 5 \times 5 \times 5 = 5^4$$

**Example 10**

Write 216 as a power of 6.

$$216 = 6 \times 6 \times 6 = 6^3$$

**Example 11**

Write 1 000 000 000 as a power of 10.
There are nine zeros after the 1 so

$$1\,000\,000\,000 = 10^9$$

**Example 12**

Work out $7^3$.

$$7^3 = 7 \times 7 \times 7 = 343$$

**Exercise 5N**

1   Write:
   (a) $3 \times 3 \times 3 \times 3$ as a power of 3
   (b) $8 \times 8 \times 8$ as a power of 8
   (c) $2 \times 2 \times 2 \times 2 \times 2$ as a power of 2
   (d) $10 \times 10 \times 10 \times 10 \times 10 \times 10$ as a power of 10
   (e) $7 \times 7$ as a power of 7
   (f) $9 \times 9 \times 9 \times 9$ as a power of 9

2   Work out:
   (a) $4^2$   (b) $2^5$   (c) $3^4$   (d) $7^3$   (e) $10^3$   (f) $3^2$
   (g) $1^4$   (h) $0^5$   (i) $3^5$   (j) $8^3$   (k) $4^4$   (l) $9^4$

**3** Write:

   **(a)** 8 as a power of 2

   **(b)** 9 as a power of 3

   **(c)** 81 as a power of 9

   **(d)** 125 as a power of 5

   **(e)** 100 000 as a power of 10

   **(f)** 64 as a power of 4

   **(g)** 16 as a power of 2

   **(h)** 1 000 000 as a power of 10

   **(i)** 27 as a power of 3

**4** Which is larger:

   **(a)** $2^3$ or $3^2$   **(b)** $3^4$ or $4^3$   **(c)** $3^3$ or $5^2$   **(d)** $4^3$ or $8^2$?

**5** Work out:

| | | |
|---|---|---|
| **(a)** 6 squared | **(b)** 2 cubed | **(c)** 5 squared |
| **(d)** 9 squared | **(e)** 4 cubed | **(f)** 10 cubed |
| **(g)** 10 squared | **(h)** 100 squared | **(i)** 1 squared |
| **(j)** 3 squared | **(k)** 3 cubed | **(l)** 5 cubed |

## Summary of key points

**1**   The multiples of 3 are the answers in the 3 times multiplication table.

    You can find the multiples of 3 by multiplying 3 by 1, 2, 3, 4, 5, ...

    They go on for ever: 3, 6, 9, 12, 15, ..., 84, 87, ...

**2**   The factors of a number are the numbers that divide into it exactly.
    For example 1, 2, 3 and 6 are the factors of 6.
    A factor is always a whole number.

**3**   When you multiply a whole number by itself you get a square number.

    $1 \times 1 = 1, \quad 2 \times 2 = 4, \quad 3 \times 3 = 9, \quad 4 \times 4 = 16, \ldots$

    1, 4, 9, 16, ... are square numbers.

**4**   A prime number is a whole number greater than 1
with only two factors: itself and 1.

    2, 3, 5, 7, 11, 13, 17, 19, 23, . . .
are prime numbers.

    1, 4, 6, 8, 9, 10, 12, 14, 15, 16, 18, 20, 21, 22, . . .
are not prime numbers.

**5**   To multiply a whole number by 10, 100, 1000 . . .
move each digit to the left by the number of zeros.

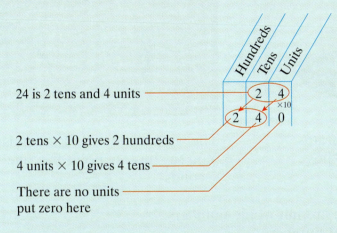

24 is 2 tens and 4 units

2 tens × 10 gives 2 hundreds

4 units × 10 gives 4 tens

There are no units
put zero here

**6**   To divide a whole number by 10, 100, 1000 . . . move
each digit to the right by the number of zeros.

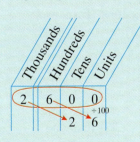

**7**   To multiply by 40, multiply by 4
then multiply your answer by 10.

**8**   $3^5$ is called '3 to the power 5
$3^5 = 3 \times 3 \times 3 \times 3 \times 3 = 243$

**9**   $4^2$ or '4 to the power 2' is also called '4 squared'.
$4^3$ or '4 to the power 3' is also called '4 cubed'.

# 6 Decimals

## 6.1 Understanding decimals

When you count things you get whole number values:

There are 12 clementines in this bag:

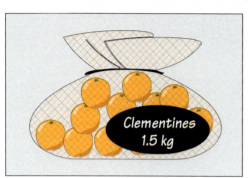

8 runners ran this race:

This bag weighs 1.5 kilograms.
You say 'one point five kilos'.

The winner took 20.51 seconds.
You say 'twenty point five one'
seconds.

Measurements like these are **not** whole numbers.
1.5 and 20.51 are **decimal numbers**.

■ **In a decimal number the decimal point separates the
whole number from the part that is less than one:**

decimal point

## 20.51

20 is the whole
number

.51 is the part
less than one

This place value diagram will help you
understand what 20.51 means:

The whole number part is 20.
There are 2 tens and zero units.

The decimal part is .51
There are 5 tenths and
1 hundredth.

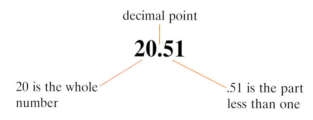

2 tens
0 units

5 tenths
1 hundredth

**Example 1**

This calculator display shows the decimal
number 325.078

(a) Show this number on a decimal place
value diagram.

(b) Write down the value of each digit.

(a)

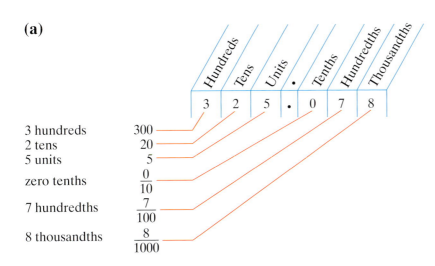

3 hundreds     300
2 tens     20
5 units     5
zero tenths     $\dfrac{0}{10}$
7 hundredths     $\dfrac{7}{100}$
8 thousandths     $\dfrac{8}{1000}$

Even though there are zero *tenths* the 0 has to be
recorded.
This keeps the 7 and the 8 in their correct place value
positions.

(b) The values of the digits are
3 hundreds, 2 tens, 5 units, 0 tenths, 7 hundredths and
8 thousandths.

**Example 2**

Write down the value of the digit underlined in each
decimal number.

(a) 82.3     (b) 3.68     (c) 4.05     (d) 0.276

(a) 2 units     (b) 8 hundredths     (c) 0 tenths     (d) 6 thousandths

> Write .276
> as 0.276
> The zero
> draws
> attention to
> the decimal
> point.

## Exercise 6A

1   Draw a decimal place value diagram like the one in Example 1 and write in these numbers.

   **(a)** 12.3   **(b)** 4.31   **(c)** 0.56   **(d)** 3.05
   **(e)** 0.082   **(f)** 930.08   **(g)** 18.62   **(h)** 0.03

2   Write down the value of the digit underlined in each decimal number.

   **(a)** 3̲7.8   **(b)** 46̲.3   **(c)** 17.6̲5   **(d)** 3.8̲1
   **(e)** 11.93̲   **(f)** 8.1̲4   **(g)** 6̲27.8   **(h)** 46̲2.9
   **(i)** 9.127̲   **(j)** 3.5̲24   **(k)** 9.273̲   **(l)** 0.09̲2

## 6.2 Adding and subtracting decimals

You can add and subtract decimals in the same way you add and subtract money in pounds and pence.

- **When adding or subtracting decimal numbers always line up the decimal points.**

### Example 3

Senga has £43.87 in her savings account and Joshua has £28.30 in his. **Without a calculator** work out the total amount that Senga and Joshua have saved. Show all your working.

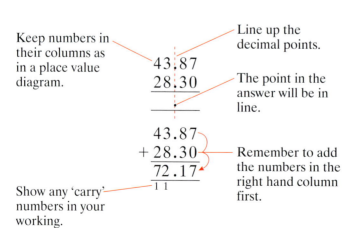

Keep numbers in their columns as in a place value diagram.

Line up the decimal points.

43.87
28.30
____

The point in the answer will be in line.

43.87
+ 28.30
72.17
 1 1

Show any 'carry' numbers in your working.

Remember to add the numbers in the right hand column first.

The answer is £72.17

**Example 4**

Work out $6.2 + 14.36 + 22.24$ without using a calculator.

$$
\begin{array}{r}
6.2 \\
14.36 \\
+\ 22.24 \\
\hline
42.80 \\
\phantom{0}1\phantom{0}\phantom{0}1
\end{array}
$$

42.80 and 42.8 have the same value. The answer is not an amount of money, so the zero in the hundredths place **can** be left out.

The answer is 42.8

**Example 5**

On Thursday evening Liam's temperature was 39.2 °C. The following morning his temperature was 36.7 °C. By how much had Liam's temperature fallen overnight?

$39.2\,°C - 36.7\,°C$

Line up the points

$$
\begin{array}{r}
39.2 \\
-\ 36.7 \\
\hline
\end{array}
$$

Put the point in the answer

$$
\begin{array}{r}
\phantom{39.}. \\
\end{array}
$$

Now subtract

$$
\begin{array}{r}
^{8}3\overset{1}{9}.2 \\
-\ 36.7 \\
\hline
2.5
\end{array}
$$

Hint: There is more about subtraction on page 42.

Liam's temperature fell by 2.5 °C.

## Exercise 6B

Show all your working.

1   (a)  £21.42 + £35.16          (b)  £4.30 + £15.48
    (c)  £3.40 + £6.50            (d)  £8.97 + £6.35
    (e)  £68.47 + £19.33          (f)  £16.39 + £97.74

2   (a)  $4.2 + 1.8$              (b)  $6 + 1.47$
    (c)  $163.7 + 0.45$           (d)  $9.9 + 9.9$
    (e)  $4.3 + 16.5 + 7.46$      (f)  $8.09 + 15 + 0.52$

**3** (a) £4.83 − £2.71    (b) £3.21 − £1.86
  (c) £15.65 − £9.28    (d) £14.72 − £8.25

**4** (a) 0.95 − 0.52    (b) 16.02 − 4.35
  (c) 200.8 − 3.4    (d) 9.237 − 4.7
  (e) 1 − 0.6    (f) 1 − 0.38

Hint: write 1 as 1.00

**5** Katie ran 1.25 km from The Bourne
  to Millbridge, 2.8 km from Millbridge
  to Rowledge and 3.24 km from
  Rowledge to The Bourne.
  Work out the total distance that
  Katie ran.

**6** The temperature in Larne at midnight was 4.8 °C.
  By noon the temperature had gone up by 4.5 °C.
  What was the temperature in Larne at noon?

**7** Eleanor sawed a length of 0.26 metres from a one
  metre piece of wood.
  Work out the length of wood left over.

**8** The temperature in Oxford at noon was 17.3 °C.
  By midnight the temperature had fallen by 7.9 °C.
  What was the temperature in Oxford at midnight?

**9** A cake weighed 1.42 kg.
  What was the weight of the cake after Sean had eaten
  a slice that weighed 0.17 kg?

**10** Asif's empty bag weighs 0.92 kg.
  One day Asif had two text books in his bag, weighing
  1.05 kg and 0.96 kg, two exercise books each weighing
  0.2 kg and a pencil case weighing 0.33 kg.
  What was the total weight of Asif's bag and its
  contents?

**11** Winford's packed rucksack weighed 21.2 kg.
  Winford removed a radio weighing 0.5 kg, a sweater
  weighing 0.7 kg and a pair of shoes weighing 1.6 kg.
  Work out the new weight of Winford's rucksack.

## 6.3  Writing decimal numbers in size order

Sometimes you need to sort measurements and decimal numbers in order of size.

**Example 6**

Write the decimal numbers 2.05, 2.4, 3.7, 2.069, 8 in order of size starting with the largest.

Look at the whole number
part of each number

2.05      2.4      3.7      2.069      8

Put the largest whole
number first …

8      3.7      2.05      2.4      2.069

2.05, 2.4, 2.069 all have
the same whole number so
look at the tenths place.

8      3.7      2.05      2.4      2.069

Put the largest
'tenth' first …

8      3.7      2.4      2.05      2.069

2.05, and 2.069 have the
same tenths so look at
the hundredths.

8      3.7      2.4      2.05      2.069

Put the largest
'hundredth' first …

8      3.7      2.4      2.069      2.05

- ■ **You can sort decimal numbers in order of size by comparing first the whole numbers, then the tenths, then the hundredths, and so on.**

### Exercise 6C

Rearrange these decimal numbers in order of size, starting with the largest:

1  2.4, 3.2, 5.1, 2.8

2  4.6, 4.8, 5.9, 5.3

3  3.8, 6.5, 7.2, 3.4, 6.3

4  2.91, 3.85, 2.78, 3.96, 4.21

5  5.94, 6.04, 6.43, 8.12, 5.29

Put these numbers in order of size, smallest first:

**6** 2.92, 4.16, 3.05, 3.74, 3.61

**7** 2.3, 5.1, 4.06, 5.09, 4.71

**8** 4, 6.8, 4.08, 6.354, 5.02

**9** 17, 9.84, 24.19, 24.3, 9.09

**10** 12.5, 17.1, 9.074, 17.08, 9.2

## 6.4 Multiplying decimals by 10, 100 and 1000

To multiply a decimal number by 10 move the digits one place to the left.

For example, $5.6 \times 10 = ?$

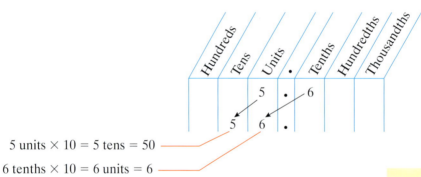

5 units $\times$ 10 = 5 tens = 50

6 tenths $\times$ 10 = 6 units = 6

So $5.6 \times 10 = 56$

> You can write 6 tenths as a
>
> - decimal 0.6
> - fraction $\frac{6}{10}$
>
> There is more about fractions on page 119.

You can use a similar method to show the rules for multiplying decimal numbers by 100 and 1000.

■ **To multiply a decimal number by 10 move each digit one place to the left.**

$25.68 \times 10 = 256.8$

■ **To multiply a decimal number by 100 move the digits two places to the left.**

$36.97 \times 100 = 3697$

■ **To multiply a decimal number by 1000 move the digits three places to the left.**

$0.23 \times 1000 = 230$

## Example 7

Work out

(a) $2.348 \times 100$                            (b) $3.67 \times 1000$

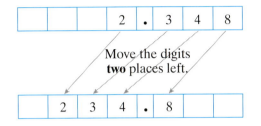 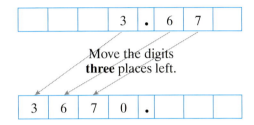

So $2.348 \times 100 = 234.8$           So $3.67 \times 1000 = 3670$

## Example 8

**Without using a calculator** find:

(a) $52.47 \times 10$    (b) $4.83 \times 100$    (c) $2.5 \times 1000$

(a) $52.47 \times 10 = 524.7$        Move the digits 1 place to the left.

(b) $4.83 \times 100 = 483$          Move the digits 2 places to the left.

(c) $2.5 \times 1000 = 2500$        Move the digits 3 places to the left.

## Exercise 6D

Write down the answers to these calculations:

Hint: draw a place value diagram to help you.

**1**   (a) $3.63 \times 10$      (b) $12.4 \times 10$      (c) $0.402 \times 10$
      (d) $0.068 \times 10$    (e) $56.28 \times 10$    (f) $0.03 \times 10$

**2**   (a) $4.72 \times 100$     (b) $21.48 \times 100$    (c) $2.568 \times 1000$
      (d) $5.38 \times 1000$    (e) $4.7 \times 100$      (f) $0.06 \times 1000$

**3**   (a) $0.065 \times 100$    (b) $5.307 \times 10$     (c) $0.0202 \times 100$
      (d) $6.88 \times 1000$    (e) $9.36 \times 10$      (f) $0.0045 \times 1000$

**4**   (a) $98.2 \times 100$     (b) $5.27 \times 1000$    (c) $0.09 \times 10$
      (d) $0.023 \times 100$    (e) $72.54 \times 10$    (f) $18.2 \times 1000$

## 6.5 Dividing decimal numbers by 10, 100 and 1000

To divide a decimal number by 10 move each digit one place to the right.

For example, $83.2 \div 10 = ?$

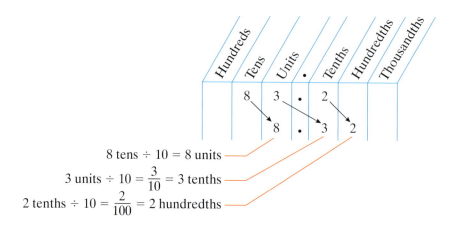

8 tens $\div$ 10 = 8 units

3 units $\div$ 10 = $\frac{3}{10}$ = 3 tenths

2 tenths $\div$ 10 = $\frac{2}{100}$ = 2 hundredths

So $83.2 \div 10 = 8.32$

> You can write 2 hundredths as a
> - decimal 0.02
> - fraction $\frac{2}{100}$

You can use a similar method to show the rules for dividing decimal numbers by 100 and 1000.

■ **To divide a decimal number by 10 move each digit one place to the right.**

$98.72 \div 10 = 9.872$

■ **To divide a decimal number by 100 move each digit two places to the right.**

$26.5 \div 100 = 0.265$

■ **To divide a decimal number by 1000 move each digit three places to the right.**

$536.8 \div 1000 = 0.5368$

$629.5 \div 100$

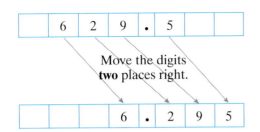

So  $629.5 \div 100 = 6.295$

$4382.7 \div 1000$

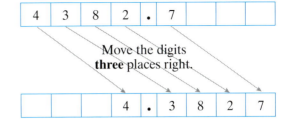

So  $4382.7 \div 1000 = 4.3827$

**Example 9**

**Without using a calculator** find:

**(a)**  $954.5 \div 10$  **(b)**  $15.26 \div 100$  **(c)**  $92.8 \div 1000$

**(a)**  $954.5 \div 10 = 95.45$     Move the digits 1 place to the right.

**(b)**  $15.26 \div 100 = 0.1526$     Move the digits 2 places to the right.

**(c)**  $92.8 \div 1000 = 0.0928$     Move the digits 3 places to the right.

 **Exercise 6E**

Write down the answers to these calculations.

**1**   **(a)** $18.5 \div 10$   **(b)** $175.4 \div 10$   **(c)** $2.84 \div 10$
    **(d)** $563.2 \div 10$   **(e)** $0.075 \div 10$   **(f)** $0.06 \div 10$

**2**   **(a)** $247.2 \div 10$   **(b)** $38.7 \div 10$   **(c)** $1852.4 \div 10$
    **(d)** $816.7 \div 1000$   **(e)** $4.6 \div 100$   **(f)** $12.5 \div 1000$

**3**   **(a)** $84.2 \div 10$   **(b)** $153.61 \div 10$   **(c)** $189.2 \div 100$
    **(d)** $568 \div 1000$   **(e)** $294 \div 100$   **(f)** $36 \div 100$

**4**   **(a)** $17.5 \div 100$   **(b)** $0.68 \div 10$   **(c)** $2.8 \div 100$
    **(d)** $5.2 \div 1000$   **(e)** $0.05 \div 100$   **(f)** $42.8 \div 1000$

# 6.6 Multiplying decimals by whole numbers

### Example 10

Find the cost of 6 books at £5.28 each.

$$
\begin{array}{r}
528 \\
\times \quad 6 \\
\hline
3168 \\
{\scriptstyle 1\,4}
\end{array}
$$

Multiply the numbers together.
Ignore the decimal point.

528 is 100 times 5.28
So 3168 is 100 times the actual cost.
To find the cost divide 3168 by 100.
The cost of the books is £31.68

## Where to put the decimal point

Look at the original question:

$$5.28 \times 6$$

There are 2 digits after
the decimal point.

The answer must also have 2 digits after the decimal point:

$$528 \times 6 = 3168$$

so $\quad 5.28 \times 6 = 31.68$

2 digits

### Example 11

**Without using a calculator** work out $7.16 \times 4$

$$
\begin{array}{r}
716 \\
\times \quad 4 \\
\hline
2864 \\
{\scriptstyle 2}
\end{array}
$$

7.16

2 digits after the
decimal point

The answer is 28.64

## Exercise 6F

Show all your working in these questions.

**1** Find the cost of:

    **(a)** 5 books at £4.37 each.

    **(b)** 4 kg of apples at £0.64 per kg.

    **(c)** 8 chocolate bars at £0.45 each.

    **(d)** 6 packets of crisps at £1.38 each.

**2**   **(a)** $7.8 \times 2$      **(b)** $5.6 \times 4$

    **(c)** $8.4 \times 5$      **(d)** $2.35 \times 3$

    **(e)** $14.6 \times 8$     **(f)** $5.29 \times 6$

**3**   **(a)** $53.67 \times 9$    **(b)** $7.6 \times 5$

    **(c)** $28.63 \times 7$    **(d)** $8.76 \times 5$

    **(e)** $9.25 \times 4$     **(f)** $15.99 \times 8$

**4** Work out the cost of 9 CDs which cost £12.99 each.

**5** Find the total length in metres of seven pieces of wood, each 0.65 metre long.

**6** Work out the total length in metres of six pieces of wire, each 0.34 metre long.

**7** Find the total cost in pounds (£) of three loaves at £0.82 each and eight cakes at £0.55 each.

**8** Calculate the total cost of five cartons of fruit juice which cost £0.70 each and seven packets of biscuits which cost £0.56 each.

## 6.7 Dividing decimals by whole numbers

### Example 12

Four friends share the cost of a meal equally.
The total bill comes to £18.32
How much should they each pay?

You need to work out      $18.32 \div 4$

First put the decimal point
in the answer.                                        Then divide.

$$4\overline{)18\,.\,32}$$                            $$\begin{array}{r} 4\,.\,5\;8 \\ 4\overline{)18\,.^{2}3^{3}2} \end{array}$$

They should each pay £4.58

### Example 13

Without a calculator, work out   **(a)** $36.3 \div 5$   **(b)** $0.24 \div 8$

**(a)**   $$\begin{array}{r} 7\,.\,2\;6 \\ 5\overline{)36\,.^{1}3^{3}0} \end{array}$$     There is a remainder of 3, so put a zero here.
(36.30 has the same value as 36.3)

The answer is 7.26

**(b)**   $$\begin{array}{r} 0\,.\,0\;3 \\ 8\overline{)0\,.\,2^{2}4} \end{array}$$     $2 \div 8 = 0$ remainder 2

The answer is 0.03

### Exercise 6G

Work these out **without a calculator**. Show all your
working.

**1**   Find one share if:
  **(a)** Four people share £5.08 equally.
  **(b)** Seven people share £215.60 equally.
  **(c)** Six people share £10.50 equally.
  **(d)** Eight people share £30.24 equally.

**2**   **(a)** $8.6 \div 2$        **(b)** $5.6 \div 4$        **(c)** $120.5 \div 5$
       **(d)** $187.2 \div 3$      **(e)** $38.82 \div 6$      **(f)** $17.28 \div 8$

**3**  (a)  $0.612 \div 6$  (b)  $0.245 \div 7$  (c)  $1.08 \div 4$

(d)  $0.0057 \div 3$  (e)  $9.054 \div 9$  (f)  $3.75 \div 5$

**4**  10.8 litres of lemonade are poured equally into six jugs.
How much lemonade is in each jug?

**5**  Four people share equally the
cost of hiring a taxi.
The taxi costs £28.60.
How much does each person pay?

**6**  A box of apples weighing 67.5 kg is packed equally
into 9 trays. Work out the weight of apples in each tray.

## Summary of key points

**1**  In a decimal number the decimal point separates
the whole number from the part that is less than
one:

$$20.51$$

20 is the whole
number

.51 is the part
less than one

**2**  When adding or subtracting decimal numbers
always line up the decimal points.

**3**  You can sort decimal numbers in order of size by
comparing first the whole numbers, then the tenths,
then the hundredths, and so on.

**4**  To multiply decimal numbers:
   - by  10 move each digit one   place to the left  $25.68 \times 10 = 256.8$
   - by  100 move each digit two   places to the left  $36.97 \times 100 = 3697$
   - by 1000 move each digit three places to the left  $0.23 \times 1000 = 230$

To divide decimal numbers
   - by  10 move each digit one   place to the right  $98.72 \div 10 = 9.872$
   - by  100 move each digit two   places to the right  $26.5 \div 100 = 0.265$
   - by 1000 move each digit three places to the right  $536.8 \div 1000 = 0.5368$

# 7 Measuring

This unit is about measuring lengths, weights and times.

## 7.1 Measuring lengths and distances

You can measure:

| very short lengths in millimetres (mm) | short lengths in centimetres (cm) | medium lengths in metres (m) | long distances in kilometres (km) |
|---|---|---|---|

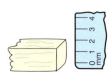 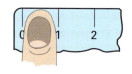 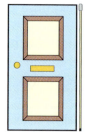 

A matchstick is about 2 mm thick. You can use a ruler to measure very short lengths.

A fingernail is about 1 cm wide. You can use a ruler to measure short lengths.

A door is about 2 m high. You can use a tape measure to measure medium lengths.

Three times round a football pitch is about 1 km. You can use a trundle wheel to measure this.

Millimetres, centimetres, metres and kilometres are all **units** of measurement. A unit is a standard amount, the same everywhere in the world.

## Exercise 7A

1   Give three examples of things you would measure in:

   (**a**) mm      (**b**) cm      (**c**) m      (**d**) km

2   What units would you measure these lengths in?

   (**a**) length of a car                    (**b**) length of a hockey pitch
   (**c**) length of a pencil                 (**d**) length of a river
   (**e**) length of a sheet of paper         (**f**) width of a staple
   (**g**) height of a building               (**h**) thickness of a piece of glass
   (**i**) width of a doorway                 (**j**) length of the M1 motorway
   (**k**) thickness of a coin                (**l**) height of a step

## 7.2  Using a ruler

You can use a ruler to measure in mm and cm.

■   **10 mm = 1 cm**
    **1 mm = 0.1 cm**

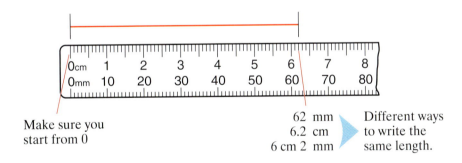

Make sure you
start from 0

62  mm
6.2  cm
6 cm 2  mm

Different ways
to write the
same length.

## Exercise 7B

1   Measure these lines:

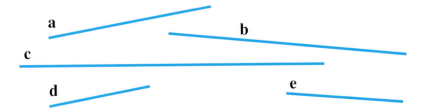

**2**  Draw these lines:

(a)  30 mm      (b)  56 mm      (c)  84 mm
(d)  2.3 cm     (e)  4.9 cm     (f)  6.5 cm
(g)  2 cm 9 mm  (h)  3 cm 4 mm

**3**  Write these lengths as centimetres in decimal form:

(a)  56 mm      (b)  120 mm     (c)  86 mm
(d)  2 cm 4 mm  (e)  10 cm 2 mm (f)  93 mm
(g)  6 cm 7 mm  (h)  7 cm 3 mm

Hint:
22 mm = 2.2 cm

**4**  Write these lengths in mm:

(a)  3.6 cm      (b)  12.8 cm    (c)  7.4 cm
(d)  14 cm 2 mm  (e)  4.3 cm     (f)  36.9 cm
(g)  29 cm 7 mm  (h)  0.4 cm

**5**  Measure these lines as accurately as you can:

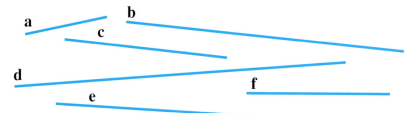

# 7.3 Longer and longer

■  **1 km = 1000 m**

■
$$1 \text{ m} = 100 \text{ cm} = 1000 \text{ mm}$$
$$0.1 \text{ m} = 10 \text{ cm} = 100 \text{ mm}$$
$$0.01 \text{ m} = 1 \text{ cm} = 10 \text{ mm}$$
$$0.001 \text{ m} = 0.1 \text{ cm} = 1 \text{ mm}$$

You can write the same length in several different ways:

| mm | 80 | 90 | 100 | 110 | 120 | 130 |
| cm | 0.8 | 0.9 | 1.0 | 1.1 | 1.2 | 1.3 |

0.87 m is in metres
0 m 87 cm is a mixed length
87 cm is in centimetres
870 mm is in millimetres

1.23 m is in metres
1 m 23 cm is a mixed length
123 cm is in centimetres
1230 mm is in millimetres

**Example 1**

Write 345 cm in as many different ways as you can.

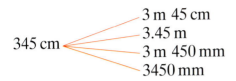

345 cm
- 3 m 45 cm
- 3.45 m
- 3 m 450 mm
- 3450 mm

## Exercise 7C

**1** Write each of these lengths in as many ways as you can.

(a) 726 cm      (b) 9 m 32 cm      (c) 5 m 270 mm

(d) 8230 mm      (e) 3.65 m      (f) 89 cm

(g) 26.9 cm      (h) 3765 mm

**2** Write in metres:

(a) 4 km 320 m          (b) 32 km 428 m

(c) 7 km 560 m          (d) 81 km 205 m

**3** Write in kilometres:

(a) 1526 m          (b) 48 743 m

(c) 201 591 m          (d) 2047 m

**4** **Activity** You need a sheet of A4 paper and a ruler.

(a) Measure the distance around the edge of an A4 sheet of paper.

(b) Fold your piece of paper in half.
Measure the distance around the half piece of paper.

(c) Fold the piece of paper in half again.
Measure the distance around the quarter piece of paper.

(d) What do you notice?

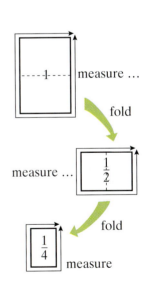

**5** **Activity** You need a metre rule or a tape measure. Find objects in the classroom which are as close as possible to these lengths:

(a) 78 cm      (b) 405 mm      (c) 1250 mm

(d) 7.8 m      (e) 0.7 cm      (f) 2 m 380 mm

(g) 19 cm 5 mm      (h) 3 m 30 cm

## 7.4 Ordering lengths

### Example 2

Write these lengths in order of size, shortest first:

4 m 53 cm    4 m 48 cm    6 m 38 cm    2 m 31 cm

First sort using the number of metres:

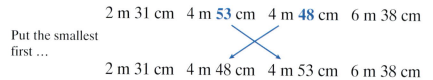

Put the smallest first …

2 m 31 cm    4 m 53 cm    4 m 48 cm    6 m 38 cm

4 m 53 cm and 4 m 48 cm have the same number of metres, so look at the number of centimetres:

2 m 31 cm    4 m **53** cm    4 m **48** cm    6 m 38 cm

Put the smallest first …

2 m 31 cm    4 m 48 cm    4 m 53 cm    6 m 38 cm

### Exercise 7D

1   William's six jumps in the long jump final were:

8 m 17 cm    7 m 94 cm    8 m 09 cm    7 m 87 cm
7 m 81 cm    8 m 03 cm

(a) Write these lengths in order of size.

(b) Which was his longest jump?

2   The table shows the six throws of competitors in a discus event.

| Name | 1st throw | 2nd throw | 3rd throw | 4th throw | 5th throw | 6th throw |
|---|---|---|---|---|---|---|
| Helena | 32.95 m | 27.64 m | 34.06 m | 29.85 m | 34.19 m | 27.94 m |
| Fatima | 33.14 m | 32.94 m | 26.85 m | 33.98 m | 33.94 m | 31.94 m |
| Dionne | 35.14 m | 35.86 m | 32.30 m | 32.30 m | 24.15 m | 36.17 m |
| Sarah | 24.83 m | 27.63 m | 30.04 m | 30.06 m | 34.24 m | 26.39 m |
| Elspeth | 26.49 m | 37.04 m | 33.46 m | 25.38 m | 22.49 m | 28.86 m |

The competitor who throws the furthest wins the event.

**(a)** Write down the longest throw for each woman.

**(b)** Copy and complete the table to find the position of each woman in the event.

| Position | Name | Longest throw |
|---|---|---|
| 1$^{st}$ | | |
| 2$^{nd}$ | | |
| 3$^{rd}$ | | |
| 4$^{th}$ | | |
| 5$^{th}$ | | |

**3** Put these lengths in order of size:

230 cm   2 m 25 cm   2060 mm   1 m 97 cm   2 m 9 mm

Hint: write each length in the same way then sort them.

## 7.5 Measuring weights

You can measure weights in:

Milligrams …       … grams (g)       … kilograms (kg)       … tonnes (t).

My dear Karen,
I write to you about a very weighty matter …

FINE SUGAR
1kg

A grain of sand weighs about 1 mg

A sheet of A4 paper weighs about 1g

A bag of sugar weighs 1 kg

A small car weighs about 1 t.

## Exercise 7E

**1** In what units would you measure these objects?
Use mg, g, kg or t.

**(a)** a sweet          **(b)** a bicycle     **(c)** a van

**(d)** a robin          **(e)** a goose       **(f)** a hippopotamus

**(g)** a grain of sugar **(h)** a brick       **(i)** this textbook

**(j)** a slipper        **(k)** a sock        **(l)** a hair

**(m)** a jacket         **(n)** a piano       **(o)** a spoon

**(p)** a snowflake      **(q)** a chair       **(r)** a cupboard

**2** Write down four things you would weigh in each of these units:

(a) milligrams  (b) grams
(c) kilograms  (d) tonnes

## 7.6 Mixing weights

■ 1000 mg = 1 g
 1000 g  = 1 kg
 1000 kg = 1 t

### Example 3

(a) Write 2360 g as a mixed weight.
(b) Write 4028 mg as a mixed weight.

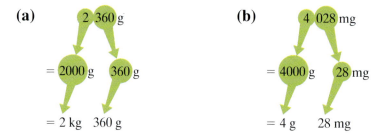

### Example 4

Ian bought a chicken weighing 1 kg 315 g, a packet of stuffing weighing 254 g and a $2\frac{1}{2}$ kg bag of potatoes.

What was the total weight of the three items?

Write each weight in kilograms as decimal numbers:

$$1\,\text{kg}\ 315\,\text{g} \rightarrow 1.315\,\text{kg}$$
$$254\,\text{g} \rightarrow 0.254\,\text{kg}$$
$$2\tfrac{1}{2}\,\text{kg} \rightarrow 2.5\,\text{kg}$$

Add the decimals:

$$
\begin{array}{r}
1.315 \\
0.254 \\
+\ 2.5 \\
\hline
4.069
\end{array}
$$

The total weight of the three items was 4.069 kg or 4 kg 69 g

## Exercise 7F

**1** Write down in grams **and** kilograms:

    **(a)** 3 kg 250 g     **(b)** 6 kg 200 g     **(c)** 9 kg 420 g

    **(d)** 3 kg 50 g     **(e)** 10 kg 350 g     **(f)** 20 kg 5 g

    **(g)** 30 000 mg     **(h)** 25 500 mg     **(i)** 14 050 mg

**2** Write each of these weights in two different ways:

    **(a)** 2750 g     **(b)** 3500 g     **(c)** 7570 kg

    **(d)** 1050 kg     **(e)** 10 024 g     **(f)** 4006 g

    **(g)** 3.455 kg     **(h)** 7.050 kg     **(i)** 16.45 kg

    **(j)** 20.02 kg     **(k)** 15.325 g     **(l)** 1.245 t

**3** What is the total weight of shopping in each basket?

**(a)**     **(b)** 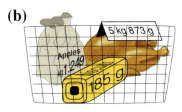    **(c)**

**4** A lorry has a maximum weight limit of 5 tonnes.
Which of these objects can be carried by the lorry in
one load?

    crate      drum      girder      cage      casting

    1.75 tonnes    987 kg      2 tonnes 465 kg    1.259 tonnes    2.394 tonnes

Find all the possible combinations.

# 7.7 Reading scales

The division marks on a scale may not go up 1 at a time.
Sometimes the divisions are 2 units, sometimes 5 units,
sometimes 10, 25 or 50 units.

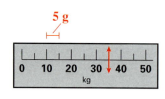

Each division on this scale
represents 10 g.
The scale shows 270 g.

Each division on this scale
represents 5 kg.
The scale shows 35 kg.

## Exercise 7G

For each scale:
- what does each division represent?
- what weight does the scale show?

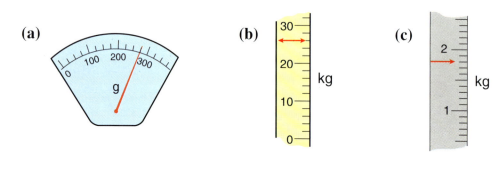

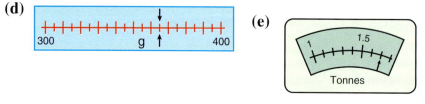

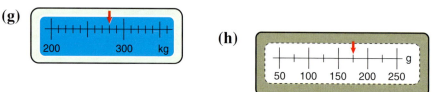

## 7.8  What time is it?

### The 24-hour clock

This clock shows 9 o'clock:

9 o'clock in the morning is 9 am

9 o'clock in the evening is 9 pm

**am**  ante **m**eridiem
before midday

**pm**  **p**ost **m**eridiem
after midday

Hint: a comes
before p in the
alphabet.

- **You use am for times between midnight and midday.**

- **You use pm for times after midday and up to midnight.**

This video clock uses the 24-hour clock

This shows 9:30 am

This shows 9:30 pm

The 24-hour clock works like this:

**12-hour clock times** use **am** or **pm** to show whether a time is before or after midday

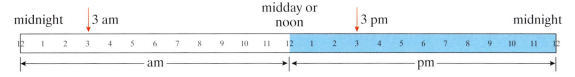

**24-hour clock times** number the hours from **0** to **23**

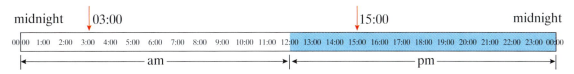

24-hour clock times must have 4 digits.
The first two digits show the hours.
The last two digits show the minutes.

■  **To change 12-hour times to 24-hour times:**

| Up to 12 noon the times are the same:<br><br>8:30 am → 08:30<br><br>24-hour time always has 4 digits | After 12 noon add 12 to the hour number:<br><br>2:57 pm → 14:57<br><br>+ 12<br><br>**except** for times from midnight to 1 am. These start with 00<br><br>12:35 am → 00:35 |
|---|---|

### Exercise 7H

**1**  Change to 24-hour clock time:
  (**a**) 8:00 am    (**b**) 8:35 pm    (**c**) 11:20 am    (**d**) 1:30 pm
  (**e**) 3:45 pm    (**f**) 4:15 pm    (**g**) 9:15 pm    (**h**) 10:00 pm
  (**i**) 11:15 pm    (**j**) midday    (**k**) 12:20 pm    (**l**) 12:35 am

**2**  Write these times as 24-hour clock times:
  (**a**) Quarter past six in the morning.  (**b**) Half past two in the afternoon.
  (**c**) Quarter to ten in the morning.    (**d**) Ten to six in the evening.

**3**  Change to 12-hour clock time:
  (**a**) 11:00    (**b**) 14:45    (**c**) 17:36    (**d**) 03:50
  (**e**) 08:15    (**f**) 21:38    (**g**) 23:17    (**h**) 00:30
  (**i**) 18:23    (**j**) 07:15    (**k**) 12:48    (**l**) 00:47

## 7.9  How long will it take?

■  **60 minutes = 1 hour**

When you are calculating times remember: there are 60 minutes in an hour **not** 100!

### Example 5

Nina takes 10 minutes to walk to the bus stop. She waits 5 minutes for the bus to arrive. She is on the bus for 50 minutes.
How long does Nina's journey take altogether?

Add the times together:

10 + 5 + 50 = 65 minutes

It takes 1 hour and 5 minutes altogether.

**Example 6**

Joe started work at 9:15 am and finished at 12:20 pm.
How long was Joe working?

You can work it out like this:

9:15 am        10:00 am        12:00 pm        12:20 pm

     add 45 minutes      add 2 hours      add 20 minutes

45 minutes + 2 hours + 20 minutes
   = 2 hours + 65 minutes
   = 3 hours and 5 minutes

He worked for 3 hours and 5 minutes.

**Exercise 7I**

**1**   Sue spends 25 minutes doing French homework, 36 minutes doing maths homework and 20 minutes doing geography homework.
How long did Sue spend doing her homework?

**2**   Vijay went on holiday. He travelled on the underground for 35 minutes. He waited in the airport for 55 minutes. The flight took 1 hour 50 minutes. The taxi to the hotel took 20 minutes.
How long did Vijay's journey take altogether?

**3**   The train takes 1 hour 31 minutes to travel from London to Eastbourne.
A train leaves London at 3:48 pm.
What time does it arrive in Eastbourne?

**4**   A History lesson is 50 minutes long.
The lesson starts at 1:25 pm. What time does it finish?

**5**   It takes Naomi 20 minutes to walk to school.
What time must she leave home to arrive by five past nine?

**6** Here is a list of jobs Gary must do this weekend.

Gary has $2\frac{1}{4}$ hours free on Saturday to complete some of the jobs.

(a) Which jobs can he do on Saturday to use up all $2\frac{1}{4}$ hours?

(b) How much time does he need to spend on Sunday to complete the jobs?

| Mow the lawn | 35 min |
| Wash the car | 20 min |
| Hoover the house | 40 min |
| Paint a door | 1 hour 10 min |
| Dust | 25 min |

## 7.10 Using timetables

This timetable shows when trains go from Morecambe to Southport in the morning:

| Morecambe | 0630 | 0730 | 0830 |
| Lancaster | 0650 | 0800 | 0900 |
| Preston | 0740 | 0900 | |
| Southport | 0850 | 0940 | 1040 |

The trains leave Morecambe at 0630, 0730 and 0830.

The 0730 train leaves Preston at 0900.

The 0830 train does not stop at Preston.

The trains arrive in Southport at these times.

### Example 7

Using the timetable:

(a) What time is the earliest train from Morecambe?

(b) What time does the 0730 train from Morecambe arrive in Lancaster?

(c) How long does the 0830 train from Morecambe take to get to Southport?

(a) The earliest train is at 0630.

(b) The 0730 train arrives in Lancaster at 0800.

(c) The 0830 train gets to Southport at 1040.

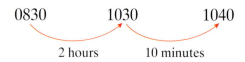

0830     1030     1040

2 hours     10 minutes

The train takes 2 hours 10 minutes.

## Exercise 7J

**1**  Here is part of a bus timetable:

| Hertford  | 0730 | 0850 | 0940 | 1055 |
|-----------|------|------|------|------|
| Hoddesdon | 0746 | 0906 | 0956 | 1111 |
| Nazeing   | 0759 | 0919 | 1009 | 1124 |
| Harlow    | 0820 | 0940 | 1030 | 1045 |

**(a)** What time does the second bus leave Hertford?

**(b)** What time does the 0940 bus from Hertford arrive at Harlow?

**(c)** A bus arrives in Harlow at 1045. When did it leave Hoddesdon?

**(d)** How long does the journey from Hoddesdon to Nazeing take?

**(e)** If I *just* miss the 0956 bus from Hoddesdon, how long will I have to wait for the next bus?

**2**  Here is part of a train timetable:

| Derby       | ---- | 0729 | 0802 | ---- | 0854 |
|-------------|------|------|------|------|------|
| Spondon     | ---- | 0734 | ---- | ---- | ---- |
| Long Eaton  | ---- | 0741 | 0811 | ---- | 0904 |
| Attenborough| 0736 | 0747 | 0817 | 0834 | ---- |
| Beeston     | 0740 | 0751 | ---- | 0837 | ---- |
| Nottingham  | 0745 | 0800 | 0824 | 0843 | 0910 |

**(a)** Which train takes the least time to travel between Derby and Nottingham?

**(b)** Which train is the last I could catch from Attenborough to be in Nottingham by 0830?

**(c)** Which trains from Attenborough stop at Beeston?

**(d)** I arrive at Derby at 0740. How could I get to Beeston?

**3**  Here is part of a train timetable:

| Kemble     | 1534 | 1634 | 1726 | 1815 |
|------------|------|------|------|------|
| Stroud     | 1549 | 1649 | 1741 | 1830 |
| Stonehouse | 1554 | 1654 | 1746 | 1835 |
| Gloucester | 1607 | 1708 | 1801 | 1847 |
| Cheltenham | 1620 | 1719 | ---- | 1906 |

**(a)** What time does the 1634 train from Kemble arrive at Stonehouse?

**(b)** I want to arrive in Gloucester before 6 pm. Which trains could I catch from Kemble?

**(c)** How long does the 1649 from Stroud take to reach Cheltenham?

**(d)** Which train travels between Stroud and Gloucester in the shortest time?

**(e)** I leave work in Kemble at 5 pm. What is the earliest I can arrive by train in Cheltenham?

**4** Here is part of a railway timetable:

| Birmingham | 2250 | 0524 | 0615 | ---- |
|---|---|---|---|---|
| Coventry | 2310 | 0546 | ---- | ---- |
| Rugby | 2324 | 0600 | ---- | 0650 |
| Milton Keynes | 0003 | 0625 | ---- | 0714 |
| Watford | 0039 | 0649 | 0734 | 0739 |
| London Euston | 0105 | 0710 | 0754 | 0800 |

(a) What time does the 2250 train from Birmingham arrive in London?

(b) How long does the journey take?

(c) Which train from Coventry arrives at Watford at 0649?

(d) The 0615 from Birmingham is running 35 minutes late. What time does it arrive at London Euston?

(e) I get off the 0546 from Coventry at Milton Keynes. How long is it until the next train to London?

## Summary of key points

**1** 10 mm = 1 cm
1 mm = 0.1 cm

**2** 1 km = 1000 m

**3**
$$1\,m = 100\,cm = 1000\,mm$$
$$0.1\,m = 10\,cm = 100\,mm$$
$$0.01\,m = 1\,cm = 10\,mm$$
$$0.001\,m = 0.1\,cm = 1\,mm$$

**4** 1000 mg = 1 g
1000 g = 1 kg
1000 kg = 1 t

**5** You use am for times between midnight and midday.

**6** You use pm for times after midday and up to midnight.

**7** To change 12-hour time to 24-hour time:

8:30 am → 08:30      24-hour time always has 4 digits.

11:25 am → 11:25     The 4 digits stay the same.

2:57 pm → 14:57      For pm times add twelve to the number of hours.

12:35 am → 00:35     Times between midnight and 1 am start with 00.

**8** 60 minutes = 1 hour

# 8 Fractions

All these things are divided into equal parts called **fractions**:

This symbol has two halves.

One part is **one half** or $\frac{1}{2}$ of the symbol.

This swimming pool has four lanes.

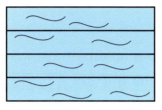

Each lane is **one quarter** or $\frac{1}{4}$ of the pool.

This pie has eight slices.

Each slice is **one eighth** or $\frac{1}{8}$ of the pie.

## 8.1 Using numbers to represent fractions

Three quarters or $\frac{3}{4}$ of this garden is grass:

■ The top number shows 3 parts are grass.

The top number is the **numerator**.

$$\frac{3}{4}$$

The bottom number shows the garden has 4 equal parts.

The bottom number is the **denominator**.

### Example 1

Write down the fraction that is shaded.

(a)

(b)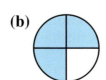

(a) $\frac{2}{5}$

(b) $\frac{3}{4}$

**When is a fraction not a fraction?**

Each slice is the same size. Each slice is $\frac{1}{3}$ or **one third**.

These slices are unequal. They are **not** thirds.

## Exercise 8A

1    Write down the fraction that is shaded.

(a) 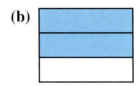    (b)     (c) 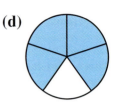    (d)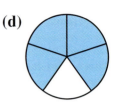

2    (a)  What is the numerator of the fraction $\frac{5}{6}$?
     (b)  What is the denominator of the fraction $\frac{3}{10}$?

3    For each shape write down
     • the fraction that is shaded
     • the fraction that is unshaded.

(a)     (b) 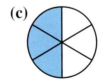    (c)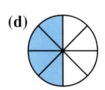

4    For each circle, write down the fraction that is shaded.

(a) 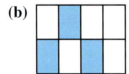    (b) 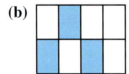    (c) 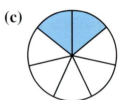    (d)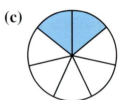

Notice that all four fractions represent the **same** amount of the circle.

5    Each shape is divided into a number of equal parts.
     Copy each shape and shade the fraction marked by it.
     Describe in words what fraction is unshaded.

(a)  $\frac{5}{8}$    (b) 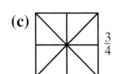 $\frac{1}{3}$    (c) $\frac{3}{4}$

6  **(a)** Copy this shape and shade in $\frac{2}{3}$ of it.

   **(b)** On another copy, shade $\frac{3}{5}$ of the shape.

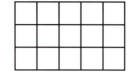

7  This number line shows three fifths. Draw a number line to show seven tenths.

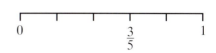

8  Lucy bought a bag of nuts. She kept three eighths of the nuts and gave the rest to her brother. What fraction did she give her brother?


## 8.2 Mixed numbers and improper fractions

Sometimes whole numbers and fractions are combined.

■ **A mixed number has a whole number part and a fraction part,** for example $1\frac{3}{4}$.

A mixed number can be written as a top heavy fraction. For example:

mixed number $1\frac{3}{4} = \frac{7}{4}$ top heavy

$\frac{7}{4}$ is top heavy because 7 is greater than 4

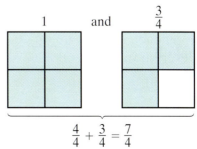

■ **Top heavy fractions are also called improper fractions. The numerator (top) is greater than the denominator (bottom).** For example $\frac{7}{4}$.

■ **A vulgar fraction's numerator is less than its denominator.** For example $\frac{3}{4}$.

Vulgar fractions are more common than improper fractions.

Vulgar comes from the Latin word *vulgaris* meaning common.

### Exercise 8B

1  Write down whether these fractions are:
   ● vulgar
   ● improper
   ● mixed numbers.

   (a) $1\frac{2}{3}$      (b) $\frac{7}{2}$      (c) $3\frac{4}{5}$      (d) $\frac{1}{7}$

   (e) $2\frac{1}{4}$      (f) $\frac{6}{4}$      (g) $\frac{2}{5}$      (h) $\frac{4}{9}$

   (i) $\frac{11}{2}$      (j) $5\frac{1}{2}$      (k) $\frac{3}{2}$      (l) $\frac{2}{3}$

2  Notice that   $1 = \frac{1}{1} = \frac{2}{2} = \frac{3}{3} = \frac{4}{4}$

   Copy and complete this with three more examples:

   $1 = \frac{8}{8} = \underline{\phantom{--}} = \underline{\phantom{--}} = \underline{\phantom{--}}$

## 8.3  Finding a fraction of a quantity

Sometimes you need to find a fraction of a quantity.

■ **You can think of the bottom part of a fraction as a division.** For example:

   **to find** $\frac{1}{2}$ **divide by 2**
   **to find** $\frac{1}{3}$ **divide by 3**
   **to find** $\frac{1}{4}$ **divide by 4**

### Example 2

Find $\frac{1}{5}$ of 30.

To find one fifth of 30, divide by 5.

   $30 \div 5 = 6$   so   $\frac{1}{5}$ of 30 is 6

$30 \div 5$ can also be written as $\frac{30}{5}$

You often have to find fractions of amounts of money, weights, times and lengths.

## Example 3

Find $\frac{1}{4}$ of 32p.

To find $\frac{1}{4}$ divide by 4

$32p \div 4 = 8p$   so   $\frac{1}{4}$ of 32p is 8p

> $32 \div 4$ can also be written as $\frac{32}{4}$

When you find a fraction of a quantity you won't always get a whole number answer.

## Example 4

Find $\frac{1}{4}$ of 3 cakes.

$3$ cakes $\div 4 = \frac{3}{4}$ of a cake

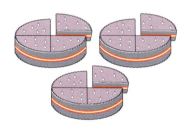

## Example 5

Divide 4 rolls equally between 3 children.

How many rolls do they get each?

The children each get one whole roll.
The fourth roll is cut into thirds.

$4 \div 3 = \frac{4}{3}$ or $1\frac{1}{3}$.   They each get $1\frac{1}{3}$ rolls.

## Exercise 8C

**1**   Find:

(a) $\frac{1}{3}$ of 12        (b) $\frac{1}{8}$ of 16        (c) $\frac{1}{4}$ of 36

(d) $\frac{1}{5}$ of 8         (e) $\frac{1}{6}$ of 5

**2** Find:

(a) $\frac{1}{3}$ of 24 records      (b) $\frac{1}{5}$ of £45

(c) $\frac{1}{4}$ of 60 kilograms      (d) $\frac{1}{4}$ of 120 minutes

(e) $\frac{1}{5}$ of 300 cm      (f) $\frac{1}{10}$ of 230p

**3** If you divide 5 oranges equally between 3 children how many oranges do they each get?

**4** Mrs Shah shares 7 bars of chocolate equally between her 4 children.
How many bars do they each get?

## 8.4 Finding more than one part

To find three quarters $\left(\frac{3}{4}\right)$ of something first find one quarter, then multiply one quarter by three.

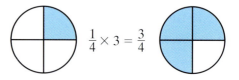

$\frac{1}{4} \times 3 = \frac{3}{4}$

### Example 6

Find $\frac{3}{4}$ of 24.

First find $\frac{1}{4}$ of 24.

     $\frac{1}{4}$ of 24    is    $24 \div 4 = 6$

If $\frac{1}{4}$ of 24 is 6    then    $\frac{3}{4}$ of 24 is    $6 \times 3 = 18$

> Here is another method:
> Find 3 lots of 24
>      $3 \times 24 = 72$
> Then find one quarter of 72
>      $72 \div 4 = 18$

### Example 7

Find $\frac{4}{5}$ of £30.

First find $\frac{1}{5}$ of £30.

     $\frac{1}{5}$ of £30    is    $£30 \div 5 = £6$

If $\frac{1}{5}$ of £30 is £6    then    $\frac{4}{5}$ of £30 is    $£6 \times 4 = £24$

■ **To find $\frac{4}{5}$ of an amount, divide by 5 then multiply by 4.**

## Exercise 8D

**1** Find:

    **(a)** $\frac{3}{4}$ of 24         **(b)** $\frac{2}{3}$ of 60         **(c)** $\frac{2}{5}$ of 35

**2** Find:

    **(a)** $\frac{5}{6}$ of 60 minutes     **(b)** $\frac{3}{4}$ of 200p     **(c)** $\frac{3}{5}$ of 100 cents

**3** $\frac{3}{5}$ of the 250 people at a disco are girls.

    **(a)** How many girls are at the disco?

    **(b)** How many boys are at the disco?

**4** Maureen and David are shopping for a picnic. They have £36. They spend $\frac{1}{6}$ of the money on drinks and $\frac{2}{3}$ of the money on snacks.

    How much do they spend on:

    **(a)** drinks

    **(b)** snacks?

**5** Akila and Andrew both get £5 pocket money each week.

    Akila spends $\frac{2}{5}$ of her money on magazines.

    Andrew spends $\frac{3}{10}$ of his money on sweets.

    **(a)** How much does Akila spend on magazines?

    **(b)** How much does Andrew spend on sweets?

**6** Steven has a dog called K9. He spends $\frac{3}{8}$ of his weekly shopping bill of £32 on food for K9. How much does he spend on K9?

**7** Morgan has a company car. His total annual mileage is 12 000 miles. $\frac{5}{8}$ of this mileage is for work.

    **(a)** How many miles does he travel for work?

    **(b)** What fraction of his 12 000 miles is for his personal use?

## 8.5 Equivalent fractions

Each of these chocolate bars is divided up a different way.
Dominic, Gary, Emma and Anne all eat the same amount.

Dominic eats $\frac{1}{2}$    Gary eats $\frac{2}{4}$    Emma eats $\frac{3}{6}$    Anne eats $\frac{4}{8}$

Notice that $\frac{1}{2}$ a bar is the same as $\frac{2}{4}$, $\frac{3}{6}$ or $\frac{4}{8}$ of a bar.

$\frac{1}{2}$, $\frac{2}{4}$, $\frac{3}{6}$ and $\frac{4}{8}$ all represent the same amount.

They are all **equivalent fractions.**

> **Equivalent** just means having the same value.

■ **Equivalent fractions have the same value.**
   For example, $\frac{2}{3} = \frac{4}{6} = \frac{6}{9} = \frac{8}{12}$

### Example 8

Draw a diagram to show that $\frac{3}{9} = \frac{1}{3}$

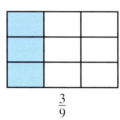    =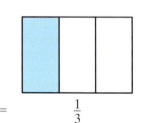

$\frac{3}{9}$    =    $\frac{1}{3}$

You can find equivalent fractions by multiplying the numerator and denominator of a fraction by the same number.

$\frac{1}{2}$    | 1 multiplied by 3 is 3 | | 2 multiplied by 3 is 6 |    $\frac{3}{6}$

so    $\frac{1}{2} = \frac{3}{6}$

You can also find equivalent fractions by dividing the numerator and denominator of a fraction by the same number.

$\frac{3}{6}$    | 3 divided by 3 is 1 | | 6 divided by 3 is 2 |    $\frac{1}{2}$

so    $\frac{3}{6} = \frac{1}{2}$

$\frac{1}{2}$ is the **simplest form** of the fraction $\frac{3}{6}$.
There is no equivalent fraction with smaller numbers on the top and bottom.

**Example 9**

Find an equivalent fraction in sixths for $\frac{2}{3}$

$$\frac{2}{3} \xlongequal{\times 2} \frac{4}{6}$$

**Example 10**

Find an equivalent fraction in fifths for $\frac{4}{10}$

$$\frac{4}{10} \xlongequal{\div 2} \frac{2}{5}$$

Notice that 2 is a factor of 4 and 10. There is more about factors on page 71

## Exercise 8E

1   Draw 4 squares the same size. Use them to show that $\frac{1}{2} = \frac{2}{4} = \frac{3}{6} = \frac{4}{8}$

Label each square with its fraction.

2   Copy and complete these fractions:

   (a) $\frac{1}{2} = \frac{}{4}$    (b) $\frac{1}{3} = \frac{}{12}$    (c) $\frac{1}{} = \frac{3}{6}$    (d) $\frac{3}{8} = \frac{9}{}$

3   Using diagrams (or any other way) find four fractions equivalent to $\frac{1}{3}$

4   John wants to share a chocolate bar between 3 people. What fraction will each person get if:

   **(a)** it is split into 12 parts    **(b)** it is split into 9 parts    **(c)** it is split into 15 parts

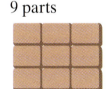 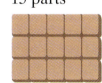

5   Andrew, Sharon and Rotna each made a cake the same size. Andrew cut his into 12 equal pieces, Sharon cut hers into 8 equal pieces and Rotna cut hers into 4 equal pieces.
   Each offered a friend exactly the same amount. Draw diagrams to show what amount this could be and describe it in words. What other amounts could you have chosen?

**6** Mary has $\frac{2}{3}$ of a bar of nougat. Keith has $\frac{4}{6}$ of an identical bar.

Are the following sentences true or false?

**(a)** Mary has more nougat than Keith.

**(b)** Keith has more nougat than Mary.

**(c)** They have the same amount of nougat.

**(d)** Keith has twice the amount of nougat as Mary.

**(e)** Keith has smaller pieces of nougat but the same amount as Mary.

**7** Pick out three equivalent fractions from this group:

$$\frac{1}{2} \qquad \frac{1}{3} \qquad \frac{3}{4} \qquad \frac{3}{6} \qquad \frac{2}{4} \qquad \frac{4}{10}$$

## 8.6 Adding and subtracting fractions

It is easy to add and subtract fractions when the denominator (bottom) is the same:

| **Adding** | | **Subtracting** | |
|---|---|---|---|
| 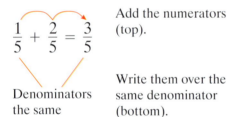 $\frac{1}{5} + \frac{2}{5} = \frac{3}{5}$ | Add the numerators (top). | $\frac{4}{5} - \frac{2}{5} = \frac{2}{5}$ $\quad 4 - 2 = 2$ | |
| Denominators the same | Write them over the same denominator (bottom). | | Keep the same denominator. |

■ **To add (or subtract) fractions with the same denominator add (or subtract) the numerators. Write the result over the same denominator.**

### Exercise 8F

**1** Add these fractions:

**(a)** $\frac{1}{5} + \frac{2}{5}$    **(b)** $\frac{3}{10} + \frac{1}{10}$    **(c)** $\frac{2}{9} + \frac{5}{9}$    **(d)** $\frac{1}{3} + \frac{2}{3}$

**(e)** Discuss your answer to part **(d)** with your neighbour.

**2**  Work out these additions:

(a) $1\frac{3}{4} + \frac{3}{4}$    (b) $\frac{4}{7} + \frac{5}{7}$    (c) $\frac{3}{5} + 2\frac{4}{5}$

**Remember:**
You can write 1 as any fraction where the top and bottom are the same:

$1 = \frac{1}{1} = \frac{2}{2} = \frac{3}{3} \cdots$

**3**  Work out these subtractions:

(a) $1 - \frac{1}{2}$    (b) $1 - \frac{3}{4}$    (c) $1 - \frac{2}{5}$

(d) $\frac{4}{5} - \frac{1}{5}$    (e) $\frac{5}{6} - \frac{1}{6}$    (f) $\frac{5}{8} - \frac{3}{8}$

**4**  Diana eats $\frac{2}{9}$ of a packet of Yum Yums and Gina eats $\frac{5}{9}$ of the packet.

(a)  What fraction do they eat altogether?

(b)  What fraction is left?

**5**  Paul's family eats $\frac{5}{8}$ of a pizza and leaves the rest for him. What fraction is this?

## 8.7  Adding and subtracting fractions with different denominators

$\frac{1}{2}$ and $\frac{1}{4}$ have **different denominators**.

To add them find equivalent fractions with the **same denominators**.

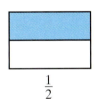

$$\frac{1}{2} \quad = \quad \frac{2}{4}$$

$\frac{1}{2}$ is equivalent to $\frac{2}{4}$

So  $\frac{1}{2} + \frac{1}{4} = \frac{2}{4} + \frac{1}{4} = \frac{3}{4}$

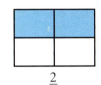

$$\frac{2}{4} \quad + \quad \frac{1}{4} \quad = \quad \frac{3}{4}$$

### Example 11

Work out $\frac{1}{3} + \frac{1}{5}$

$$\frac{1}{3} + \frac{1}{5} = \frac{5}{15} + \frac{3}{15} = \frac{8}{15}$$

  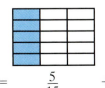  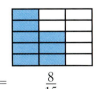

$$\frac{1}{3} \quad + \quad \frac{1}{5} \quad = \quad \frac{5}{15} \quad + \quad \frac{3}{15} \quad = \quad \frac{8}{15}$$

■ **To add (or subtract) fractions with different denominators find equivalent fractions with the same denominators.**

---

**Example 12**

Work out $\frac{1}{3} + \frac{1}{4}$

Notice that 3 and 4 are factors of 12.

$\frac{1}{3} = \frac{4}{12}$  and  $\frac{1}{4} = \frac{3}{12}$

So  $\frac{1}{3} + \frac{1}{4} = \frac{4}{12} + \frac{3}{12} = \frac{7}{12}$

---

**Example 13**

Work out $\frac{2}{5} - \frac{1}{4}$

4 and 5 are factors of 20.

$\frac{2}{5} = \frac{8}{20}$  and  $\frac{1}{4} = \frac{5}{20}$

So  $\frac{2}{5} - \frac{1}{4} = \frac{8}{20} - \frac{5}{20} = \frac{3}{20}$

---

## Exercise 8G

**1** Work out:

    **(a)** $\frac{1}{4} + \frac{1}{8}$
    **(b)** $\frac{1}{3} + \frac{1}{6}$
    **(c)** $\frac{2}{5} - \frac{3}{10}$

    **(d)** $\frac{2}{9} + \frac{1}{18}$
    **(e)** $\frac{3}{4} + \frac{1}{20}$
    **(f)** $\frac{1}{5} - \frac{1}{6}$

    **(g)** $\frac{2}{3} - \frac{1}{4}$
    **(h)** $\frac{3}{8} + \frac{1}{2}$
    **(i)** $\frac{1}{6} + \frac{2}{9}$

**2** An architect is designing a play area. $\frac{1}{3}$ of the area will be used as a swimming pool and $\frac{1}{5}$ as tennis courts.

    **(a)** How much of the area has the architect used?

    **(b)** How much space does the architect have left? Explain how you worked this out.

**3** On Angela and Ian's stall $\frac{1}{4}$ of the space is used for vegetables and $\frac{3}{10}$ is used for fruit.

    **(a)** What fraction of the space has been used up?

    **(b)** The rest is used for flowers. What fraction is this? Show how you worked out your answer.

## 8.8 Comparing fractions

You can compare fractions with different denominators to see which is the largest.

### Example 14

Jane and Henry ran in a marathon. Jane ran $\frac{2}{3}$ of the way and Henry ran $\frac{3}{4}$ of the way.

Who ran the furthest?

Rewrite the fractions so they both have the same denominator.

$\frac{2}{3}$ and $\frac{3}{4}$ can both be rewritten with a denominator of 12.

$$\text{Jane} \quad \frac{2}{3} \overset{\times 4}{\underset{\times 4}{=}} \frac{8}{12} \qquad \text{Henry} \quad \frac{3}{4} \overset{\times 3}{\underset{\times 3}{=}} \frac{9}{12}$$

$\frac{9}{12}$ is larger than $\frac{8}{12}$ so $\frac{3}{4}$ is larger than $\frac{2}{3}$

Henry ran further than Jane.

### Exercise 8H

1   Tom feeds both his cats the same tinned food.
    Each day Christobel eats $\frac{3}{8}$ of a tin and Tiny eats $\frac{1}{2}$ a tin.
    Which cat eats more food?

2   Would you prefer $\frac{2}{5}$ of a bag of sweets or $\frac{3}{10}$ of the same bag of sweets? Show your working.

3   Are the following statements true or false? Show your working.
    (a) $\frac{12}{15}$ is 3 times as big as $\frac{3}{5}$
    (b) $\frac{3}{5}$ is smaller than $\frac{12}{15}$
    (c) $\frac{12}{15}$ is equivalent to $\frac{3}{5}$
    (d) $\frac{3}{5}$ is larger than $\frac{12}{15}$

4   Put the following fractions in order of size, smallest first:
    (a) $\frac{2}{3}, \frac{3}{5}, \frac{4}{15}$          (b) $\frac{3}{10}, \frac{2}{15}, \frac{1}{2}$

## Summary of key points

1   You can use numbers to represent a fraction:

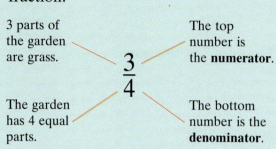

3 parts of the garden are grass.

The garden has 4 equal parts.

$\dfrac{3}{4}$

The top number is the **numerator**.

The bottom number is the **denominator**.

2   A mixed number has a whole number part and a fraction part, for example $1\frac{3}{4}$

3   Top heavy fractions are also called improper fractions. The numerator (top) is greater than the denominator (bottom), for example $\frac{7}{4}$

4   A vulgar fraction's numerator is less than its denominator, for example $\frac{3}{4}$

5   You can think of the bottom part of a fraction as a division. For example:

to find $\frac{1}{2}$ divide by 2

to find $\frac{1}{3}$ divide by 3

to find $\frac{1}{4}$ divide by 4

6   To find $\frac{4}{5}$ of an amount, divide by 5 then multiply by 4.

7   Equivalent fractions have the same value, for example, $\frac{2}{3} = \frac{4}{6} = \frac{6}{9} = \frac{8}{12}$

8   To add (or subtract) fractions with the same denominator, add (or subtract) the numerators. Write the result over the same denominator.

9   To add (or subtract) fractions with different denominators find equivalent fractions with the same denominators.

# 9 Working with algebra

Algebra is a branch of mathematics in which letters are used to represent numbers.

You can use it to solve many mathematical problems.

If phonecalls cost 20p a minute you can find the cost of a call using this algebra:

$$c = 20 \times t$$

cost in pence = 20p × time in minutes

Quite complicated algebra can be used to calculate the speed at which a skydiver falls, and to work out when to open the parachute.

## 9.1 Using letters to represent numbers

You can use letters to represent numbers even when you don't know what the numbers are yet:

**Example 1**

Celine has some videos.

You don't know how many videos she has.

Using algebra you could say:

'Celine has $x$ videos.'

## Example 2

John has $d$ computer games. Julie has 12 computer games.
How many computer games do they have altogether?

They have $d + 12$ computer games altogether.

## Example 3

Fiona has $x$ videos and Marsha has $y$ videos.
How many videos do they have altogether?

They have $x + y$ videos altogether.

## Exercise 9A

1 Matthew has $a$ sweets and Bridgit has $b$ sweets.
How many sweets do they have altogether?

2 Pulin has $x$ pets and Harsha has $y$ pets.
How many pets do they have altogether?

3 Anthony has $a$ pairs of socks and Phillip has $b$ pairs of socks.
How many pairs of socks do they have altogether?

4 Esther has $p$ posters and Ailsa has 5 posters.
How many posters do they have altogether?

5 Daniel has 23 marbles and Victoria has $m$ marbles.
How many marbles do they have altogether?

6 Francoise has $x$ rings and Dylan has 2 rings.
How many rings do they have altogether?

7 Ben has $m$ pounds. His uncle gives him 3 pounds.
How many pounds does he have now?

8 Andrea has $x$ pens. Michelle has 2 more pens than Andrea.
How many pens does Michelle have?

9 Pulin has $x$ books, Harsha has $y$ books and Neil has 6 books. How many books do they have altogether?

10 Sarah earns $d$ pounds. Jane earns 4 pounds less than Sarah. How much does Jane earn?

## 9.2 Collecting up letters

The sugar factory's printer has broken down.
None of the bags have weight labels.

Jim has to find out how many kilograms of sugar there are in stock.

Say there are *l* kilograms of sugar in a large bag.

The large bags contain $l + l + l + l + l$ kilograms altogether.

Jim writes this as 5*l* meaning 5 lots of *l*.

There are *m* kilograms of sugar in a medium bag.

$m + m + m + m = 4m$ kilograms altogether.

4*m* means 4 lots of *m*.

There are *s* kilograms of sugar in a small bag.

He writes this as *s* meaning 1 lot of *s*.

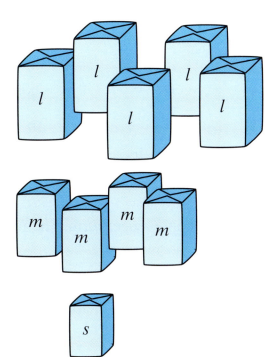

■   **In algebra you write 1 lot of *x* as *x*.
   *x* means 1*x*. You don't write 1*x*.**

Altogether Jim has   $5l + 4m + s$   kilograms of sugar.

Once he knows how much is in each bag he can give the answer as a number.

## Example 4

Write in a shorter form:

(a)  $x + x$     (b)  $y + y + y + y + y$

(a)  $x + x$ is 2 lots of $x$
$$= 2x$$
(b)  $y + y + y + y + y$ is 5 lots of $y$
$$= 5y$$

## Example 5

Write in a longer form:

(a)  $5w$     (b)  $7t$

(a)  $5w$ is 5 lots of $w$
$$= w + w + w + w + w$$
(b)  $7t$ is 7 lots of $t$
$$= t + t + t + t + t + t + t$$

## Exercise 9B

Write these in a shorter form:

**1**  $t + t$

**2**  $s + s$

**3**  $w + w$

**4**  $y + y + y$

**5**  $n + n + n + n$

**6**  $t + t + t + t + t$

**7**  $s + s + s$

**8**  $w + w + w + w$

**9**  $y + y + y + y + y + y + y$

**10**  $p + p + p + p + p + p + p$

**11**  $x + x + x + x + x$

**12**  $r + r + r + r + r + r + r + r$

**13**  $t + t + t + t$

**14**  $n + n + n + n + n + n + n$

Write these in a longer form. The first one has been done for you.

**15**  $3z = z + z + z$

**16**  $4p$

**17**  $2y$

**18**  $6x$

**19**  $5n$

**20**  $7y$

**21**  $4r$

**22**  $3t$

**23**  $5y$

**24**  $7x$

**25**  $6t$

**26**  $4s$

**29**  Write down the length of each line as simply as possible:

**Hint:** simply means in as short a form as possible.

(a)

(b)

## 9.3 Collecting like terms

Jim had $5l + 4m + s$ kilograms of sugar
in his warehouse.

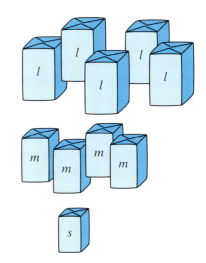

■ **$5l + 4m + s$ is an algebraic expression.**

Each part is called a ***term***.

■ **Terms which use the same letter are called
*like terms*.** For example, $2x$ and $8x$ are like
terms. They both use the letter $x$.

Sometimes you can make algebraic expressions
simpler by adding or subtracting like terms.

**Example 6**

Simplify these expressions by adding or subtracting like
terms:

**(a)** $2x + 3x$    **(b)** $6t - 4t$    **(c)** $3y + 4x$    **(d)** $9f - f$

**(a)** $2x$ and $3x$ are like terms.

   2 lots of $x$  +  3 lots of $x$  =  5 lots of $x$

   so $2x + 3x = 5x$

**(b)** $6t$ and $4t$ are like terms.

   6 lots of $t$  −  4 lots of $t$  =  2 lots of $t$

   so $6t - 4t = 2t$

**(c)** $3y$ and $4x$ use different letters
   so $3y + 4x$ cannot be simplified.

**(d)** $9f$ and $f$ are like terms.

   9 lots of $f$  −  1 lot of $f$  =  8 lots of $f$

   so $9f - f = 8f$

## Exercise 9C

Simplify these expressions by adding or subtracting like terms:

1  $2x + 3x$          2  $4x - 2x$          3  $5y + 3y$

4  $5t + 3t$          5  $6y - 5y$          6  $y + 7y$

7  $3x + 5x$          8  $7x - 4x$          9  $8p + 2p$

10  $9s - 6s$          11  $2p - p$          12  $3r + 5r$

13  $2r + 3r$          14  $7t + 9t$          15  $2x + 3x + 5x$

16  $5y + 6y - 2y$     17  $5t + 7t - t$     18  $21p + 10p - 17p$

19  $6y + 7y - 3y$     20  $7x - 6x + 4x$    21  $4t + 6t - 3t$

Simplify if possible:

22  $6a - 2a$          23  $6a - 2b$          24  $9b - 2$

25  $x + 2x$           26  $x + 2$            27  $s + 6s$

28  $5l + l + 2l$      29  $5 + l + 2m$       30  $m + 3m$

## 9.4 Simplifying more complicated expressions

Sometimes you can simplify expressions by collecting
several like terms together.

**Example 7**

Simplify $2x + 3y + 4x + 5y$

Imagine the $x$ terms are
bags containing $x$ coins …     … and the $y$ terms are
bags containing $y$ coins.

$2x + 3y + 4x + 5y$ looks like this:

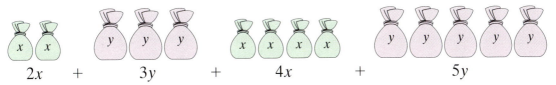

$$2x \quad + \quad 3y \quad + \quad 4x \quad + \quad 5y$$

Collect like terms together:

$$2x \quad + \quad 4x \quad + \quad 3y \quad + \quad 5y$$

Add like terms:

$$6x \quad + \quad 8y$$

So $\quad 2x + 3y + 4x + 5y \; = \; 2x + 4x + 3y + 5y \; = \; 6x + 8y$

So $\quad 2x + 3y + 4x + 5y \; = \; 6x + 8y$

## Example 8

Simplify $4p + 3q - 2p + q$

Collect like terms:

$$4p + 3q - 2p + q$$

$$4p - 2p + 3q + q$$

$$2p + 4q$$

## Example 9

Simplify $4x + 2y + 3x - y + x$

Collect like terms:

$$4x + 2y + 3x - y + x$$

$$4x + 3x + x + 2y - y$$

$$8x + y$$

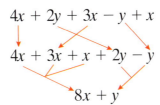

Notice that the $+$ or $-$ sign is part of each term.

$-y$ is a term.

## Exercise 9D

Simplify these expressions by collecting like terms:

**1** $\quad 2x + 5y + 2x + 3y$

**2** $\quad 3p + 2q + 2p + 3q$

**3** $\quad 3w + 9t + 5w + 6t$

**4** $\quad 4m + 7n + 3m + 3n$

**5** $\quad 5x + 9 + 6x + 7$

**6** $\quad 3a + 4d + 3d + a + d$

**7** $\quad 5s + 2t - 2s + 3t$

**8** $\quad p + 4q + 3p - q$

**9** $9x + 4y - 5x + 7y$  **10** $9y + 3 - 5y + 8$

**11** $3x + 2x + 7x - 5x$  **12** $5s + 9t - 4s - 8t$

**13** $6s + 5s - 3s + s$  **14** $9t - 4t + 5t - t$

**15** $5m + 6n + 6m - 3m$  **16** $5x + 7y + 2t - 3x + 2y$

**17** $8y + 3t + 3y + 2t - y$  **18** $7b + 5 + 3b - b + 2$

**19** $9x + 3y + 4y + 9y + x$  **20** $7t + 6r + 3r - 5t$

**21** $4a + 5b - 2b + 6b$  **22** $7p + 2p + 1 - 3p + 5$

**23** $3a + 4b - 3a + 4b$  **24** $11a + 7d - 7a - 5d + 1$

**25** $6x + 2 - 3x - 1 + 3x$  **26** $11x + 3y - 2x + 4y + 2$

**27** $e + 7d + 2c - 6d + c$  **28** $11p + 9r - 3p - 4p + 2r$

**29** $11x + 7y + 8x - 9x + y - 2x$  **30** $3x + 4x - 5x + 6y - 2x - y$

## 9.5 Multiplying with algebra

Remember $2x$ also means:

$x + x$    or    2 lots of $x$    or    $2 \times x$

It's easy to confuse $x$ with $\times$ so in algebra leave out the multiplication sign. Write:

$2 \times x$  as  $2x$    and    $a \times b$  as  $ab$

**Example 10**

Write these expressions without multiplication signs:

**(a)** $3 \times b$    **(b)** $6 \times y$    **(c)** $f \times 4$

**(d)** $x \times y$    **(e)** $2 \times s \times t$    **(f)** $h \times 3 \times s$

**(g)** $\frac{1}{2} \times x$    **(h)** $\frac{2}{5} \times a \times b$    **(i)** $d \times \frac{4}{7} \times e$

Always write the number in front of the letters. It's much easier to read $4xy$ than $y4x$

**(a)** $3 \times b$ is $3b$    **(b)** $6 \times y$ is $6y$    **(c)** $f \times 4$ is $4f$

**(d)** $x \times y$ is $xy$    **(e)** $2 \times s \times t$ is $2st$    **(f)** $h \times 3 \times s$ is $3hs$

**(g)** $\frac{1}{2}x$    **(h)** $\frac{2}{5}ab$    **(i)** $\frac{4}{7}de$

## Exercise 9E

Write these expressions with multiplication signs.
The first one is done for you.

| | | | |
|---|---|---|---|
| **1** $cd = c \times d$ | **2** $st$ | **3** $wx$ | **4** $mn$ |
| **5** $bcd$ | **6** $3a$ | **7** $4x$ | **8** $5xy$ |
| **9** $2st$ | **10** $4mnp$ | **11** $10abc$ | **12** $9xyz$ |
| **13** $15abcd$ | **14** $11efgh$ | | |

Write these expressions without multiplication signs.
The first one is done for you.

| | | | |
|---|---|---|---|
| **15** $b \times c = bc$ | **16** $d \times e$ | **17** $f \times g \times h$ | **18** $2 \times b$ |
| **19** $5 \times a$ | **20** $3 \times x$ | **21** $2 \times x \times y$ | **22** $5 \times a \times b$ |
| **23** $10 \times s \times t$ | **24** $11 \times x \times y \times z$ | **25** $v \times 3$ | **26** $b \times 3 \times a$ |
| **27** $k \times 2 \times j \times l$ | **28** $z \times 6 \times y \times w$ | **29** $\frac{1}{2} \times y$ | **30** $\frac{4}{7} \times b \times c$ |
| **31** $9 \times x \times \frac{2}{3} \times y$ | **32** $6 \times a \times \frac{1}{2} \times b$ | | |

## 9.6 Multiplying terms together

The area of a rectangle is the length times the width.

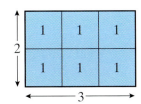

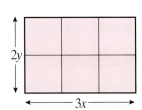

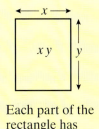

Each part of the rectangle has area $xy$.

There is more about area on page 152.

The area of this rectangle is: $3 \times 2 = 6$ square units.

The area of this rectangle is: $3x \times 2y$ square units.

To multiply   $3x \times 2y$

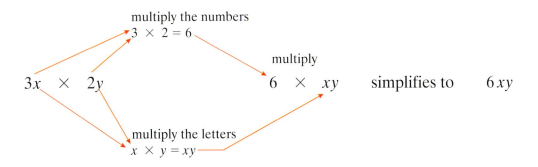

simplifies to      $6xy$

■ To multiply terms together first multiply the numbers, then multiply the letters.
   Write the letters in alphabetical order.

**Example 11**

Simplify:

**(a)** $3ab \times 4c$

$\qquad 3 \times 4 = 12$

$\qquad ab \times c = abc$

so $\quad 3ab \times 4c = 12abc$

**(b)** $2y \times 5xz$

$\qquad 2 \times 5 = 10$

$\qquad y \times xz = yxz = xyz$

so $\quad 2y \times 5xz = 10xyz$

### Exercise 9F

Simplify:

**1** $3a \times 2b$

**2** $3x \times 4y$

**3** $2s \times 4t$

**4** $3a \times b$

**5** $2a \times 6d$

**6** $5x \times 6y$

**7** $4m \times 7n$

**81** $5e \times 10f$

**9** $7g \times 8h$

**10** $2ab \times 3c$

**11** $3xy \times 4z$

**12** $5ab \times 2cd$

**13** $10ab \times cd$

**14** $3bc \times 2ad$

**15** $5mps \times 5nrt$

## 9.7 Using brackets in algebra

Brackets are often used in algebra. For example:

$\quad 2 \times (a + b)$ means add $a$ to $b$ *before* multiplying by 2

Usually this is written: $2(a + b)$ without the $\times$.
This avoids confusion with the letter $x$ which is used a lot in algebra.

$\quad 2(a + b)$ means $2 \times a + 2 \times b = 2a + 2b$

Working this out is called **expanding the brackets**.
Actually the brackets disappear!

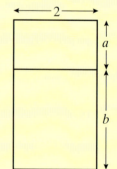

What could $2(a + b)$ represent?

The area of the whole rectangle is $2(a + b)$

There is more about area on page 152.

■ **To expand brackets multiply each term inside the brackets by the term outside.**
For example:

To expand   $3(a + 2b)\ldots$

$3 \times 2b = 6b$

$3(a + 2b) = 3a + 6b$

$3 \times a = 3a$

## Example 12

Expand:

**(a)** $3(2x + 1)$

$= 3 \times 2x + 3 \times 1$

$= 6x + 3$

**(b)** $4(b - 3c)$

$= 4 \times b - 4 \times 3c$

$= 4b - 12c$

## Exercise 9G

Expand these brackets:

**1** $2(a + b)$

**2** $4(x + y)$

**3** $3(s - t)$

**4** $2(c - d)$

**5** $4(2x + 5y)$

**6** $3(3p + q)$

**7** $2(4x + 3y)$

**8** $8(2p + 3s)$

**9** $7(2p - 7q)$

**10** $5(3m - 7n)$

**11** $4(3r - 2s)$

**12** $2(a + b + c)$

**13** $3(2p + 4q - 3r)$

**14** $2(2x + 3y - 2z)$

**15** $3(2a - 3b + 5c)$

**16** $4(2x - y - 5z)$

## 9.8 Powers in algebra

Page 86 shows you a short way of writing numbers like 1 000 000

$$1\,000\,000 = 10 \times 10 \times 10 \times 10 \times 10 \times 10$$
$$= 10^6$$

**How you say it:** "10 to the power 6"

$$10^6$$

This number is the **power** or **index**.

The power tells you how many times the number is multiplied by itself.

You can use powers in algebra too.

$$x^6 = x \times x \times x \times x \times x \times x$$

**How you say it:** "x to the power 6"

### Example 13

Write, using powers:

(a) $x \times x$    (b) $y \times y \times y \times y$    (c) $3 \times p \times p \times p \times p \times p$

(a) $x$ is multiplied by itself 2 times

   $x \times x = x^2$

(b) $y$ is multiplied by itself 4 times

   $y \times y \times y \times y = y^4$

(c) $p$ is multiplied by itself 5 times

   $3 \times p \times p \times p \times p \times p = 3 \times p^5 = 3p^5$

**Example 14**

Simplify these algebraic expressions using powers:

(a) $2x \times 3x \times y \times x$  (b) $f \times 3f \times g \times 2f \times 2g$

(a) $2x \times 3x \times y \times x$
$= 2 \times x \times 3 \times x \times y \times x$
$= 2 \times 3 \times x \times x \times x \times y$
$= 6 \times x^3 \times y$
$= 6x^3y$

(b) $f \times 3f \times g \times 2f \times 2g$
You may find it is quicker to do it this way:
multiply the numbers:  $3 \times 2 \times 2 = 12$
multiply the $f$ terms:  $f \times f \times f = f^3$
multiply the $g$ terms:  $g \times g = g^2$
so $f \times 3f \times g \times 2f \times 2g = 12 \times f^3 \times g^2$
$= 12f^3g^2$

■ $y^5$ **means $y$ multiplied by itself 5 times:**
$$y^5 = y \times y \times y \times y \times y$$

**Exercise 9H**

**1** Write using powers:
(a) $2 \times 2$  (b) $4 \times 4 \times 4 \times 4 \times 4 \times 4$
(c) $3 \times 3 \times 3 \times 3$  (d) $5 \times 5 \times 5$
(e) $2 \times 2 \times 2 \times 2 \times 2$  (f) $3 \times 3 \times 3 \times 3 \times 3 \times 3 \times 3$

For a reminder on using powers with numbers see page 87.

**2** Write using powers:
(a) $a \times a$  (b) $b \times b \times b$
(c) $c \times c \times c \times c$  (d) $x \times x \times x \times x$
(e) $y \times y \times y \times y \times y$  (f) $s \times s \times s \times s \times s \times s$
(g) $w \times w \times w$  (h) $z \times z$
(i) $p \times p \times p \times p \times p \times p$  (j) $m \times m \times m \times m$
(k) $t \times t \times t \times t \times t$  (l) $c \times c \times c$
(m) $a \times a \times a \times a$  (n) $d \times d \times d \times d \times d \times d$

**3** Write without powers:
(a) $x^2$  (b) $y^3$  (c) $s^2$  (d) $t^4$  (e) $m^3$
(f) $n^5$  (g) $a^7$  (h) $b^5$  (i) $c^4$  (j) $d^8$
(k) $r^5$  (l) $p^4$  (m) $q^9$  (n) $z^5$

4 Simplify these algebraic expressions:

(a) $2x \times 3x$        (b) $3y \times 4y$

(c) $y \times 2y \times 3y$      (d) $2b \times b \times 3b \times b$

(e) $6t \times t \times 3t \times 2t$    (f) $2p \times p^2$

(g) $x \times 2y \times 3x \times y$    (h) $2f \times 3g \times f \times 2g$

(i) $5m \times n \times 2n \times m$    (j) $2a \times 3a \times b \times a \times 2b$

(k) $3y \times y \times x \times y \times 2x$    (l) $p \times 2q \times 3p \times q \times p$

## Summary of key points

1 In algebra you write 1 lot of $x$ as $x$.
$x$ means $1x$. You don't write $1x$.

2 $5l + 4m + s$ is an algebraic expression.

Each part is called a *term*.

3 Terms which use the same letter are called *like terms*.

4 To multiply terms together first multiply the numbers, then multiply the letters.
Write the letters in alphabetical order.

5 To expand brackets, multiply each term inside the brackets by the term outside. For example:

$$3(a + 2b) = 3a + 6b$$

6 $y^5$ means $y$ multiplied by itself 5 times:

$$y^5 = y \times y \times y \times y \times y$$

# 10 Perimeter, area and volume

## 10.1 What is a perimeter?

Naomi wants to frame her new picture.
She measures the distance around the
edge in centimetres.
Now she knows how much wood to buy.

■ **The distance around the edge of a
shape is called the perimeter.**

Remember: you can measure distances
using mm, cm, m or km.

You would measure the perimeter
of this garden in metres.

You would measure the perimeter
of this lake in kilometres.

### Example 1

Find the perimeters of these shapes:

**(a)**

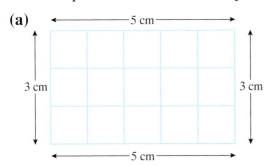

**(b)**

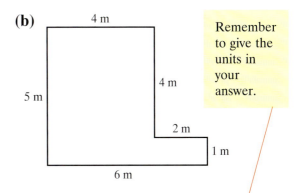

Remember
to give the
units in
your
answer.

**(a)** Add the lengths of the edges:

$5 + 3 + 5 + 3 = 16\,\text{cm}$

**(b)** Add the lengths of the edges:

$5 + 4 + 4 + 2 + 1 + 6 = 22\,\text{m}$

# Exercise 10A

1   What is the most sensible unit to use to measure the perimeter of:

   (a) a page of this book   (b) the room you are in

   (c) the coastline of Ireland   (d) an envelope

   (e) the hem of a dress   (f) a leaf?

> mm, cm, m and km are all units of length.
>
> There is more about these on page 104.

2   These shapes are drawn on centimetre squared paper.
   Find the perimeter of each shape.

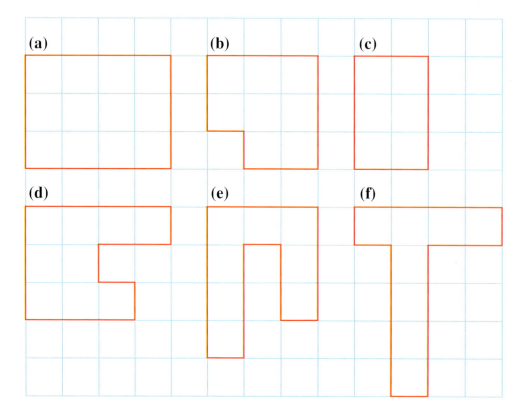

3   Find the perimeters of these shapes.
   Remember to give the units in your answer.

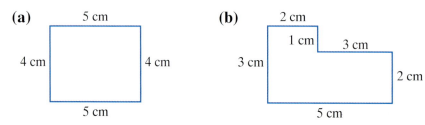

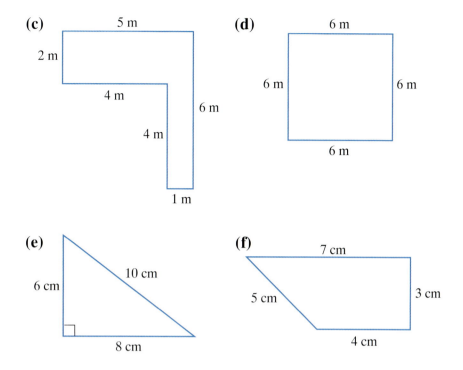

**4** A rectangular carpet measures 3 m by 5 m.
Find the perimeter of the carpet.

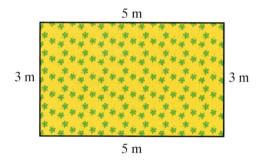

**5** Find the perimeters of these triangles:

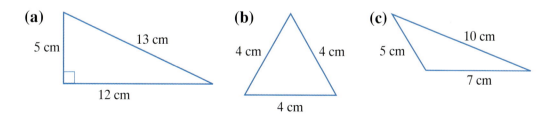

**6** A rectangular field is 120 m long and 50 m wide.
Find the perimeter of the field.

## 10.2 Perimeter of a rectangle

The opposite sides of a rectangle are the same length.
This makes it easy to work out the perimeter.

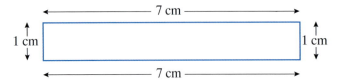

$$\text{Perimeter} = 1 + 1 \ + \ 7 + 7 \qquad \text{or} \qquad \text{Perimeter} = 1 + 7 + 1 + 7$$
$$\text{Perimeter} = (2 \times 1) + (2 \times 7) \qquad \text{or} \qquad \text{Perimeter} = 2 \times (1 + 7)$$
$$= 2 + 14 = 16\,\text{cm} \qquad\qquad\qquad = 2 \times 8 = 16\,\text{cm}$$

■ **For any rectangle:**

**Perimeter = (2 × length) + (2 × width)**
**or**
**Perimeter = 2 × (length + width)**

### Example 2

Find the perimeter of a 4 m by 7 m rectangle.

length = 7 m     width = 4 m

Sketch the rectangle:

7 m

4 m                              4 m

7 m

$$\text{Perimeter} = (2 \times \text{length}) + (2 \times \text{width}) \quad \text{or} \quad \text{Perimeter} = 2 \times (\text{length} + \text{width})$$
$$= (2 \times 7) + (2 \times 4) \qquad\qquad\qquad = 2 \times (7 + 4)$$
$$= 22\,\text{m} \qquad\qquad\qquad\qquad = 2 \times 11$$
$$\qquad\qquad\qquad\qquad = 22\,\text{m}$$

## Exercise 10B

**1** Find the perimeters of these rectangles:

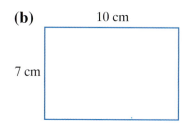

**(a)** 6 cm
4 cm

**(b)** 10 cm
7 cm

**(c)** 9 cm
4 cm

**2** Work out the perimeter of:

**(a)** a rectangular carpet with sides 6 m and 4 m

**(b)** a rectangular field with length 120 m and width 60 m

**(c)** a square with of sides 5 cm long

**(d)** a rectangular table cloth which measures 70 cm by 80 cm

**(e)** a rectangular football pitch with length 110 m and width 65 m

**(f)** the front cover of this book. (You will need to make some measurements.)

**3** The perimeter of a rectangle is 24 cm.
One side measures 9 cm.
How long is the other side?

**4** Find these perimeters:

**(a)** Square of side 4 cm

**(b)** Square of side 3 cm

**(c)** Square of side 6 cm

**(d)** Square of side 8 cm

> **of side 4 cm** means each side is 4 cm long.

**5** Using your answers to question **4**, write down a formula for the perimeter of a square.

## 10.3 Area

How many tiles will Joe need to cover the walls?

How much carpet will Gina need for her bedroom?

Joe and Gina each need to measure an **area**.

■ **Area is the amount of space covered by a shape.**

You use squares to measure area:

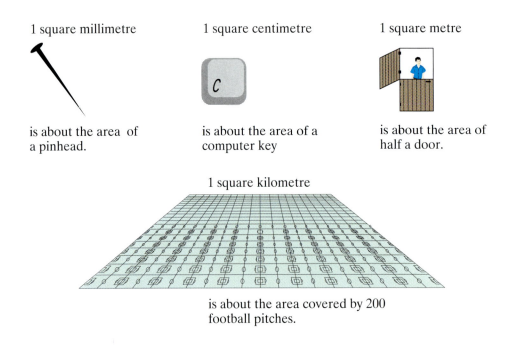

1 square millimetre

is about the area of a pinhead.

1 square centimetre

is about the area of a computer key

1 square metre

is about the area of half a door.

1 square kilometre

is about the area covered by 200 football pitches.

You will also see measures of area written like this:

1 square millimetre:  1 sq mm  or  $1\,mm^2$
1 square centimetre:  1 sq cm  or  $1\,cm^2$
1 square metre:  1 sq m  or  $1\,m^2$
1 square kilometre:  1 sq km  or  $1\,km^2$

Remember: You write $3 \times 3$ as $3^2$.

You say '3 squared'.

**Example 3**

Find the areas of these shapes:

(a) 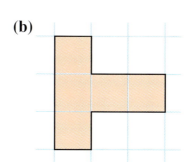   (b)

Remember to
write the units
in your answer.

(a) Count the squares: $12\,\text{cm}^2$     (b) Count the squares: $5\,\text{cm}^2$

## Exercise 10C

**1**   Which units of area would you use to measure the
area of:

mm², cm², m² and
km² are all units of
area.

  (a) a page of this book  (b) the floor of your classroom
  (c) a leaf                     (d) a small oil droplet
  (e) the top of a table    (f) Wales?

**2**   Write these areas in order of size.
Start with the smallest.
        $10\,\text{cm}^2$   $5\,\text{km}^2$   $20\,\text{mm}^2$   $6\,\text{m}^2$   $100\,\text{m}^2$

**3**   Find the areas of these shapes. They are drawn on
centimetre squared paper.

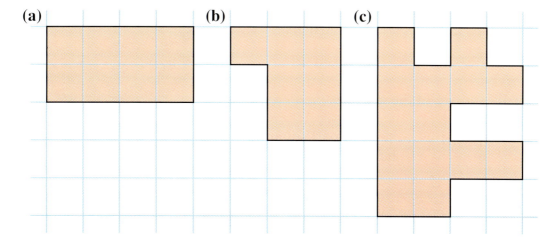

(a)                          (b)                          (c)

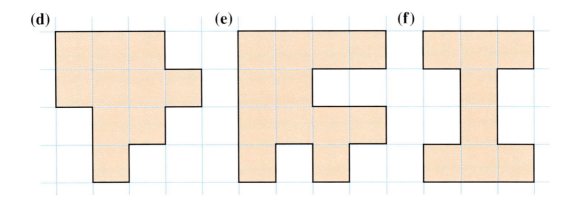

(d)   (e)   (f)

## 10.4 Estimating areas

To find the area of a curved shape, you need to estimate the number of squares that it covers.

**Example 4**

Estimate the area of this leaf:

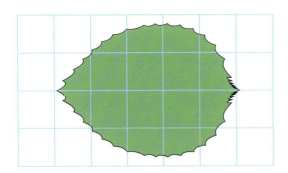

Count the whole squares first:

There are 6 whole squares marked ○

There are 12 part squares marked ×

A good estimate of the area is:

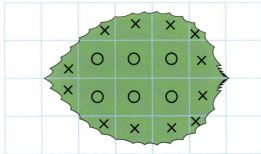

The whole squares + half the part squares.
$$= \quad 6 \qquad + \text{ half of } 12$$

$$= 6 + 6 = 12$$

The area of the leaf is about $12\,\text{cm}^2$.

Remember the units!

## Exercise 10D

Estimate the areas of these shapes.

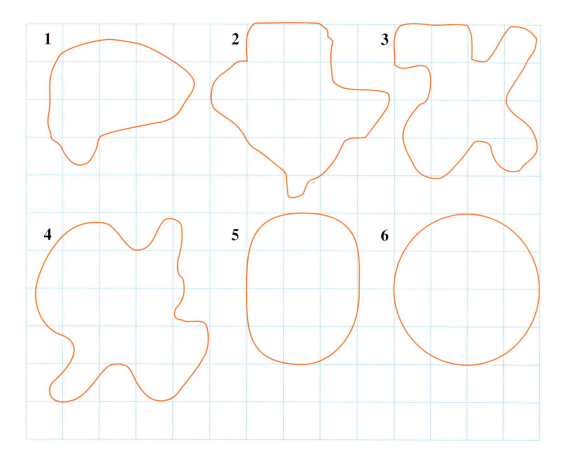

## 10.5  Areas by multiplying

It can take a long time to count squares.

Sometimes it is quicker to use
multiplication:

This rectangle measures
6 mm by 15 mm

By counting squares:
the area is 90 mm$^2$

There are 6 rows of 15 mm

By multiplying:
the area is $6 \times 15 = 90$ mm$^2$

■ **For any rectangle:**
  **Area = length × width**

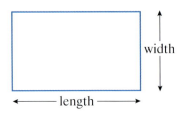

The length and width must be measured in the same units.

## Example 5

Find the area of each rectangle:

**(a)**

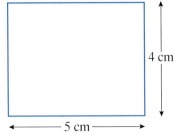

4 cm

5 cm

**(b)**

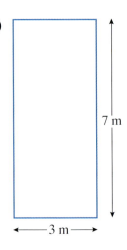

7 m

3 m

**(a)** length = 5 cm
width = 4 cm
The units are both cm so use:

area = length × width
    = 5 × 4
    = 20 cm²

**(b)** length = 7 m
width = 3 m
The units are both m so use:

area = length × width
    = 7 × 3
    = 21 m²

## Exercise 10E

**1** Find the areas of these rectangles:

**(a)** 6 cm

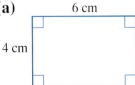

4 cm

**(b)** 2 cm

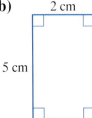

5 cm

**(c)** 3 cm

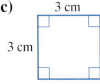

3 cm

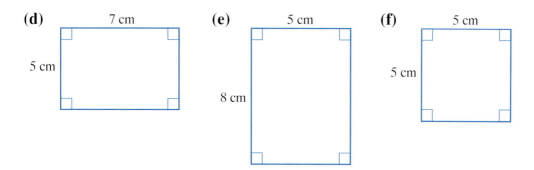

**(d)** 7 cm · 5 cm

**(e)** 5 cm · 8 cm

**(f)** 5 cm · 5 cm

**2** This table shows the lengths and widths of some rectangles. Copy and complete the table.

| Length in cm | Width in cm | Perimeter in cm | Area in cm$^2$ |
|---|---|---|---|
| 5 | 2 | 14 | 10 |
| 4 | 3 | | |
| 5 | 5 | | |
| 6 | 4 | | |
| 4 | 4 | | |
| 7 | 3 | | |
| 6 | 3 | | |
| 10 | 2 | | |
| 5 | 4 | | |
| 6 | 10 | | |
| 12 | 5 | | |

**3** A rectangle has a length of 12 cm and a width of 7 cm. Work out:

**(a)** the perimeter of the rectangle

**(b)** the area of the rectangle

**4** A rectangular wall measures 4 m by 7 m. Work out:

**(a)** the perimeter of the wall

**(b)** the area of the wall

**5** The width of a rectangle is 8 cm.
The perimeter of the rectangle is 20 cm.
Work out the area of the rectangle.

**6** The area of a rectangle is 30 cm$^2$.
The width of the rectangle is 3 cm.
Find the length of the rectangle.

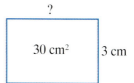

?

30 cm² · 3 cm

7 **Investigation** You may want to use squared paper.
The diagram shows a rectangle. Its perimeter is 24 cm.

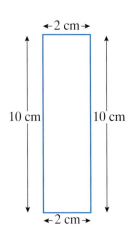

- Draw as many rectangles as you can which have a perimeter of 24 cm.

- Write down the length and width of each rectangle.

- Work out the area of each rectangle. Which of the rectangles has the largest area?

Repeat this investigation for rectangles with a perimeter of:

(a) 12 cm    (b) 20 cm    (c) 36 cm    (d) 40 cm

Each time find which rectangle gives the largest area.

8 Find the areas of these shapes made from rectangles.

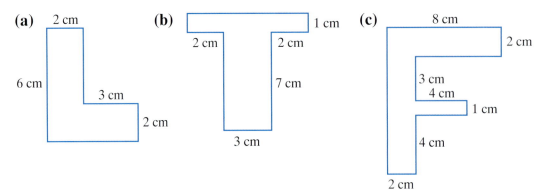

# 10.6 Area of a right-angled triangle

| This triangle has a right angle: | It fits inside a rectangle: | The area of the rectangle is: base × height | The area of the triangle is: $\frac{1}{2}$ × base × height |
|---|---|---|---|

right angle

■ **The area of a right-angled triangle is:**
$\frac{1}{2}$ × **base** × **height**

## Example 6

Find the area of this triangle:

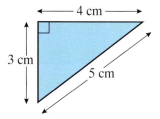

The triangle fits inside a rectangle:

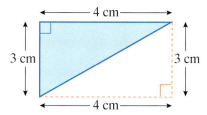

area of rectangle $= 3 \times 4 = 12\,\text{cm}^2$

area of triangle $= \frac{1}{2} \times 3 \times 4 = 6\,\text{cm}^2$

The area of the triangle is $6\,\text{cm}^2$.

## Exercise 10F θ

These triangles are drawn on centimetre squared paper.
For each triangle:

(a) write down the lengths of the perpendicular sides
(b) find the area of the triangle.

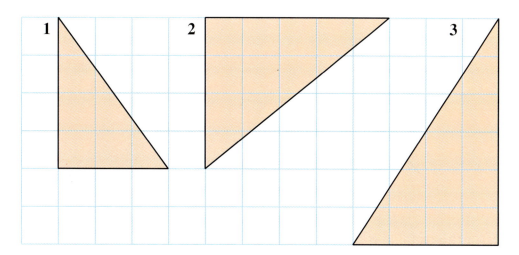

**4** Find the area of these triangles. All measurements are in cm.

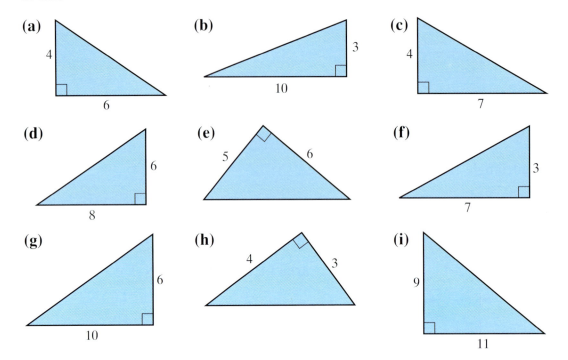

## 10.7 Areas of more complex triangles

You can find the area of a triangle like this by splitting it into two right-angled triangles.

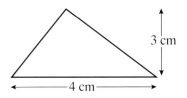

| Split it into two right-angled triangles: | Each triangle fits inside a rectangle: | The area of the large rectangle is: area = 3 × 4 = 12 cm² | The area of the triangle is: area = $\frac{1}{2}$ × 3 × 4 = 6 cm² |
|---|---|---|---|

   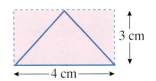 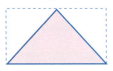

The area of the triangle is 6 cm².

■ **The area of a triangle is half the area of the surrounding rectangle:**

**Area** $= \frac{1}{2} \times$ **base** $\times$ **height**

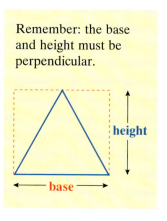

Remember: the base and height must be perpendicular.

## Example 7

Find the area of this triangle:

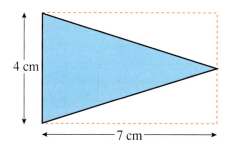

The triangle fits inside a rectangle with sides 4 cm and 7 cm.

The area is $\frac{1}{2} \times 4 \times 7 = 14 \,\text{cm}^2$

## Exercise 10G

1   Find the area of each triangle.

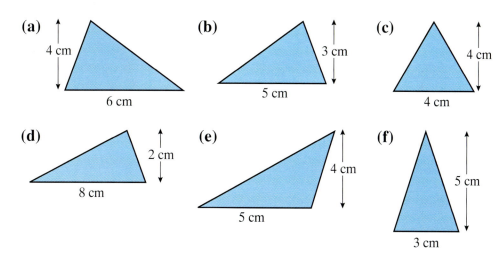

**(g)**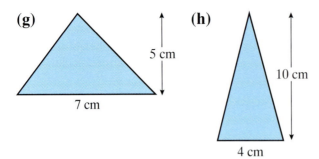

5 cm

7 cm

**(h)**

10 cm

4 cm

**(i)**

2 cm

5 cm

**2** Here is another triangle

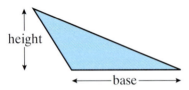

height

base

Use pictures to show why the formula

Area $= \frac{1}{2} \times$ base $\times$ height

still works for this triangle.

## 10.8 Putting it all together

Nadia is tiling her kitchen floor.

How many tiles should she buy?

She draws a plan of her kitchen to work out the area:

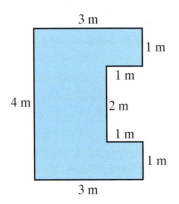

3 m

1 m

1 m

4 m

2 m

1 m

1 m

3 m

Nadia can work out the area of her floor in two ways:

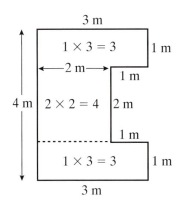

Split it into 3 rectangles.
Then add their areas:

$$3 + 4 + 3 = 10\,\text{m}^2$$

Complete the large rectangle.
Take away the shaded area:

$$12 - 2 = 10\,\text{m}^2$$

A shape you can break into simpler shapes is called a
**composite shape**.

■ **To find the area of a composite shape break it into simpler shapes, for example: rectangles and triangles.**

## Exercise 10H

**1** Find the area of each shape. All units are in cm.

**(a)**

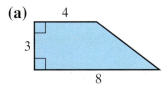

**(b)**

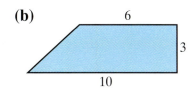

**(c)**

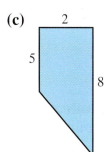

**(d)**

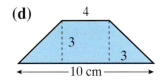

**(e)**

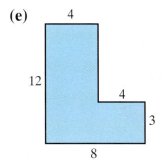

**(f)**

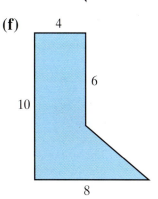

**2** Find the shaded area in each shape:

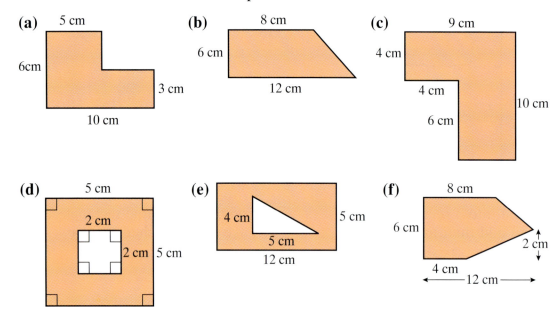

**(a)** 5 cm
6cm
3 cm
10 cm

**(b)** 8 cm
6 cm
12 cm

**(c)** 9 cm
4 cm
4 cm
6 cm
10 cm

**(d)** 5 cm
2 cm
2 cm 5 cm

Hint: find the whole area.
Subtract the unshaded part.

**(e)** 4 cm
5 cm
5 cm
12 cm

**(f)** 8 cm
6 cm
2 cm
4 cm
12 cm

# 10.9 Volume

How much space will Vic's
CD collection occupy?

■ **The volume of an object is the
amount of space it occupies.**

You can use cubes to measure volume:

1 millimetre
cube

The size of a
grain of sand.

1 centimetre
cube

The size of a
sugar cube
or dice.

1 metre
cube

The size of a
large washing
machine.

1 kilometre
cube

Bigger than the
biggest mountain
in Britain.

You will also see measures of volume written like this:

| 1 millimetre cube: | 1 cubic mm | or | $1\,mm^3$ |
| 1 centimetre cube: | 1 cubic cm | or | $1\,cm^3$ |
| 1 metre cube: | 1 cubic m | or | $1\,m^3$ |
| 1 kilometre cube: | 1 cubic km | or | $1\,km^3$ |

> The 3 shows there are 3 dimensions: length, width and height.

1 cm
1 cm
1 cm

**Example 9**

Find the volume of this box:

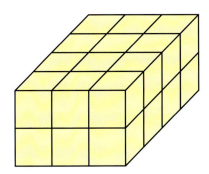

Count the centimetre cubes:
There are 12 cubes in each layer, and 2 layers.

So the volume is $12 \times 2 = 24\,cm^3$

> Remember to use the correct units.

## Exercise 10I

1  Which shape has
   **(a)** the largest volume?
   **(b)** the smallest volume?

A 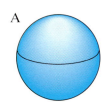    B     C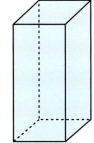

2  Write these objects in order of size.
   Start with the largest volume.

   Brick    Pencil    This book    Loaf of bread    Pin    Orange

**3**   These objects are made of centimetre cubes.
Find the volume of each object:

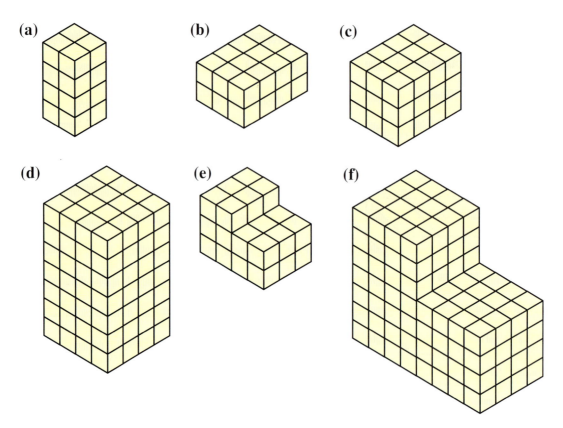

(a)   (b)   (c)

(d)   (e)   (f)

## 10.10  Volume of a cuboid

A cuboid is a solid shape with rectangular faces:

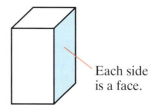

Each side
is a face.

**Example 10**

Work out the volume of this cuboid:

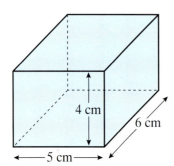

4 cm

6 cm

5 cm

You can fit

| 5 centimetre cubes in the width | 6 centimetre cubes in the length | $6 \times 5 = 30$ centimetre cubes in the base | 4 layers like the base |
|---|---|---|---|

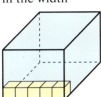 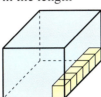 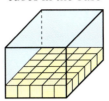 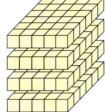

The volume is
$30 \times 4 = 120$ centimetre cubes.

The quick way is: $6 \times 5 \times 4 = 120\,cm^3$.

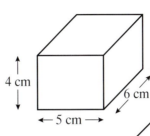
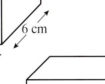

■ **For any cuboid:**

**Volume = length × width × height**

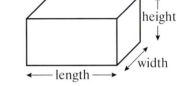

## Exercise 10J

Find the volume of each cuboid. All lengths are in cm.

**(a)**

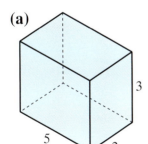

3
5
2

**(b)**

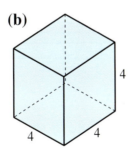

4
4
4

**(c)**

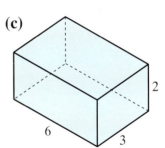

2
6
3

**(d)**

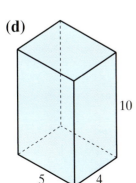

10
5
4

**(e)**

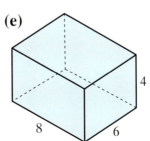

4
8
6

**(f)**

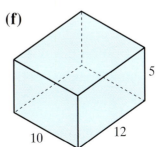

5
10
12

# 10.11 Capacity

■ **The volume of space inside a hollow object is called its *capacity*.**

You can find the capacity of …

… an empty box          … an empty glass          … a car boot

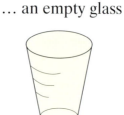

Imagine the space inside these objects:

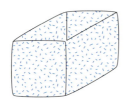

## Example 11

Find the capacities of these boxes:

**(a)**

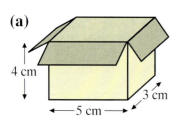

**(b)**

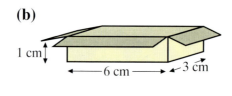

The capacity of an empty box is the volume of space inside it.

The boxes are both cuboids so you can use the formula:

$$\text{Volume} = \text{length} \times \text{width} \times \text{height}$$

**(a)**     Volume $= 4 \times 5 \times 3 = 60 \, \text{cm}^3$
so  Capacity $= 60 \, \text{cm}^3$

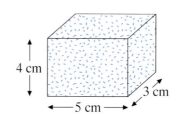

**(b)**     Volume $= 6 \times 3 \times 1 = 18 \, \text{cm}^3$
so  Capacity $= 18 \, \text{cm}^3$

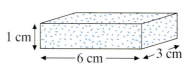

## Exercise 10K

1 These objects can all hold liquid.
Write the objects in order of size.
Start with the greatest capacity.

Teacup     Teaspoon     Washing up bowl     Swimming pool

2 All these boxes are empty.
Find the capacity of each box.

**(a)**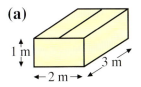

**(b)**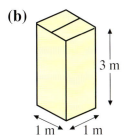

**(c)**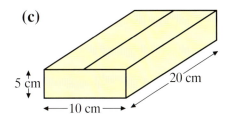

**(d)**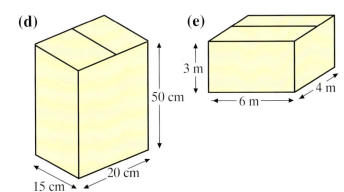

**(e)**

**(c)**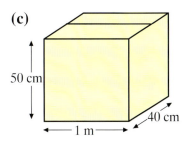

## Summary of key points

1 The distance around the edge of a shape is its perimeter.

2 For any rectangle:
Perimeter = (2 × length) + (2 × width)
or
Perimeter = 2 × (length + width)

3 Area is the amount of space covered by a shape.

**4** For any rectangle:

Area = length × width

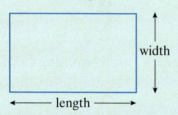

The length and width must be measured in the same units.

**5** The area of a right-angled triangle is: $\frac{1}{2}$ × base × height

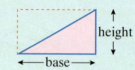

**6** Area of a triangle is half the area of the surrounding rectangle:

Area = $\frac{1}{2}$ × base × height

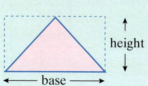

**7** You can find the area of a composite shape by breaking it into simpler shapes, for example: rectangles and triangles.

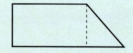

**8** The volume of an object is the amount of space it occupies.

**9** For any cuboid:

Volume = length × width × height

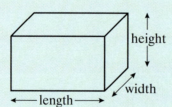

**10** The volume of space inside a hollow object is called its **capacity**.

# 11 Formulae and equations

This unit shows you how to use formulae and equations to help solve problems.

## 11.1 Using word formulae

■ **A formula is a sentence describing a rule or relationship.**
**It must contain an equals (=) sign.**
For example:

$$\text{speed} = \frac{\text{distance}}{\text{time}}$$

$E = mc^2$ is the famous formula which shows how much energy is released when matter is converted into energy.

### Example 1

Helen buys ice creams from a shop. This formula describes the total cost:

cost of ice creams = cost of one ice cream × number bought

Helen buys 4 ice creams at 80p each.
Put these numbers into the word formula:

cost of ice creams = cost of one ice cream × number bought

$$= \qquad 80p \qquad \times \qquad 4$$
$$= 320p$$
$$= £3.20$$

## Exercise 11A

1   Andrew buys some pens. He uses the formula:
    cost of pens = cost of one pen × number bought
    The cost of one pen is 25p. Andrew buys 2 pens. Find the total cost of the pens.

2   Diana buys some buns. She uses the formula:
    cost of buns = cost of one bun × number bought
    The cost of one bun is 55p. Diana buys 4 buns. Find the total cost of the buns.

3   Narinder buys some bags of sweets. She uses the formula:
    cost of sweets = cost of one bag × number bought
    The cost of one bag of sweets is 85p. Narinder buys 6 bags. Find the cost of the sweets.

**4**   Sam buys some choc bars. He uses the formula:
    cost of choc bars = cost of one choc bar × number bought
The cost of one choc bar is 25p. Sam buys 3 choc bars.
Work out the cost of the choc bars.

**5**   Mrs Akeya shares out some money equally among her
family. She uses the formula:
    amount each person gets = amount of money ÷ number in family
Work out how much each person gets when Mrs Akeya
shares out £20 among:
**(a)** 2 people    **(b)** 4 people    **(c)** 5 people

**6**   The formula to work out the number of people in a
school is:
    number of people = number of staff + number of pupils
Work out the number of people in a school which has
47 staff and 1083 pupils.

**7**   The formula to work out the temperature difference
between Greece and England is:
    temperature difference = temperature in − temperature in
                              Greece          England

Work out the temperature
difference when the
temperatures in Greece
and England are:

|     | Greece | England |
|-----|--------|---------|
| **(a)** | 19°C | 7°C |
| **(b)** | 10°C | 0°C |
| **(c)** | 30°C | 16°C |

## 11.2  Using letters to represent numbers

You can fit a
green rod and
a red rod
together ...

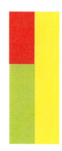

... to make the
same length as
a yellow rod.

This mathematical sentence connects the lengths of the rods:

length of yellow = length of red + length of green

You can write this in letters for short:

$$y = r + g$$

You can fit other rods together to match the length of the yellow rod:

length of yellow = length of white + length of white + length of green

In letters this is:

| $y$ | = | $w$ | + | $w$ | + | $g$ |

or:

| $y$ | = | $2w$ | + | $g$ |

$2w$ means $2 \times w$
or $w + w$

### Exercise 11B

In this exercise either use a set of Cuisenaire rods or trace the rods below.

Using these letters to stand for the lengths of the rods:

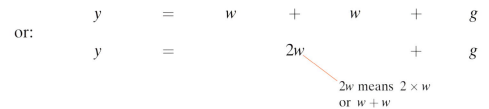

| $w$ | $r$ | $g$ | $p$ | $y$ |

**1** Write each of these as a sentence using letters.
( The first one is: $r = 2w$ )

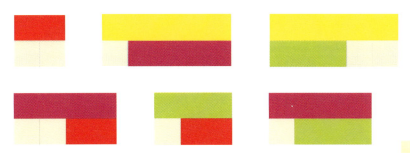

**2** Find the three different rod trains equal to the length of the green rod.
Write each one as a sentence using letters.

**3** Find all the different rod trains equal to the length of the yellow rod.
Write each one as a sentence using letters.

A **rod train** is any combination of rods in a row.
For example:

## 11.3 Using letters in formulae

You can shorten formulae by using letters to stand for unknown amounts.

### Example 2

The formula for the total distance Joan travels to school is:

total distance = distance travelled by car + distance walked

Write this formula using these letters:

$d$ for total distance travelled
$c$ for distance travelled by car
$w$ for distance walked

The formula is: $d = c + w$

### Example 3

Alex works in a sports shop.
He gets £5 for each hour he works.
The formula for his pay is:

pay = 5 × number of hours worked

Write this formula using the letters:

$p$ for pay
$n$ for number of hours worked

The formula is: $p = 5 \times n$   or   $p = 5n$

### Exercise 11C

1   Write a formula for the cost $c$ of $b$ buns at 35 pence each.

2   Ben has $p$ pens and Bill has $q$ pens. Together Ben and Bill have a total of $t$ pens.
Write a formula for the total number of pens they have.

3   David has $s$ sweets. He divides them equally between his 5 friends. Write down a formula for the number of sweets $n$ each of them receives.

**4**   The temperature in Greece is $g$ °C.
The temperature in England is $e$ °C.
The difference between the temperatures in Greece
and England is $d$ °C.
Write a formula connecting $d$, $g$ and $e$.

**5**   Savita sells cameras.
She earns a commission of £6 for every sale she makes.
Last month she made 5 sales and her commission was £$c$.
Write a formula connecting $c$ and 5.

**6**   **(a)**

This rod has three equal sections.
Each section is $a$ cm long.
The total length of the rod is 2 cm.
Write a formula connecting 2 and $a$.

   **(b)**   A pencil is five times as long as the rod above.
The length of the pencil is $L$ cm

   (i)   Write a formula connecting $L$ and 2.

   (ii)   Write a formula connecting $L$ and $a$.

**7**   The perimeter of a flat shape is the total distance
around the edge of the shape. Write formulae for the
perimeters $P$ of these shapes.

> Each formula
> should begin:
>
> $P =$

(i) 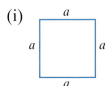   (ii) 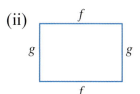   (iii)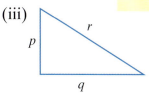

**8**   Jessica is $x$ years old today.
In 10 years time she will be $a$ years old.
Write a formula connecting $x$ and $a$.

## 11.4 Formulae with two operations

length of yellow $= 2 \times$ length of white $+$ length of green

This formula contains two operations: $\times$ and $+$.
You always $\times$ before you $+$

### Example 4

Tony is a mechanic. To mend a car he charges the cost of the spare parts plus £15 for each hour he works.

(a) Write this as a word formula.
(b) Find out how much he charges if the spare parts cost £100 and the work takes 6 hours.

(a) charge $=$ cost of spare parts $+ 15 \times$ number of hours worked
(b) charge $= 100 + 15 \times 6$
$= 100 + \quad 90$     multiply first ...
$= 190$     ... then add.

Tony charges £190

### Exercise 11D

1   Jaqui joins a video club.
She has to pay a membership fee and then £2 for each video she hires.

(a) Write this as a formula in words.
(b) Work out the total amount Jaqui will pay if the membership fee is £5 and she hires 15 videos.

2   The instructions for cooking a turkey are
'Allow 45 minutes for each kilogram the turkey weighs, then add another 30 minutes.'

(a) Copy and complete this formula in words:

    time to cook a turkey $=$

(b) How many minutes will it take to cook a turkey weighing 10 kilograms?

**3**   The total monthly cost of using a mobile phone is the monthly line rental plus £12 for each hour the phone is used.

   **(a)** Write this as a formula in words.

   **(b)** If line rental is £40, find the total monthly cost of using a mobile phone for:
       (i) 5 hours       (ii) $\frac{1}{2}$ an hour

## 11.5 Using algebraic formulae

Tony's formula for working out how much to charge is:

   charge $=$ cost of spare parts $+\ 15 \times$ number of hours worked

It's quicker to write this using letters:

Use $c$ for the charge
   $s$ for the cost of spare parts
   $n$ for the number of hours worked.

The formula becomes:

   $c = s + 15\,n$

### Example 5

Samantha went to the school disco. She paid 50p for her ticket, then 30p for each drink she bought.

Write a formula for the total cost of going to the school disco:

**(a)** in words       **(b)** using letters

**(a)** In words the formula is:

   cost of going $=$ price of ticket $+\ 30 \times$ number of drinks bought
   Or       cost $=$       50       $+\ 30 \times$ number of drinks bought

**(b)** Use $c$ for cost
       $n$ for number of drinks bought.
   The formula is:
       $c = 50 + 30n$

> Remember:
> You can only collect terms with the same letters.
>
> $50 + 30n$ is **not** $80n$

### Exercise 11E

1   The instructions for cooking a joint of beef are:

'allow 45 minutes for each kilogram then add a further 30 minutes.'

A joint of beef weighs $w$ kilograms. The total time to cook it is $t$ minutes.
Using letters write a formula connecting $w$ and $t$.

2   In this diagram, the length of each side is in centimetres:

The perimeter of the triangle is $p$ cm.

Write a formula connecting $p$ and $x$.

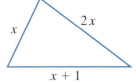

Remember: the perimeter of a flat shape is the total distance around the edge of the shape.

3   A football team gets 3 points for a win and 1 point for a draw.
Last season they got $p$ points.
They won $w$ games and drew $d$ games.
Using letters write a formula connecting $p$, $w$ and $d$.

## 11.6 Solving equations

■  **Equations and formulae are different:**

| Equation | Formula |
|---|---|
| $2 + m = 8$ | cost = price × number bought |
| This **equation** is **only true** when $m = 6$ | $c = p \times n$ |
| 6 is a **solution** of the equation. Finding the value of $m$ is called **solving the equation**. | You can put **any values** into these parts of the **formula** and get a result for the cost. |

**Equations** may be true for one value (like $m = 6$) or several values but are not generally true for any value.

## Using number machines to solve equations

To solve the equation $p + 3 = 10$
you need to find the value of $p$

First write $p + 3 = 10$
as a number machine:

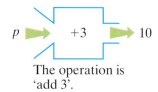

The operation is
'add 3'.

Now find a number machine
to 'undo' the operation 'add 3':

This is an **inverse number machine**.

The operation is
'subtract 3'.

Use the inverse number machine
to find the value of $p$:

$p = 7$ is a solution of the equation
$p + 3 = 10$

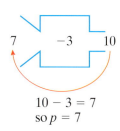

$10 - 3 = 7$
so $p = 7$

## Exercise 11F

Solve these equations using inverse number machines:

(a) $a + 4 = 6$      (b) $b + 3 = 7$

(c) $c + 2 = 7$      (d) $d + 3 = 8$

(e) $r + 2 = 12$      (f) $s + 5 = 10$

(g) $t + 8 = 12$      (h) $u + 7 = 8$

(i) $e - 6 = 1$      (j) $f - 5 = 6$

(k) $g - 3 = 1$      (l) $h - 4 = 4$

(m) $7e = 21$      (n) $3f = 18$

(o) $2g = 10$      (p) $5h = 25$

(q) $5i = 0$      (r) $6j = 24$

(s) $8k = 16$      (t) $2l = 20$

(u) $t \div 4 = 0$      (v) $j \div 3 = 4$

(w) $k \div 4 = 6$      (x) $l \div 5 = 20$

(y) $\dfrac{m}{3} = 2$      (z) $\dfrac{n}{4} = 2$

## Solving more complex equations

To solve the equation $3x - 2 = 13$
you need a two step number machine.

First write $3x - 2 = 13$
as a number machine:

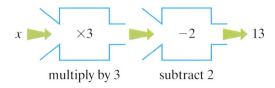

Now find an inverse number
machine to undo the operations
'multiply by 3' and 'subtract 2':

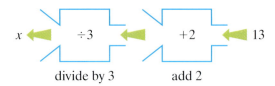

Use the inverse number
machine to find the value
of $x$:

$x = 5$ is a solution of the equation $3x - 2 = 13$

Check:
$3 \times 5 - 2 = 15 - 2$
$= 13$
So $x = 5$ is correct.

### Exercise 11G

Solve each of these equations:

(a) $2x - 1 = 9$      (b) $4p - 3 = 5$      (c) $3z + 2 = 17$

(d) $3t + 1 = 19$      (e) $4g - 2 = 22$      (f) $5x - 3 = 32$

(g) $4p - 3 = 7$      (h) $5n - 3 = 2$      (i) $6p - 1 = 20$

(j) $4x - 2 = 20$      (k) $2t - 1 = 0$      (l) $3t - 7 = 11$

(m) $5p + 4 = 19$      (n) $2 + 5x = 22$      (o) $10x - 100 = 0$

## 11.7  Using algebra to solve equations

To solve $3x - 4 = 11$ you need to get $x$ on its own on one side of the scales.

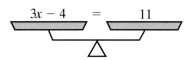

First add 4 to both sides:

adding 4 to **both** sides means the scales still balance

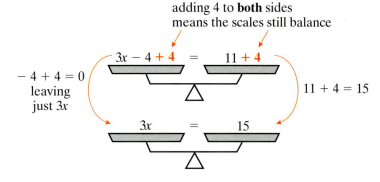

$-4 + 4 = 0$ leaving just $3x$

$11 + 4 = 15$

To get $x$ on its own divide both sides by 3:

dividing both sides by 3 means that the scales still balance

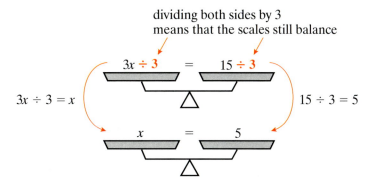

$3x \div 3 = x$

$15 \div 3 = 5$

The scales balance when $x = 5$

$x = 5$ is a solution of $3x - 4 = 11$

### Exercise 11H

Solve each of these equations:

(a) $3x - 2 = 16$      (b) $2y + 1 = 9$      (c) $5t - 2 = 8$

(d) $4x - 3 = 21$      (e) $5n + 3 = 13$      (f) $7p - 1 = 20$

(g) $8y + 2 = 58$      (h) $4p - 1 = 9$      (i) $6n + 3 = 30$

(j) $5t - 3 = 17$      (k) $8n - 3 = 9$      (l) $4x - 3 = 6$

(m) $6x - 7 = 5$      (n) $5 + 4x = 17$      (o) $7q - 35 = 0$

## 11.8 Writing equations

Sometimes you will need to write an equation to find an unknown value.

### Example 9

The perimeter of this triangle is 12 cm.

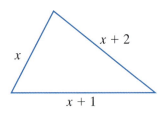

(a) Write down an equation for the perimeter.
(b) Solve the equation.
(c) Write down the length of each side of the triangle.

(a) The equation is:  $x + x + 1 + x + 2 = 12$

Collect like terms:  $3x + 3 = 12$

(b) Subtract 3 from both sides:  $3x + 3 - 3 = 12 - 3$
$$3x = 9$$

Divide both sides by 3:  $3x \div 3 = 9 \div 3$
$$x = 3$$

Check:
$3 + 4 + 5 = 12$
So $x = 3$ is correct.

(c) The sides are $x$, $x + 1$ and $x + 2$
so the sides are 3 cm, 4 cm and 5 cm.

### Exercise 11I

1   The perimeter of this quadrilateral is 33 cm.

   (a) Write an equation for the perimeter.
   (b) Solve the equation.

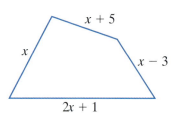

2   Jaqui is $a$ years old.
   Her mum's age is $3 \times$ Jaqui's age plus another 4 years.
   Jaqui's mum is 40 years old.

   (a) Write down an equation for Jaqui's age using $a$.
   (b) Find the value of $a$.

3   The cost of a choc-bar is *n* pence.
Asif buys 4 choc bars.
He pays for them with a £2 coin
and gets 60p change.
By writing down and solving an
equation, find the cost of one
choc bar.

4   Ken thinks of a number.
He multiplies it by 3.
Then he takes away 5.
His answer is then 7.
Write an equation and use it to find the number Ken
thought of. Use *n* for the number Ken thought of
originally.

## Summary of key points

1   A formula is a sentence describing a rule or relationship. It must
contain an equals ($=$) sign.
For example

$$\text{speed} = \frac{\text{distance}}{\text{time}}$$

2   Equations and formulae are different:

| Equation | Formula |
|---|---|
| $2 + m = 8$ | cost = price × number bought |
| This **equation** is **only true** when $m = 6$ | $c = p \times n$ |
| 6 is a **solution** of the equation. Finding the value of $m$ is called **solving the equation**. | You can put **any values** into these parts of the **formula** and get a result for the cost. |

**Equations** may be true for one value (like $m = 6$) or several values but
are not generally true for any value.

# 12 Negative numbers

## 12.1 Measuring temperatures

This thermometer measures temperatures in degrees
Celsius, written °C for short.

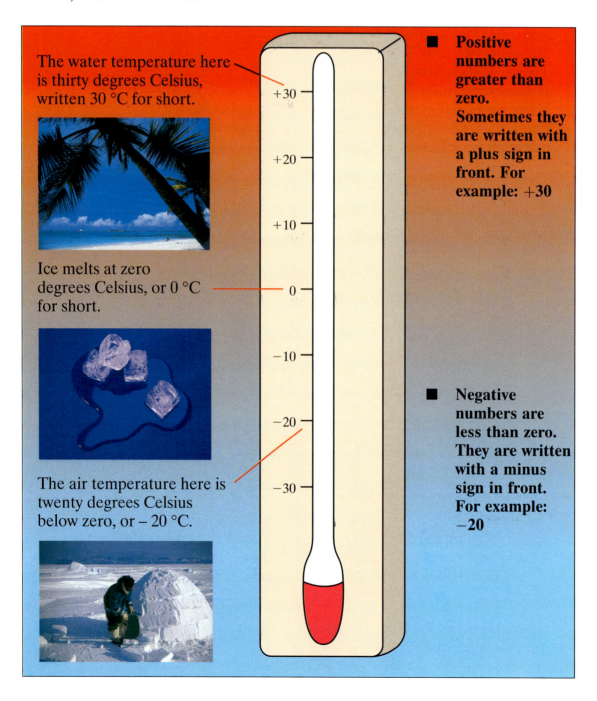

The water temperature here
is thirty degrees Celsius,
written 30 °C for short.

Ice melts at zero
degrees Celsius, or 0 °C
for short.

The air temperature here is
twenty degrees Celsius
below zero, or – 20 °C.

■ **Positive
numbers are
greater than
zero.
Sometimes they
are written with
a plus sign in
front. For
example: +30**

■ **Negative
numbers are
less than zero.
They are written
with a minus
sign in front.
For example:
–20**

**Example 1**

What temperature does the thermometer show?
Write your answer:

**(a)** in words

**(b)** in figures.

**(a)** minus eight degrees Celsius

**(b)** $-8\,°\text{C}$

**Example 2**

Mark these temperatures on the thermometer activity sheet:

**(a)** $+3\,°\text{C}$     **(b)** $-4\,°\text{C}$

**(a)** The temperature $+3\,°\text{C}$ means three degrees Celsius above zero. This is what it looks like on a thermometer.

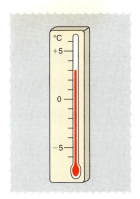

**(b)** The temperature $-4\,°\text{C}$ means four degrees Celsius below zero. This is what it looks like on a thermometer.

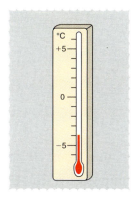

**Exercise 12A**

**1**   Look at the thermometers. Write down each temperature:
   **(i)**  in words        **(ii)** in figures.

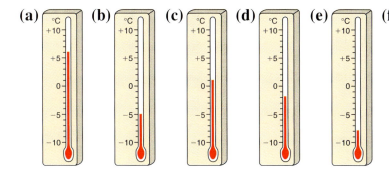

**2** You need Activity sheet 8. On it show these temperatures.

The symbol ° is short for degrees.

(a) $+5\,°C$    (b) $-3\,°C$    (c) $-6\,°C$    (d) $+9\,°C$

(e) $-2\,°C$    (f) $-4\,°C$    (g) $+6\,°C$    (h) $-7\,°C$

(i) $-1\,°C$    (j) $-11\,°C$    (k) $+4\,°C$    (l) $-8\,°C$

## 12.2 Writing temperatures in order of size

You need to be able to sort a list of temperatures in order of size.

On this weather map the numbers are temperatures in degrees Celsius.

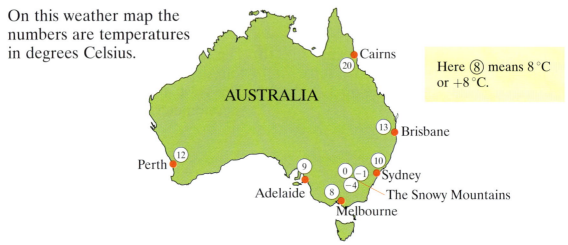

Here ⑧ means $8\,°C$ or $+8\,°C$.

### Example 3

From the weather map write down

(a) the highest temperature in °C,

(b) the lowest temperature in °C,

(c) all the temperatures in order of size, starting with the highest.

(a) The highest temperature is $20\,°C$.

(b) The lowest temperature is $-4\,°C$.

(c) Sketch a thermometer scale going from $20\,°C$ to $-5\,°C$.
Mark each temperature on the scale. Then write the temperatures in order, starting from the top of the scale:

$20\,°C$, $13\,°C$, $12\,°C$, $10\,°C$, $9\,°C$, $8\,°C$, $0\,°C$, $-1\,°C$, $-4\,°C$.

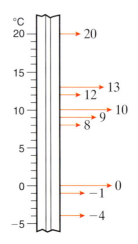

$-4\,°C$ is below $-1\,°C$, $0\,°C$, $8\,°C$ and all the other temperatures.

## Exercise 12B

On the weather maps in questions **1** and **2** the numbers are temperatures in degrees Celsius.

**1** From the weather map write down:

(a) the hottest place,

(b) the coldest place,

(c) all the temperatures in order of size, starting with the highest.

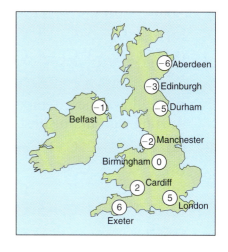

**2** Look at the weather map and write down:

(a) the highest temperature,

(b) the lowest temperature,

(c) all the temperatures in order of size, starting with the lowest.

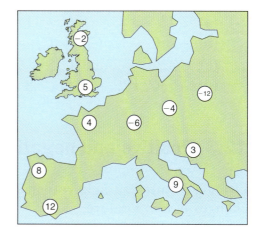

**3** Write down the higher of the two temperatures:

(a) 1 °C and 4 °C          (b) −9 °C and 3 °C

(c) −1 °C and 0 °C         (d) −2 °C and 4 °C

(e) −5 °C and −3 °C        (f) −2 °C and −5 °C

**4** Write down the lower of the two temperatures:

(a) 3 °C and 1 °C          (b) 0 °C and −2 °C

(c) −4 °C and 3 °C         (d) −3 °C and −4 °C

(e) −6 °C and −4 °C        (f) −5 °C and −9 °C

**5** Write down the highest temperature in each list:
  **(a)** $+2\,°C$, $-3\,°C$, $+3\,°C$, $-7\,°C$, $+9\,°C$, $-6\,°C$
  **(b)** $+1\,°C$, $+3\,°C$, $-4\,°C$, $-8\,°C$, $-1\,°C$, $+4\,°C$
  **(c)** $-3\,°C$, $-6\,°C$, $-1\,°C$, $-5\,°C$, $-9\,°C$, $-4\,°C$

**6** Write down the lowest temperature in each list:
  **(a)** $+2\,°C$, $-3\,°C$, $+3\,°C$, $-7\,°C$, $+9\,°C$, $-6\,°C$
  **(b)** $+1\,°C$, $+3\,°C$, $-4\,°C$, $-8\,°C$, $-1\,°C$, $+4\,°C$
  **(c)** $-3\,°C$, $-2\,°C$, $-9\,°C$, $-8\,°C$, $0\,°C$, $-7\,°C$

**7** Write down these temperatures in order of size, starting with the highest.
  **(a)** $-5\,°C$, $-2\,°C$, $2\,°C$, $-4\,°C$, $-8\,°C$, $9\,°C$
  **(b)** $2\,°C$, $-5\,°C$, $0\,°C$, $-9\,°C$, $-8\,°C$, $-1\,°C$
  **(c)** $-5\,°C$, $-2\,°C$, $-3\,°C$, $-8\,°C$, $-7\,°C$, $-1\,°C$
  **(d)** $-9\,°C$, $-4\,°C$, $-5\,°C$, $-2\,°C$, $-1\,°C$, $-11\,°C$

**8** Write down these temperatures in order of size, starting with the lowest.
  **(a)** $2\,°C$, $-3\,°C$, $-7\,°C$, $-11\,°C$, $-1\,°C$, $-6\,°C$
  **(b)** $-7\,°C$, $-12\,°C$, $-1\,°C$, $-4\,°C$, $5\,°C$, $2\,°C$
  **(c)** $-2\,°C$, $-7\,°C$, $0\,°C$, $-8\,°C$, $3\,°C$, $-13\,°C$
  **(d)** $-5\,°C$, $1\,°C$, $-11\,°C$, $-8\,°C$, $-4\,°C$, $2\,°C$

## 12.3 Positive and negative temperatures

Using a picture can help you answer questions involving changes in temperature.

**Example 4**

The temperature in Derby at midnight was $-3\,°C$. By noon the following day the temperature had gone up to $4\,°C$. How much did the temperature rise?

Start at the $-3\,°C$ mark.

To get to the $4\,°C$ mark you go up 7 degrees.

The temperature rise was $7\,°C$.

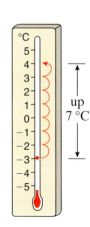

### Example 5

The temperature in Leeds at midday was $2\,°C$.
By midnight the temperature had gone down by $6\,°C$.
Work out the temperature in Leeds at midnight.

Start at the $2\,°C$ mark and go down $6\,°C$.

You end up at $-4\,°C$.

The temperature in Leeds at midnight was $-4\,°C$.

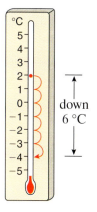

### Exercise 12C

**1** The temperature in Bangor at midnight was $-4\,°C$.
By noon the next day the temperature had gone up to
$5\,°C$. How much did the temperature rise?

**2** The temperature in Watford at noon was $4\,°C$. By $8\,pm$
the same day the temperature had gone down to $-1\,°C$.
Work out the fall in temperature.

**3** The temperature in Guildford at midnight was $-6\,°C$.
By noon the next day the temperature had gone up by
eight degrees. Work out the temperature in Guildford
at noon.

**4** The temperature in Bolton at noon was $-2\,°C$. By midnight the temperature had gone down by seven degrees.
What was the temperature in Bolton at midnight?

Copy and complete the tables for questions **5** and **6**.

**5**

| Town | Temperature at midnight | Temperature at noon the next day | Rise in temperature |
|---|---|---|---|
| Maidstone | $-3\,°C$ | $5\,°C$ | |
| Taunton | $-1\,°C$ | $6\,°C$ | |
| Luton | $-5\,°C$ | $-1\,°C$ | |
| Preston | $-2\,°C$ | | $7\,°C$ |
| Newmarket | $-4\,°C$ | | $5\,°C$ |
| Darlington | $-6\,°C$ | | $3\,°C$ |

**6**

| Town | Temperature at noon | Temperature at 2 a.m. the next day | Fall in temperature |
|------|---------------------|-----------------------------------|---------------------|
| Hatfield | $5\,°C$ | $1\,°C$ | |
| Oldham | $4\,°C$ | $-3\,°C$ | |
| Matlock | $-3\,°C$ | $-9\,°C$ | |
| Oxford | $-2\,°C$ | | $6\,°C$ |
| Brighton | $1\,°C$ | | $3\,°C$ |
| Norwich | $-4\,°C$ | | $2\,°C$ |

## 12.4 Using number lines

■ **You can use a number line to help you answer questions involving negative numbers.**

**Example 6**

Find the value of:

**(a)** $2 + 6$      **(b)** $-2 + 6$      **(c)** $2 - 6$      **(d)** $-2 - 6$

**(a)** $2 + 6 = 8$

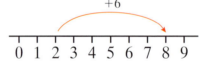

**(b)** $-2 + 6 = 4$

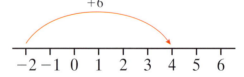

**(c)** $2 - 6 = -4$

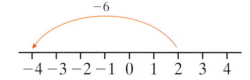

**(d)** $-2 - 6 = -8$

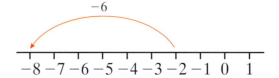

### Example 7

Write down all the whole numbers that are larger than $-8$, smaller than 6 and are even.

You need numbers smaller than 6 so 6 is not included.

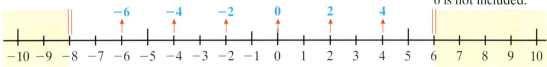

You need numbers larger than $-8$, so $-8$ is not included.

The numbers you need are $-6$, $-4$, $-2$, 0, 2 and 4.

### Exercise 12D

1   Use the number line at the top of the page to find the number that is:
   **(a)** 6 more than 3      **(b)** 7 more than $-2$
   **(c)** 9 less than $-5$   **(d)** 4 less than $-2$
   **(e)** 8 more than $-5$   **(f)** 5 less than 0
   **(g)** 7 more than $-4$   **(h)** 5 more than $-3$
   **(i)** 6 more than $-6$   **(j)** 9 more than $-4$
   **(k)** 3 more than $-8$   **(l)** 6 more than $-5$

2   Write down all the whole numbers that are larger than $-5$ and smaller than 4.

3   Write down all the numbers that are larger than $-7$, smaller than 9 and are odd.

4   Write down all the numbers that are smaller than 8, larger than $-5$ and are even.

5   Use a number line to find the value of:
   **(a)** $8 - 3$       **(b)** $3 - 5$       **(c)** $4 - 9$
   **(d)** $3 - 7$       **(e)** $-5 + 2$      **(f)** $-3 + 9$
   **(g)** $-2 + 6$      **(h)** $-3 - 6$      **(i)** $-6 - 3$
   **(j)** $-8 + 5$      **(k)** $2 - 6$       **(l)** $-9 + 5$

6   Find the value of:
   **(a)** $7 - 2$       **(b)** $3 - 9$       **(c)** $2 - 8$
   **(d)** $5 - 9$       **(e)** $-6 + 2$      **(f)** $-4 + 9$
   **(g)** $-2 + 6$      **(h)** $-3 - 7$      **(i)** $-5 - 8$
   **(j)** $-11 + 4$     **(k)** $1 - 7$       **(l)** $-23 + 6$

**7**  Liam chose a number that is smaller than −3, larger than −8 and is a multiple of 3. What is the number Liam chose?

**8**  Write down the next two numbers in each pattern:

(a)  9, 5, 1, −3,...          (b)  7, 4, 1, −2,...

(c)  12, 9, 6, 3,...          (d)  5, 3, 1, −1,...

(e)  3, −1, −5, −9,...          (f)  −3, −5, −7, −9,...

(g)  −11, −8, −5, −2,...          (h)  −13, −8, −3, 2,...

**9**  You need a calculator.

(a)  Step 1:  Enter the number 10 on the calculator.

Step 2:  Use the calculator to subtract 3 and record the result from the calculator display.

Step 3:  Continue to subtract 3 and record the results.

Step 4:  Write down what you notice about the results.

(b)  Repeat part (a), but subtract 4 each time instead of 3.

(c)  Compare the results you obtain in parts (a) and (b).

**10**  You need a calculator.

(a)  Step 1:  Enter the number −90 on the calculator.

Step 2:  Use the calculator to add 4 and record the result from the calculator display.

Step 3:  Continue to add 4 and record the results.

Step 4:  Write down what you notice about the results.

To enter '−90' on your calculator: Key in 90 then press the $\boxed{\pm}$ key.

(b)  Repeat part (a), but add 5 each time instead of 4.

(c)  Compare the results you obtain in parts (a) and (b).

**11**  What number is:

(a)  20 more than −50          (b)  30 less than −10

(c)  70 greater than −30          (d)  80 smaller than 20

(e)  120 smaller than −40          (f)  50 greater than 300

(g)  400 greater than −100          (h)  170 greater than −200

(i)  130 more than −20          (j)  300 less than −300

(k)  18 more than −33          (l)  29 more than −16

## 12.5 Ordering positive and negative numbers

■ **You can use a number line to help you sort numbers in order of size.**

### Example 8

Write down these numbers in order of size, starting with the smallest:

5,  2, −3, −8,  0,  1, −2, −6

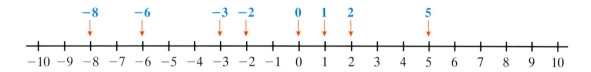

The order is  −8, −6, −3, −2,  0,  1,  2,  5

### Example 9

Write down the two missing numbers in each sequence:

**(a)** 7, 5, 3, 1, ___ , ___ , −5
**(b)** −14, −11, −8, −5, ___ , ___ , 4

**(a)** The numbers go down by 2 each time.
The missing numbers are −1 and −3

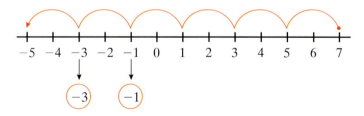

**(b)** The numbers go up 3 each time.
The missing numbers are −2 and 1

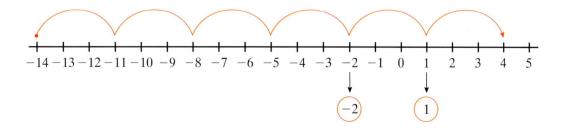

1   Write down these numbers in order of size, starting
    with the smallest:
    **(a)** 3, −9, −1, 0, 6, −5
    **(b)** 7, −2, 4, −3, 3, −8
    **(c)** −4, 8, −7, 2, −1, 0
    **(d)** −1, 5, 10, −8, 2, −3
    **(e)** 5, −9, 2, 8, −12, −1
    **(f)** 22, 71, 0, −89, −98, −3
    **(g)** −68, 43, 2, 101, −19, 72
    **(h)** −19, 5, 18, −21, −3, −4

2   Write down the two missing numbers in each sequence:
    **(a)** 13, 10, 7, 4, ___, ___, −5
    **(b)** −9, −7, −5, −3, ___, ___, 3
    **(c)** 19, 15, 11, 7, ___, ___, −5
    **(d)** −13, −9, −5, −1, ___, ___, 11
    **(e)** 15, 14, 12, 9, ___, ___, −6
    **(f)** −18, −16, −12, −6, ___, ___, 24

3   Priyah starts with the number −18 and keeps adding 4.
    Write down in order all the numbers she gets that are
    smaller than 40.

    Samir starts with the number −18 and keeps adding 5.
    Write down in order all the numbers he gets that are
    smaller than 40.

    Compare the numbers that Priyah gets with the
    numbers that Samir gets.

4   Jaspal starts with the number 50 and keeps subtracting
    6. Write down in order all the numbers she gets that
    are larger than −50.
    Martin starts with the number 50 and keeps subtracting
    5. Write down in order all the numbers he gets that are
    bigger than −50.
    Compare the numbers that Jaspal gets with the
    numbers that Martin gets.

5   Natalie works out 9 more than −3. Then she works out 7
    less than her result. What number does she end up with?

## 12.6 Adding and subtracting negative numbers

### Adding negative numbers

■ **When you add two negative numbers the result is a negative number.**

$-2 + -3$     is the same as     $-2 - 3 = -5$

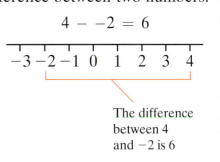

### Subtracting negative numbers

| Subtracting involves finding the difference between two numbers: |
|---|

$$5 - 3 = 2$$

The difference between 5 and 3 is 2

Subtracting a negative number also involves finding the difference between two numbers:

$$4 - -2 = 6$$

The difference between 4 and $-2$ is 6

■ **Subtracting a negative number has the same effect as adding a positive number.**

For example

$4 - -2$     is the same as     $4 + 2 = 6$
$-3 - -2$     is the same as     $-3 + 2 = -1$

### Exercise 12F

**1**   Copy and complete the subtractions on these number lines. The first one is done for you:

**(a)** $2 - 3 = -1$          **(b)** $1 - 6 =$

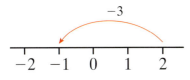

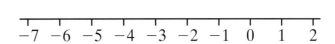

**2**  Do these subtractions:

(**a**) $3 - 1$    (**b**) $1 - 4$    (**c**) $2 - 3$    (**d**) $3 - 5$

(**e**) $-2 - 3$    (**f**) $-5 - 2$    (**g**) $-3 - 5$    (**h**) $-4 - 1$

**3**  Sketch a number line to help you answer these questions:

(**a**) $-2 + 5$    (**b**) $-2 - 5$    (**c**) $3 + -4$    (**d**) $3 - 4$

(**e**) $1 - 5$    (**f**) $1 + -5$    (**g**) $-1 - 4$    (**h**) $-1 + -4$

**4**  Copy and complete these subtractions. The first one is done for you:

(**a**) $2 - -3 = 5$                    (**b**) $4 - -4 =$

    $2 - -3$ is the same
    as $2 + 3 = 5$

(**c**) $3 - -1 =$                    (**d**) $0 - -2 =$

**5**  Work out:

(**a**) $7 - -2$    (**b**) $6 - -1$    (**c**) $4 - -5$

(**d**) $5 - -5$    (**e**) $3 - -4$    (**f**) $0 - -4$

(**g**) $4 - -6$    (**h**) $9 - -8$    (**i**) $-2 - -3$

**6**  Work out:

(**a**) $-3 + 7$    (**b**) $7 - -3$    (**c**) $5 - -1$    (**d**) $4 + -3$

(**e**) $7 + -3$    (**f**) $-3 + -7$    (**g**) $-2 + 5$    (**h**) $-1 + -1$

(**i**) $-3 + -5$    (**j**) $-5 + -7$    (**k**) $-2 + -3$    (**l**) $-1 + 7$

(**m**) $-7 + -3$    (**n**) $-2 - -5$    (**o**) $5 - -2$    (**p**) $-8 - -2$

**7**  Work out:

(**a**) $10 - -7$    (**b**) $100 + -70$    (**c**) $23 - -17$    (**d**) $-8 - -16$

(**e**) $-5 - -11$    (**f**) $-11 - -5$    (**g**) $-19 - -9$    (**h**) $-23 - 23$

(**i**) $-15 - -8$    (**j**) $-13 - -19$    (**k**) $19 - -19$    (**l**) $47 - -100$

# Summary of key points

**1**  Positive numbers are greater than zero. Sometimes they are written with a plus sign in front. For example: +30

**2**  Negative numbers are less than zero. They are written with a minus sign in front. For example: −30

The temperature here is thirty degrees Celsius, written 30 °C for short.

Water freezes at zero degrees Celsius, or 0 °C for short.

The temperature here is twenty degrees Celsius below zero, or − 20 °C.

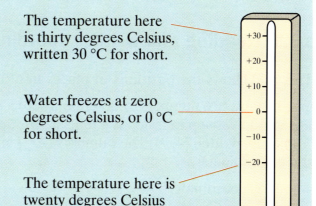

**3**  You can use a number line to help you answer questions involving negative numbers.

$2 - 6 = -4$

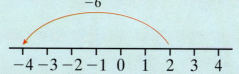

**4**  When you add two negative numbers the result is a negative number.

$-2 + -3$    is the same as    $-2 - 3 = -5$

**5**  Subtracting a negative number has the same effect as adding a positive number:

$4 - -6$    is the same as    $4 + 6 = 10$

# 13 Graphs

## 13.1 Reading and writing coordinates

This grid shows the positions of places in a theme park.

You can use two numbers to describe where a place is. For example, the pirate ship is 4 units across and 7 units up, written (4, 7). The numbers (4, 7) are the pirate ship's coordinates.

4 is the *x*-coordinate.
7 is the *y*-coordinate.

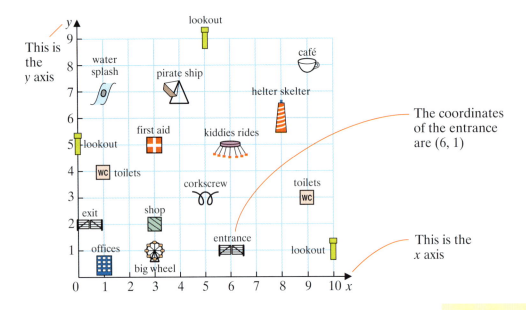

The coordinates of the entrance are (6, 1)

This is the *x* axis

You always give the *x*-coordinate before the *y*-coordinate. *x* comes before *y* in the alphabet.

■ **You can give the position of a place on a grid using coordinates.**

### Exercise 13A

1   Look at the map of the theme park. What can be found at:
   (a) (10, 1)      (b) (8, 6)      (c) (5, 3)
   (d) (0, 5)       (e) (1, 0)      (f) (3, 5)

**2** What are the coordinates of these places on the map of the theme park?

(**a**) kiddies rides     (**b**) big wheel
(**c**) pirate ship     (**d**) café
(**e**) water splash     (**f**) each lookout post
(**g**) shop     (**h**) both toilets

**3** Look at the map of the zoo. What can be found at:

(**a**) (8, 2)     (**b**) (5, 0)
(**c**) (8, 9)     (**d**) (4, 5)
(**e**) (4, 2)

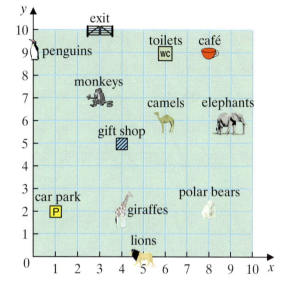

**4** What are the coordinates of:

(**a**) the exit
(**b**) the camels
(**c**) the car park
(**d**) the monkeys
(**e**) the penguins

**5** A new enclosure is placed half-way between the giraffes and the polar bears.
What are the coordinates of the new enclosure?

**6** A lifeboat starts from the position (1, 6).

The map shows the route it takes.

It goes to the wreck then on to the hospital.

Copy and complete these directions:

From (1, 6) to (1, 2)
From (1, 2) to ( , )
From ( , ) to ( , )
From ( , ) to ( , )
From ( , ) to (8, 7).

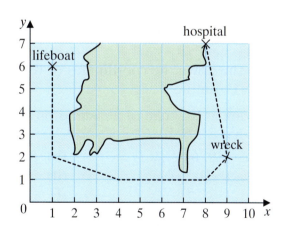

## 13.2 Extending the coordinate grid

This radar screen shows aircraft positions.

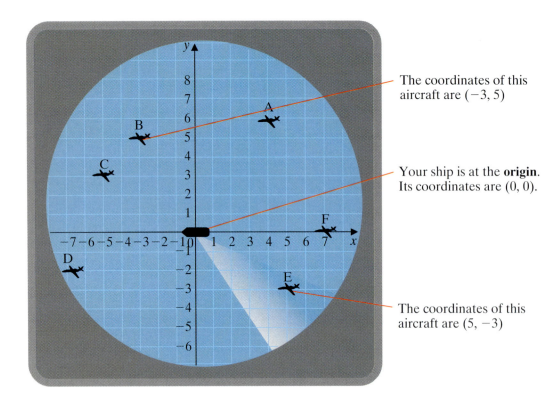

The coordinates of this aircraft are $(-3, 5)$

Your ship is at the **origin**. Its coordinates are $(0, 0)$.

The coordinates of this aircraft are $(5, -3)$

## Exercise 13B

1  Write down the coordinates of the aircraft marked A, C, D and F.

2  Look at the map of an island on page 201.
   What is at:
   **(a)** $(10, 6)$              **(b)** $(8, -6)$
   **(c)** $(-10, -4)$           **(d)** $(0, 0)$
   **(e)** $(-8, 5)$             **(f)** $(7, -1)$
   **(g)** $(0, 4)$              **(h)** $(0, -5)$

3  What are the coordinates of the:
   **(a)** shops (2 answers)     **(b)** lighthouse
   **(c)** hospital              **(d)** radio station
   **(e)** caves                 **(f)** pier
   **(g)** harbour               **(h)** castle

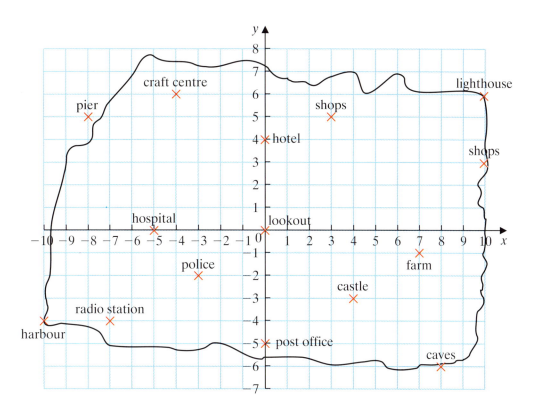

**4**   This grid shows a game of 'battleships'.

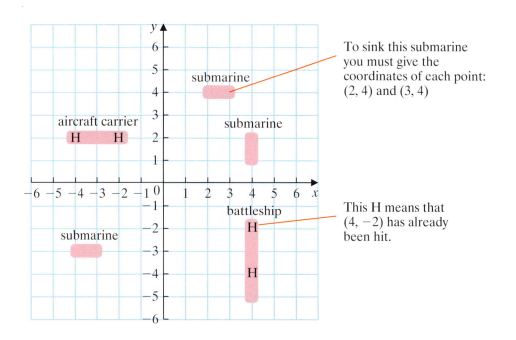

To sink this submarine you must give the coordinates of each point: (2, 4) and (3, 4)

This H means that (4, −2) has already been hit.

What coordinates should be given to sink:
**(a)**  the aircraft carrier  **(b)**  the battleship  **(c)**  each submarine?

# 13.3 Drawing coordinate grids

Sometimes you will need to draw your own coordinate grid.

Draw two perpendicular **axes** long enough for all the points you need to plot.

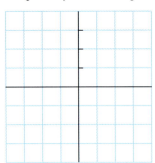

Number the axes. Write 0 where they meet.

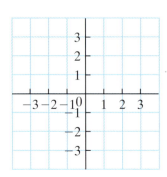

Label the horizontal axis $x$ and the vertical axis $y$.

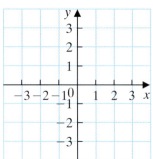

## Exercise 13C

1   Draw a coordinate grid on squared paper. Number each axis from $-10$ to 10. Plot these points and draw the shapes by joining the points in order. Shade each shape.

> Marking points on a coordinate grid is called plotting the points.

(a)  (6, 10) (9, 10) (9, 7) (6, 7) (6, 10)
(b)  (1, 0) (1, 3) (6, 3) (6, 0) (1, 0)
(c)  (−8, 8), (−8, 4), (−5, 8), (−8, 8)
(d)  (−2, 3), (−2, 1), (2, −4), (2, 3), (−2, 3)
(e)  (−5, 4), (−4, 7), (2, 7), (1, 4), (−5, 4)

Name as many of these shapes as you can.

2   Draw a coordinate grid on squared paper. Number each axis from $-10$ to 10.
Plot these points and complete the shapes.
Each shape has one corner missing.
Write down the missing coordinates.

(a)  square: (1, 1), (5, 1), (1, 5), (__ , __)
(b)  rectangle: (2, 7), (7, 7), (7, 10), (__ , __)
(c)  parallelogram: (−9, 10), (−7, 10), (−6, 7), (__ , __)
(d)  square: (4, −2), (7, −5), (4, −8), (__ , __)
(e)  rectangle: (2, −1), (9, −1), (9, 2), (__ , __)
(f)  octagon: (−6, −1), (−4, −3), (−2, −3), (0, −1),
          (0, 1), (−2, 3), (−4, 3), (__ , __)

**3    Mid points**

Draw a coordinate grid from $-10$ to $10$ in both directions.

On your grid, draw the square with corners: A(8, 8), B(8, $-8$), C($-8$, $-8$) and D($-8$, 8).

Mark the mid points of each of the sides.

Write down the coordinates of the mid points.

Join these 4 points together to make a new shape.

Find the mid points of each side of the new shape.

Join them and make a second new shape.

Repeat.

What do you notice?

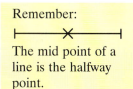

Remember:

The mid point of a line is the halfway point.

# 13.4 Line them up

### Example 1: four in a row

Two people take turns to put a counter on the grid.

To win the game, get four of your counters in a straight line.
The line can be horizontal, vertical or slanted.

This game has been started. It is blue's turn.
Can blue win the game with the next counter?
Write down the coordinates of the points that make a winning line.

Yes. If they put a counter at (3, 2) they can win the game.

(3, 1), (3, 2), (3, 3) and (3, 4) make a vertical line.

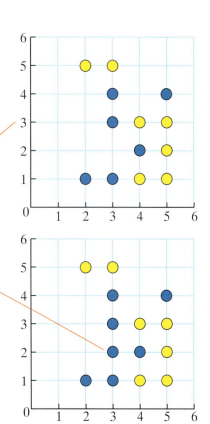

## Exercise 13D

**1** Look at this game of four in a row. Where could yellow go to win the game? Write down the coordinates of the points that make a winning line.

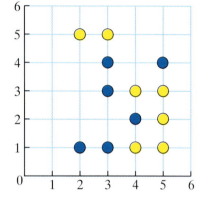

**2** Copy the grid and play your own game of four in a row. Write down the coordinates of the points that make a winning line. Write down whether the line is horizontal, vertical or slanted. Play the game 10 times.

**3** Write down what you notice about the coordinates of

(a) a horizontal winning line

(b) a vertical winning line

(c) a slanted winning line

## 13.5 Naming straight lines

These points are all on a straight line.

Their coordinates show a pattern:

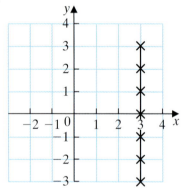

(3, −3)  (3, −2)  (3, −1)  (3, 0)  (3, 1)  (3, 2)  (3, 3)

The $x$ coordinate of each points is always 3.

The line is called $x = 3$.

$x = 3$ is the **equation of the line**.

## Example 2

From the grid, write down:

**(a)** the coordinates of the points A, C and F

**(b)** the equation of the line joining A, C and F

**(c)** the coordinates of the points G, F and J

**(d)** the equation of the line joining G, F and J

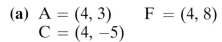

**(a)** A = (4, 3)    F = (4, 8)
C = (4, −5)

**(b)** All the $x$-coordinates are 4.
The equation of the line is $x = 4$.

**(c)** G = (−4, 8)    F = (4, 8)
J  = (7, 8)

**(d)** All the $y$-coordinates are 8.
The equation of the line is $y = 8$.

■ **You can use an equation to describe a straight line.**
For example:
$$x = 3$$

## Exercise 13E

**1**  Look at the grid at the top of this page.
Find the equation of the line joining the points:

**(a)** G  B  H

**(b)** H  D  I

**(c)** B  A  E

**(d)** J  E  I

> Hint:
> List the coordinates of each point.

**2**  Find the equation of the line connecting these points:

**(a)** (3, 0), (5, 0), (−6, 0)

**(b)** (0, 5), (0, 8), (0, −6), (0, −1)

**(c)** (2, 3), (2, −1), (2, 6)

**(d)** (5, 4), (5, 5), (5, 7)

**(e)** (3, 6), (4, 6), (−1, 6)

**(f)** (0, 7), (1, 7), (7, 7)

**(g)** (4, −1), (5, −1), (7, −1)

**(h)** (−3, 4), (−3, 6), (−3, 8)

**3** Look at the coordinate grid below. Find the equations of each of the lines shown. (Each will start with $x =$ or $y =$)

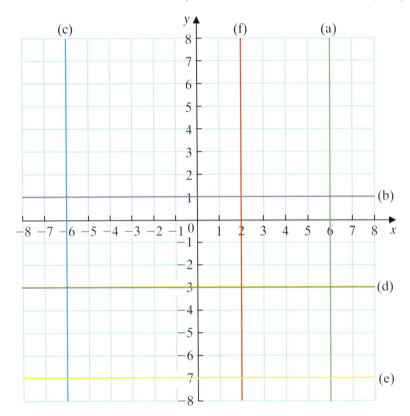

## 13.6 Naming slanted lines

The points A, B and C on this grid are on a straight line. They have coordinates (1, 1), (3, 3) and (6, 6).

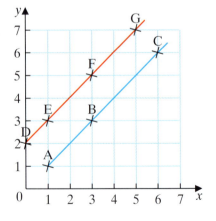

The $y$-coordinate is the same as the $x$-coordinate. So $y$-coordinate $= x$-coordinate. The equation of the line is $y = x$.

The points D, E, F and G have coordinates (0, 2), (1, 3), (3, 5) and (5, 7).

To name the line, find a rule connecting the $x$-coordinate and the $y$-coordinate:

$$(0, 2) \quad (1, 3) \quad (3, 5) \quad (5, 7)$$
$$+2 \qquad +2 \qquad +2 \qquad +2$$

The rule is 'add 2 to the $x$-coordinate'
The equation is $y = x + 2$.

$y$-coordinate is
$x$-coordinate $+ 2$

**Example 3**

Find the equations of the lines on this grid.

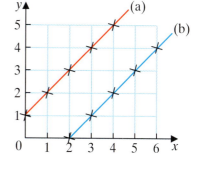

(a)  Write down the coordinates of the points on the line:

$(0, 1)$     $(1, 2)$     $(2, 3)$     $(3, 4)$

$+1$         $+1$         $+1$         $+1$

The rule is 'add 1 to the $x$-coordinate'
The equation is $y = x + 1$.

(b)  The coordinates are:

$(2, 0)$     $(3, 1)$     $(4, 2)$     $(5, 3)$

$-2$         $-2$         $-2$         $-2$

The rule is 'subtract 2 from the $x$-coordinate'.
The equation is $y = x - 2$.

■   **The equation of a vertical line is $x =$ a number.**
     **The equation of a horizontal line is $y =$ a number.**

■   **To find the equation of a slanted line find a rule connecting the $x$-coordinate and the $y$-coordinate.**

**Exercise 13F**

1    Find the equations of the lines on this grid:

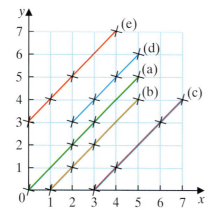

**2** Find the equations of these lines:

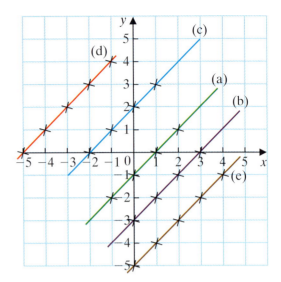

**3** Find the equations of these lines:

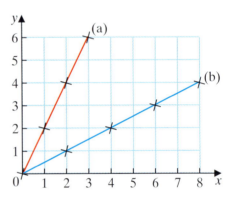

## 13.7 Drawing a line from its equation

Sometimes you will be given the equation of a line and asked to draw it.

You use the equation to find the coordinates of points on the line.

### Example 4

**(a)** Draw the line with equation $x = 1$.

You need the coordinates of any three points on the line. These will do:

$$(1, 0) \quad (1, 2) \quad (1, 5)$$

Now plot these points and join them up with a straight line:

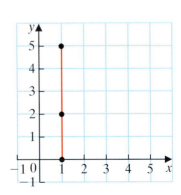

**(b)** Draw the line with equation $y = x + 3$.

You need the coordinates of any three points on the line.

To find these points, give $x$ three different values:

When   $x = 0$   $y = 0 + 3$   $y = 3$

When   $x = 1$   $y = 1 + 3$   $y = 4$

When   $x = 3$   $y = 3 + 3$   $y = 6$

So the three points are:

(0, 3)   (1, 4)   (3, 6)

Now plot these points and join them up with a straight line:

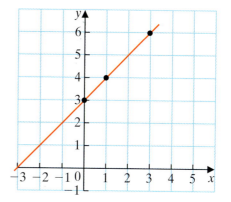

## Using a table of values

When you need to draw a sloping line like $y = x - 1$ use a table of values.

Choose some values for $x$, such as 1, 2, 3, 4 and 5. Draw a table like this:

| $x$ | 1 | 2 | 3 | 4 | 5 |
|---|---|---|---|---|---|
| $y$ |  |  |  |  |  |

Work out $x - 1$ for each $x$ value. For example:

When   $x = 1$   $y = 1 - 1$   $y = 0$

Put the answers in the table:

| $x$ | 1 | 2 | 3 | 4 | 5 |
|---|---|---|---|---|---|
| $y$ | 0 | 1 | 2 | 3 | 4 |

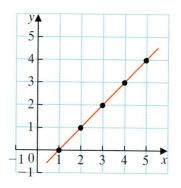

The coordinates are:

(1, 0) (2, 1) (3, 2) (4, 3) (5, 4)

## Exercise 13G

**1**   Draw a coordinate grid labelling the axes from $-8$ to 8 in each direction.
Plot each line on the same grid and label them:

**(a)** $x = 2$   **(b)** $x = 6$   **(c)** $x = 4$   **(d)** $y = 3$
**(e)** $y = 4$   **(f)** $x = -5$   **(g)** $y = -6$   **(h)** $x = 0$

**2**   Draw the straight line for each of these equations.

**(a)** $y = x + 1$   **(b)** $y = x - 2$   **(c)** $y = x + 4$
**(d)** $y = 2x$   **(e)** $y = 5 + x$

> Remember:
> $2x$ means $2 \times x$

**3**   For each equation:
Copy and complete the table of values.
Plot the points on a coordinate grid and draw the line.

**(a)** $y = x + 6$

| $x$ | $-3$ | $-2$ | $-1$ | 0 | 1 | 2 | 3 | 4 |
|---|---|---|---|---|---|---|---|---|
| $y$ | | 4 | | 6 | | | | 10 |

**(b)** $y = x + 3$

| $x$ | $-3$ | $-2$ | $-1$ | 0 | 1 | 2 | 3 | 4 |
|---|---|---|---|---|---|---|---|---|
| $y$ | 0 | | | 3 | | 5 | | |

**(c)** $y = x - 1$

| $x$ | $-3$ | $-2$ | $-1$ | 0 | 1 | 2 | 3 | 4 |
|---|---|---|---|---|---|---|---|---|
| $y$ | | $-3$ | | $-1$ | | 1 | | |

**(d)** $y = x - 3$

| $x$ | $-3$ | $-2$ | $-1$ | 0 | 1 | 2 | 3 | 4 |
|---|---|---|---|---|---|---|---|---|
| $y$ | | $-5$ | | | $-2$ | | | 1 |

**(e)** $y = 2 + x$

| $x$ | $-3$ | $-2$ | $-1$ | 0 | 1 | 2 | 3 | 4 |
|---|---|---|---|---|---|---|---|---|
| $y$ | $-1$ | | | 2 | | | | 6 |

# 13.8  Conversion graphs

When you draw the line $y = x + 3$ on a coordinate grid, it is called the **graph** of $y = x + 3$.

■   **A graph shows a relationship on a coordinate grid.**

This graph shows the relationship between miles and kilometres:

On this scale:
  10 squares  represent   20 kilometres
so  1 square  represents  20 ÷ 10
                = 2 kilometres

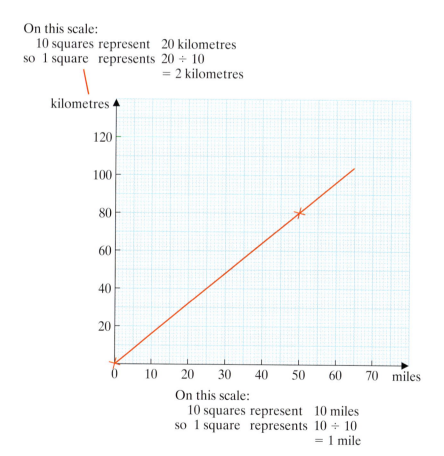

On this scale:
    10 squares  represent   10 miles
  so  1 square  represents  10 ÷ 10
                  = 1 mile

You can use the graph to convert from one measurement to another.

## Example 5

Use the graph to convert:

**(a)** 50 miles to kilometres

**(b)** 100 kilometres to miles

**(a)**

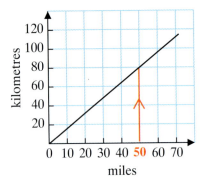

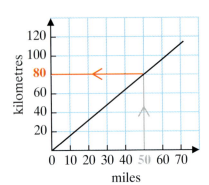

Find 50 on the miles axis.
Draw a line up to the graph.

Draw a line from the graph
to the kilometres axis.

Read off the value:
50 miles = 80 kilometres

**(b)**

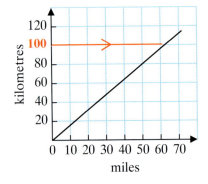

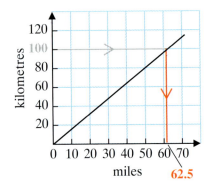

Find 100 on the kilometres axis.
Draw a line up to the graph.

Draw a line from the graph
to the miles axis.

Read off the value:
100 kilometres = 62.5 miles

## Using scales

The scales on these axes are different.

On the *y*-axis:
    10 small squares represent 50 units
so   1 small square represents 50 ÷ 10
                        = 5 units

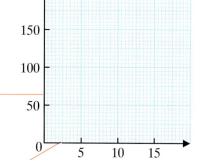

On the *x*-axis,
    10 small squares represent 5 units
so   1 small square represents 5 ÷ 10
                        = 0.5 units

The most common scales to use are the factors of 10: 1, 2, 5, 10 and multiples of 10: 10, 20, 50, 100

For example, if you use 10 small squares for 5 units, count in 5s: 5, 10, 15,...

If you use 10 small squares for 50 units, count in 50s: 50, 100, 150, 200,...

### Exercise 13H

**1**   You can use this graph to convert weights between kilograms and pounds.

(a) Work out the scale on each axis. (What does 1 small square represent?)

Use the graph to convert:

(b) 50 kilograms to pounds

(c) 30 kilograms to pounds

(d) 66 pounds to kilograms

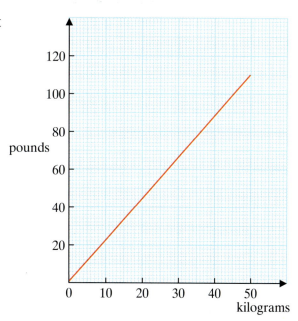

**2** This graph converts between inches and centimetres.

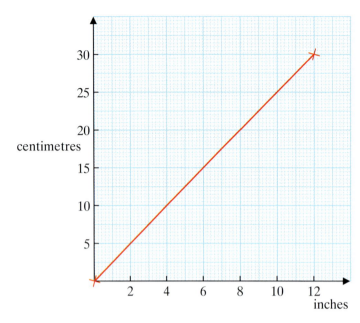

(a) Work out the scale on each axis. (What does 1 small square represent?)

Use the graph to convert:

(b) 6 inches to centimetres

(c) 20 centimetres to inches

(d) 1 inch to centimetres

(e) 1 centimetre to inches

**3** Draw two axes.
Label the *x*-axis litres and the *y*-axis pints.

Use 10 small squares to represent 5 litres on the *x*-axis and 10 small squares to represent 10 pints on the *y*-axis.

Plot two points: (0, 0) and (20, 35).
Join them up.

You can use this graph to convert between litres and pints.

> 20 litres = 35 pints so you can plot the point (20, 35) on your graph.

Use the graph to convert:

(a) 10 litres to pints        (b) 20 pints to litres

(c) 1 pint to litres          (d) 1 litre to pints

**4** Draw two axes on a large piece of graph paper. Label the *x*-axis °C and the *y*-axis °F.

Use 10 small squares to represent 10 °C on the *x*-axis and 10 small squares to represent 20 °F on the *y*-axis.

Plot the points (0, 32) and (80, 176) and join them up.

This graph converts between degrees Celsius (°C) and degrees Fahrenheit (°F).

Use your graph to convert, roughly:

**(a)** 10 °C to °F  **(b)** 100 °F to °C
**(c)** 35 °C to °F  **(d)** 40 °F to °C

**5** Draw a graph to convert between old pence (d) and new pence (p).

Use these facts:
0p = 0d  (plot (0, 0))
100p = 240d  (plot (100, 240))

Plot new pence (p) on the *x*-axis and old pence (d) on the *y*-axis.
Choose your own scales.
Use your graph to convert:

**(a)** 30p to d  **(b)** 100d to p

## Summary of key points

**1** You can give the position of a place on a grid using coordinates.

**2** You can use an equation to describe a straight line. For example: $x = 3$

**3** The equation of a vertical line is $x = $ a number

The equation of a horizontal line is $y = $ a number.

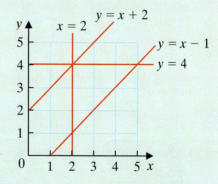

**4** To find the equation of a slanted line find a rule connecting the *x*-coordinate and the *y*-coordinate.

**5** A graph shows a relationship on a coordinate grid.

# 14 Angles

The disco light is turning:

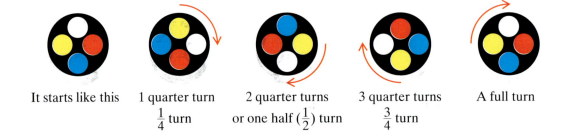

It starts like this    1 quarter turn $\frac{1}{4}$ turn    2 quarter turns or one half ($\frac{1}{2}$) turn    3 quarter turns $\frac{3}{4}$ turn    A full turn

This unit shows you how to measure turns.

## 14.1 Turning shapes

You can turn a shape clockwise or anticlockwise.

### Example 1

Draw this flag when it has turned:

(a) $\frac{1}{4}$ turn clockwise

(b) $\frac{1}{4}$ turn anticlockwise

(c) $1\frac{1}{2}$ turns.

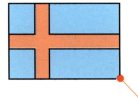

turn the shape around this dot

Trace the shape.

Turn it:

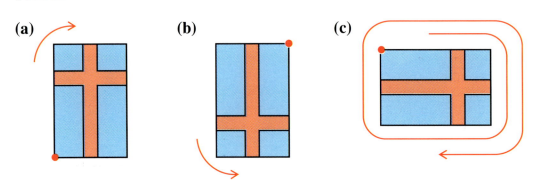

(a)     (b)     (c)

## Exercise 14A

1 Trace each of these shapes.
Draw each shape when it has turned clockwise through:

- $\frac{1}{4}$ turn
- $\frac{1}{2}$ turn
- $\frac{3}{4}$ turn

a    b    c

d    e    f

2 Write down the letter the arrow will
point to after each of these turns:

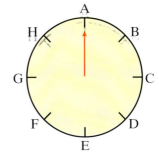

(a) $\frac{1}{4}$ turn clockwise from F

(b) $\frac{1}{2}$ turn from C

(c) $\frac{1}{4}$ turn clockwise from B

(d) $\frac{1}{4}$ turn anticlockwise from A

(e) $\frac{1}{4}$ turn anticlockwise from E

3 Using the diagram from question **2**, describe the turn
needed to move from:

(a) B to D  (b) H to D  (c) D to B

(d) G to A  (e) E to G

## 14.2 Rotational symmetry

This shape is **rotating** – another word for turning:

Start    $\frac{1}{4}$ turn    $\frac{1}{2}$ turn    $\frac{3}{4}$ turn    Full turn

1    2

In a full turn these **two** positions look exactly the same.
This shape has rotational symmetry of order 2.

- **A shape has rotational symmetry if it looks exactly the same <u>two or more times</u> in a full turn.**

- **The order of rotational symmetry is the number of times it looks exactly the same in a full turn.**

Any irregular shape – like this – must have rotational symmetry of order 1. It looks the same if you rotate it a full turn. But we usually say that such a shape does *not* have rotational symmetry.

### Example 2

For each shape:

- Does it have rotational symmetry?

- If it does, what is the order of rotational symmetry?

**(a)**    **(b)**

**(a)** Trace the shape. Make a mark in one corner. Rotate the shape this way ⤵ around the dot ●

  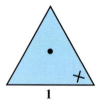  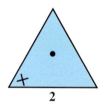  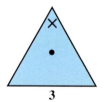
                                          1               2               3

It looks exactly the same in 3 positions so it has rotational symmetry of order 3.

> Remember not to count the full turn as different. It's the same as the start!

**(b)** Trace the shape and rotate it:

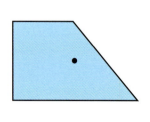  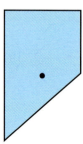  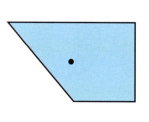  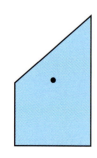

This shape does **not** have rotational symmetry.

## Exercise 14B

For each of these shapes

- Does the shape have rotational symmetry?
- If it does, what is the order of rotational symmetry?

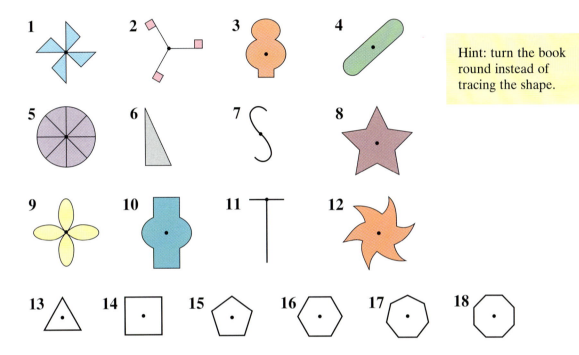

Hint: turn the book round instead of tracing the shape.

19  The shapes in questions **13** to **18** are all regular polygons: the sizes of each of their angles and the lengths of each of their sides is the same. Write down a rule about the rotational symmetry of a regular polygon.

## 14.3 Angles

Most rotations are not simple fractions of a turn:

This is about $\frac{1}{10}$ of a turn.

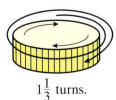

$1\frac{1}{3}$ turns.

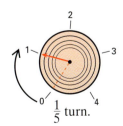

$\frac{1}{5}$ turn.

Instead of fractions you can use **angles** to describe the rotation.

■ **An angle is a measure of turn.**
 **An angle is usually measured in degrees, ° for short.**

■ **There are 360° in a full turn.**

You can use a protractor to measure angles
in degrees:

**Angle measurer**
You can use an angle measurer
instead of a protractor.

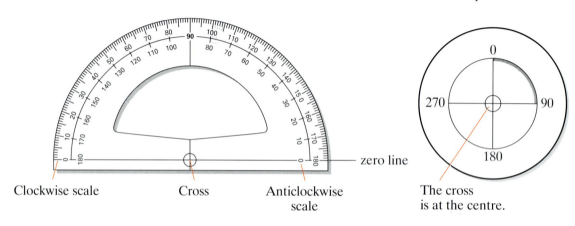

Clockwise scale          Cross          Anticlockwise
                                          scale

zero line

The cross
is at the centre.

## Example 3

Measure the angle between
these lines:

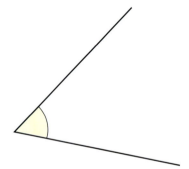

Place the protractor over one line like this:

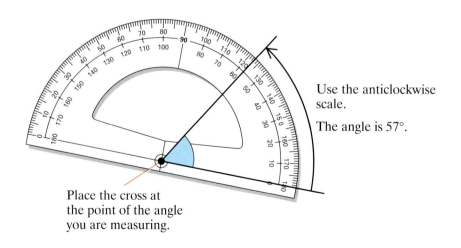

Use the anticlockwise
scale.

The angle is 57°.

Place the cross at
the point of the angle
you are measuring.

## Exercise 14C

**1** Use a protractor to measure these angles:

**(a)**

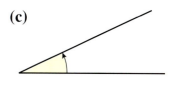
anticlockwise scale

**(b)**

clockwise scale

**(c)**

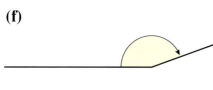

**(d)**

**(e)**

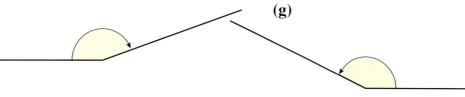

**(f)**

**(g)**

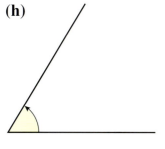
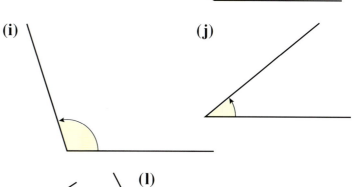

**(h)**

**(i)**

**(j)**

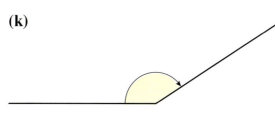
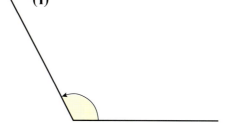

**(k)**

**(l)**

**2** How many degrees are there in:
**(a)** $\frac{1}{4}$ turn      **(b)** $\frac{1}{2}$ turn      **(c)** $\frac{3}{4}$ turn

## 14.4 Types of angles

The angle between these lines is 90°.

The angle between these lines is 180°.

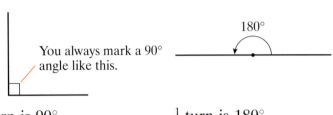

You always mark a 90° angle like this.

180°

$\frac{1}{4}$ turn is 90°

$\frac{1}{2}$ turn is 180°

You name an angle depending on its size:

■ **$\frac{1}{4}$ turn or 90°**     **smaller than 90°**     **larger than 90°**     **larger than 180°**

**Right** angle     **Acute** angle     **Obtuse** angle     **Reflex** angle

### Example 4

For each of these angles choose the correct description from the list:

**(a)** 35°    **(b)** 72°    **(c)** 108°    **(d)** 184°    **(e)** 220°

**acute angle    obtuse angle    reflex angle    right angle**

Hint: compare each angle with 90° and 180°.

**(a)** acute angle    **(b)** acute angle    **(c)** obtuse angle
**(d)** reflex angle    **(e)** reflex angle

### Exercise 14D

Write down the correct description for each angle:

1
2
3
4

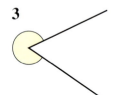
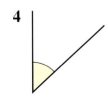

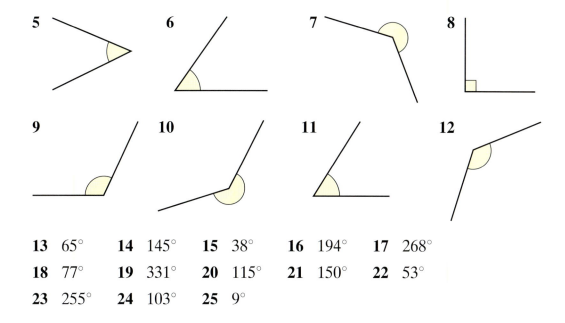

13  65°    14  145°    15  38°    16  194°    17  268°

18  77°    19  331°    20  115°    21  150°    22  53°

23  255°   24  103°    25  9°

## 14.5 Estimating angles

You can estimate the size of an angle by comparing it with
a right angle.

### Example 5

For each angle:

- What type of angle is it?
- Estimate the size of the angle.

**(a)** 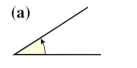  **(b)**   **(c)** 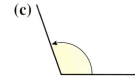  **(d)**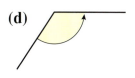

**(a)** Compare this angle with a right
angle like the corner of your page.
It is roughly $\frac{1}{3}$ of the right angle.

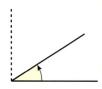

$\frac{1}{3}$ of 90° is 30°

The angle is acute. It is about 30°

**(b)** This is an acute angle.
It is roughly $\frac{1}{2}$ a right angle.

$\frac{1}{2}$ of $90°$ is $45°$

The angle is acute. It is about $45°$

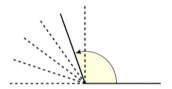

**(c)** This angle is obtuse.
You need to estimate the part that is over $90°$.
It is about $\frac{1}{5}$ of $90° = 18°$
So the angle is roughly

$$90 + 18 = 108°$$

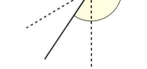

**(d)** This angle is obtuse.
The part greater than $90°$ is approximately $\frac{1}{3}$ of $90° = 30°$
So the angle is

$$90 + 30 = 120°$$

### Exercise 14E

Estimate the sizes of these angles and write down whether they are acute or obtuse:

**1**

**2**

**3**

**4**

**5**

**6**

**7**

**8**

**9**

**10**

**11**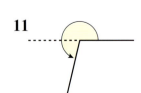

**12**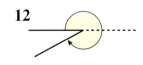

## 14.6 It all adds up

You can put 2 or more angles together to make a right angle:

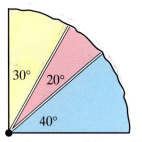

The angles must add up to 90°

You can also put 2 or more angles together to make a straight line:

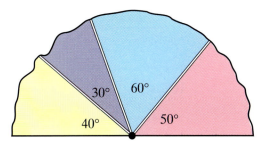

The angles must add up to 180°

Hint: Compare this with a protractor.

■ **Angles in a right angle add up to 90°.**

■ **Angles on a straight line add up to 180°.**

### Example 6

In these diagrams what angles do the letters represent?

**(a)**

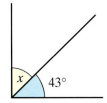

**(b)**

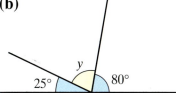

There is more about using letters to represent numbers on page 133.

**(a)** Angles add up to 90°
so $x + 43 = 90$
$x = 90 - 43$
$x = 47°$

**(b)** Angles add up to 180°
$y + 25 + 80 = 180$
$y + 105 = 180$
$y = 180 - 105$
$y = 75°$

## Exercise 14F

What angles do the letters represent?

**1**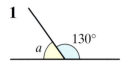

**2**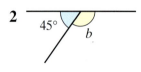

**3**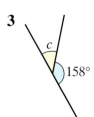

**4**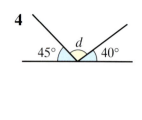

**5**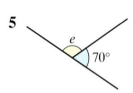

**6**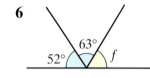

**7**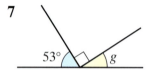

**8**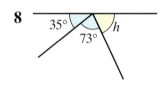

**9**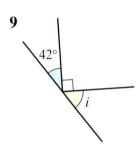

**10**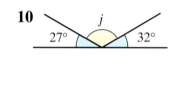

## 14.7 Angles at a point

You can put 2 or more angles together to make a full turn.

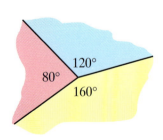

These 4 angles add up to 360°:

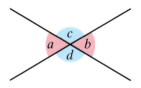

$a$ and $b$ are opposite each other: $a = b$
$c$ and $d$ are opposite each other: $c = d$

■ **Angles at a point add up to 360°.**

■ **When two straight lines cross, the opposite angles are equal.**

## Example 7

What angles do the letters represent? Explain your working.

**(a)**

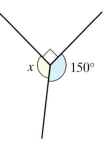

**(b)**

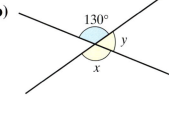

**(a)** Angles at a point
add up to 360°

$$x + 150 + 90 = 360$$
$$x + 240 = 360$$
$$x = 360 - 240$$
$$x = 120°$$

**(b)** Opposite angles are
equal

$$x = 130°$$
$$y + 130 = 180 \quad \text{(angles on a straight line)}$$
$$y = 180 - 130$$
$$y = 50°$$

## Exercise 14G

What angles do the letters represent? Explain your working:

**1**

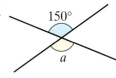

**2**

**3**

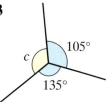

**4**

**5**

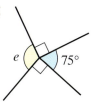

**6**

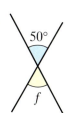

**7**

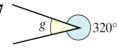

**8**

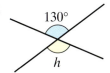

**9**

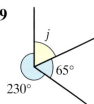

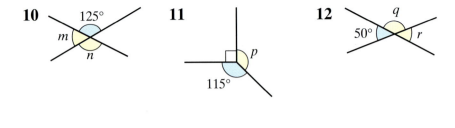

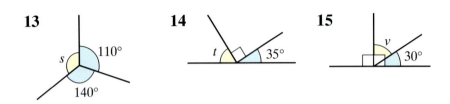

16  Using a pencil and ruler draw
a triangle on a piece of paper.
Cut out the triangle.
Colour the three angles.
Cut out the angles.
Fit them together.
What do you notice?

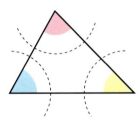

## 14.8 Angles in shapes

If you cut out the corners of a triangle and put them
together like this they make a straight line:

180°

Remember: the angles on a
straight line add up to 180°.

■ **The angles of a triangle add up to 180°.**

## Example 8

What angles do these letters represent?

**(a)**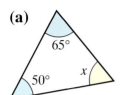
65°
50°
x

**(b)**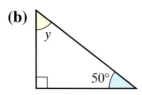
y
50°

**(c)**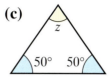
z
50° 50°

**(a)**

Angles add to 180°

$x + 50 + 65 = 180$

$x + 115 = 180$

$x = 180 - 115$

$x = 65°$

**(b)**

Angles add to 180°

$y + 50 + 90 = 180$

$y + 140 = 180$

$y = 180 - 140$

$y = 40°$

**(c)**

Angles add to 180°

$z + 50 + 50 = 180$

$z + 100 = 180$

$z = 180 - 100$

$z = 80°$

## Exercise 14H

What angles do these letters represent?

**1**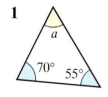
a
70° 55°

**2**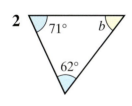
71° b
62°

**3**
c
48°

**4**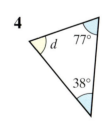
d 77°
38°

**5**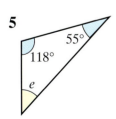
55°
118°
e

**6**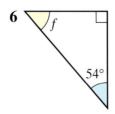
f
54°

**7**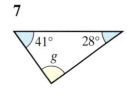
41° 28°
g

**8**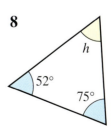
h
52°
75°

**9**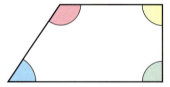

i  82°  26°

**10** 130°  j  30°

**11** k  34°

**12** 58°  l  68°

**13** Using a pencil and ruler draw a quadrilateral on a
piece of paper.
Cut it out.
Colour the four angles.
Cut out the angles and
fit them together.
What do you notice?

## 14.9 Drawing angles

You can use a protractor to help you draw an angle.

### Example 9

Draw an angle of 67°.

Draw a straight line

Put the protractor on
the line like this:

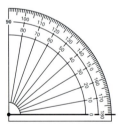

Remember to put
the cross at one end.

Use the anticlockwise
scale.
Make a mark at 67°

Join up the mark
to the end of the line.

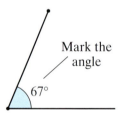

Mark the
angle

67°

### Exercise 14I

**1** Draw these angles using a protractor or angle measurer.

    **(a)** 40°    **(b)** 65°    **(c)** 50°    **(d)** 135°    **(e)** 15°

    **(f)** 34°    **(g)** 170°    **(h)** 75°    **(i)** 123°    **(j)** 27°

    **(k)** 164°    **(l)** 105°    **(m)** 46°    **(n)** 82°    **(o)** 155°

# 14.10 Constructing triangles

Engineers and architects use triangular shapes in their designs because they are strong.

You can use a ruler and compasses to help you draw triangles.

## How to construct a triangle

Construct a triangle with sides 3 cm, 5 cm and 6 cm.

The longest side is 6 cm.
Draw this using a ruler:

Set the compasses to 5 cm.
With the point at one end of the line draw an arc like this:

Set the compasses to 3 cm.
With the point at the other end of the line draw an arc:

Join the ends of the line to the point where the arcs cross:

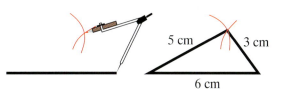

An accurate drawing like this is called a **construction**.

## Exercise 14J

**1**   Construct triangles with sides of length:

(a)  3 cm, 4 cm, 5 cm          (b)  8 cm, 10 cm, 4 cm

(c)  7 cm, 2 cm, 6 cm          (d)  2 cm, 4 cm, 5 cm

(e)  6 cm, 8 cm, 5 cm          (f)  9 cm, 7 cm, 4 cm

# Summary of key points

**1**   A shape has rotational symmetry if it looks exactly the same <u>two or more times</u> in a full turn.

**2**   The order of rotational symmetry is the number of times it looks exactly the same in a full turn.

**3**   An angle is a measure of turn.
An angle is usually measured in degrees, ° for short.

**4**   There are 360° in a full turn.

**5**   $\frac{1}{4}$ turn is 90°

**6**   $\frac{1}{2}$ turn is 180°

**7**

| **Right** angle | **Acute** angle | **Obtuse** angle | **Reflex** angle |
|---|---|---|---|
| $\frac{1}{4}$ turn: 90° | less than 90° | between 90° and 180° | more than 180° |

**8**   Angles in a right angle add up to 90°.

**9**   Angles on a straight line add up to 180°.

**10**   When two straight lines cross, the opposite angles are equal.

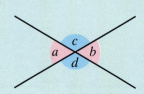

**11**   Angles at a point add up to 360°.

**12**   The angles of a triangle add up to 180°.

# 15 Handling data

You often see information given in charts like these:

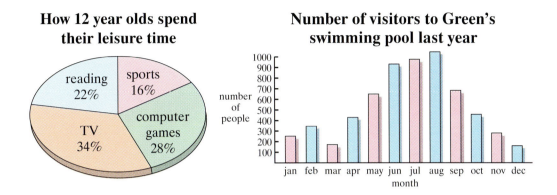

**How 12 year olds spend their leisure time**

reading 22%
sports 16%
computer games 28%
TV 34%

**Number of visitors to Green's swimming pool last year**

■ **Another word for information is data.**

Data can come from many different sources. For example:

- from a **survey** – of how people use their leisure time.
- from an **experiment** – to find out how quickly plants grow.
- from a **database** – a store of information such as test results.

This unit shows you some ways of organizing and presenting data that make it easier to work with and to spot patterns.

## 15.1 Organizing data

A data collection sheet is a good way of organizing data collected in a survey or experiment.

Ahmed asked 40 people:

'Where did you go on holiday this year?'

He used this table to collect the data:

| Country | |
|---------|---|
| England | |
| Wales | |
| Ireland | |

This is a data collection sheet.

Ahmed made a **tally mark** | for each person's answer on his record sheet:

| Country | Tally | Frequency |
|---------|-------|-----------|
| England | JHT JHT I | 11 |
| Wales | JHT I | 6 |
| Ireland | JHT III | 8 |
| Scotland | IIII | 4 |
| Spain | II | 2 |
| Italy | JHT | 5 |
| Others | IIII | 4 |

This column shows the frequency of each answer – how often each answer occurred.

Remember:
JHT means 5.

This is called a tally chart or a frequency table.

The frequency is the number of times an answer occurs. For example, two people said they went to Spain. The frequency of the answer "Spain" is 2.

■ **You can use a tally chart (or frequency table) to collect and organize data.**

### Exercise 15A

1 Copy and complete this frequency table.

| Goals | Tally | Frequency |
|-------|-------|-----------|
| 0 | JHT JHT JHT JHT | |
| 1 | JHT JHT JHT JHT | |
| 2 | | 18 |
| 3 | | 11 |
| 4 | JHT JHT | |
| 5 | | 7 |
| 6 | II | |

**2**   This table shows the number of times pupils in 7C were late each day during one half-term.

| Mon. | Tues. | Wed. | Thurs. | Fri. |
|------|-------|------|--------|------|
| 2 | 3 | 1 | 2 | 4 |
| 3 | 0 | 2 | 3 | 3 |
| 5 | 1 | 0 | 4 | 2 |
| 3 | 2 | 0 | 2 | 3 |
| 1 | 1 | 3 | 2 | 2 |
| 2 | 1 | 1 | 2 | 3 |

Copy and complete this frequency table; Monday is done for you.

| Day | Tally | Frequency |
|-----|-------|-----------|
| Mon. | ⅢⅠ Ⅲ Ⅲ Ⅰ | 16 |
| Tues. | | |
| Wed. | | |
| Thur. | | |
| Fri. | | |

**3**   At breaktime the first fifty sales from the tuck shop were:

crisps, sweets, drink, drink, roll, crisps, roll, cake, roll, crisps, fruit, roll, sweets, drink, roll, fruit, drink, sweets, roll, cake, crisps, roll, cake, fruit, roll, drink, fruit, crisps, cake, crisps, roll, roll, sweets, crisps, cake, roll, crisps, drink, cake, cake, crisps, roll, fruit, sweets, roll, drink, crisps, sweets, roll, cake.

Draw a frequency table for this data.

4    Lester did a traffic survey to find the most popular
     make of car.

His results were:

Ford, Rover, Ford, Volvo, Nissan, Peugeot, BMW,
Ford, BMW, Vauxhall, Nissan, VW, Peugeot,
Ford, Nissan, Honda, Rover, VW, Vauxhall, Ford,
Daewoo, BMW, Peugeot, VW, Volvo, Vauxhall,
Ford, Vauxhall, Rover, Ford, VW, Nissan, Ford,
Peugeot, Vauxhall, Ford, Honda, BMW, Ford,
VW, Ford, Vauxhall, Rover, Honda, VW, Nissan,
Rover, Ford, Nissan, VW, Peugeot, Ford, Nissan,
VW, Ford, Rover, Volvo, Honda, Nissan.

Draw a frequency chart for his results.

5    (a)  Roll a dice.
          Record the number shown on the top face.
          Repeat 60 times.
          Draw a frequency table.

     (b)  Roll two dice.
          Record the difference between the two numbers.
          Repeat 60 times,
          Draw a frequency table.

## 15.2 Pictograms

Reyhana did a survey to find out the way people travelled
on holiday. She asked 40 people: 'How did you get to your
holiday destination?'

This frequency table shows her data:

| Way of travelling | Frequency |
|---|---|
| Car | 16 |
| Plane | 14 |
| Train | 6 |
| Boat | 4 |

The same information can be shown more visually by using pictures or symbols to represent data:

| Way of travelling | Key: ⏢ = 4 people |
|---|---|
| Car | ⏢ ⏢ ⏢ ⏢ |
| Plane | ⏢ ⏢ ⏢ ⏝ |
| Train | ⏢ ⏝ |
| Boat | ⏢ |

> Each boat ⏢ represents 4 people. So 4 × 4 = 16 people travelled by car.

■  **A pictogram uses pictures or symbols to show data.**

## Exercise 15B

1   The pictogram shows how much pocket money six people get each week.

🪙   represents one pound (£1).

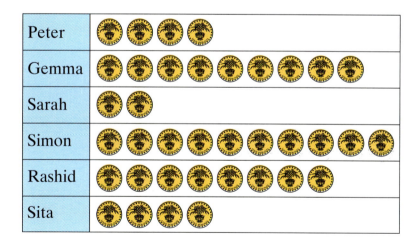

(a) Without counting: who gets the worst deal from her parents?

(b) How much money did they get altogether? (Count this time.)

(c) Who gets exactly £8?

(d) How much does Gemma get?

**2** This pictogram shows the number of cars using the station car park one week.

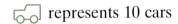 represents 10 cars

| Monday | 🚗 🚗 🚗 🚗 🚗 🚗 🚗 🚗 |
|---|---|
| Tuesday | 🚗 🚗 🚗 🚗 🚗 🚗 |
| Wednesday | 🚗 🚗 🚗 🚗 🚗 |
| Thursday | 🚗 🚗 🚗 🚗 🚗 🚗 🚗 |
| Friday | 🚗 🚗 🚗 🚗 🚗 |
| Saturday | 🚗 🚗 🚗 🚗 |

**(a)** How many cars used the car park on Wednesday?

**(b)** How many cars altogether used the car park during the week?

**(c)** It costs £1.50 to park Monday–Friday but Saturday is free.
How much money was taken that week?

**3** This pictogram shows the number of letters delivered one week.

✉ represents 4 letters.

| Monday | ✉ ✉ ✉ ✉ ✉ ✉ ✉ ✉ |
|---|---|
| Tuesday | ✉ ✉ ✉ ✉ ✉ |
| Wednesday | ✉ ✉ ✉ ✉ ✉ ✉ ✉ ✉ ✉ ✉ |
| Thursday | ✉ ✉ ✉ ✉ ✉ ✉ ✉ ✉ ✉ |
| Friday | ✉ ✉ ✉ ✉ ✉ ✉ ✉ |
| Saturday | ✉ ✉ ✉ ✉ ✉ |

**(a)** How many letters were delivered on Tuesday?

**(b)** How many letters were delivered altogether that week?

## 15.3  Bar charts

Ahmed's data about the places people went to on holiday is:

| Country | Frequency |
|---------|-----------|
| England | 11 |
| Wales | 6 |
| Ireland | 8 |
| Scotland | 4 |
| Spain | 2 |
| Italy | 5 |
| Others | 4 |

He can display his data on a bar chart.

■  **A bar chart uses bars, blocks or lines to show data.**

Here are three different types of bar charts Ahmed can use to display his data.

**1**  Horizontal bar chart:

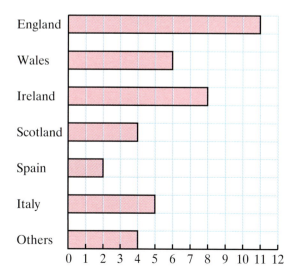

**2** Vertical bar chart:

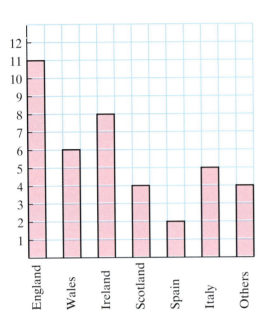

**3** Bar-line graph or Stick graph:

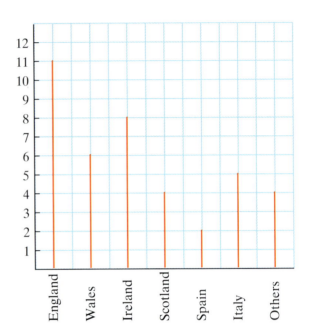

### Exercise 15C

**1** Gwen asked people 'What is your favourite colour?'
She listed the replies:

green, red, red, blue, yellow, blue, green, white, red,
green, red, yellow, blue, blue, red, green, red, green,
yellow, white, blue, red, orange, blue, red, yellow, blue,
blue, red, green.

Draw a bar chart to show her results. (You may find it
helpful to draw a tally chart first.)

**2** Jason emptied a tube of Tasties on a plate and noted
the colours:

| | | | | | |
|---|---|---|---|---|---|
| Blue | 6 | Red | 8 | Mauve | 4 |
| Yellow | 10 | White | 3 | Brown | 7 |
| Pink | 2 | Orange | 5 | | |

Draw a bar chart to represent this data.

**3**   This table shows the number of goals scored in league matches one Saturday.

| Number of goals | 0 | 1 | 2 | 3 | 4 | 5 | 6 |
|---|---|---|---|---|---|---|---|
| Number of matches | 5 | 8 | 11 | 14 | 9 | 3 | 2 |

Illustrate this information using a bar-line graph.

**4**   Employees of a supermarket were asked how they came to work. The results were:

Walk   22          Car   24          Bus          18
Train   10          Cycle   6          Motorcycle   8

(a) Draw a horizontal bar chart to show this data.
(b) Draw a vertical bar-line graph for the same data.
(c) Which did you find easier to draw?
     Give your reason.

**5**   The marks in a spelling test are shown in this table.

(a) Draw a bar-line graph to represent this data.
(b) Which mark did most pupils get?
(c) How many pupils scored 7 or more?

| 10 | 6 | 7 | 9 | 5 | 7 | 9 | 3 |
|---|---|---|---|---|---|---|---|
| 3 | 9 | 8 | 7 | 6 | 10 | 7 | 6 |
| 9 | 5 | 10 | 3 | 8 | 8 | 5 | 9 |
| 7 | 8 | 6 | 5 | 9 | 6 | 7 | 5 |
| 4 | 9 | 8 | 7 | 6 | 8 | 10 | 7 |

## 15.4  Dual bar charts

■   **Dual bar charts are used to compare two sets of similar data.**

**Example 1**

The number of students in 7G arriving late for school is shown in the table.

|  | Monday | Tuesday | Wednesday | Thursday | Friday |
|---|---|---|---|---|---|
| Week 1 | 4 | 5 | 2 | 3 | 2 |
| Week 2 | 6 | 3 | 4 | 1 | 2 |

Draw a dual bar chart to show this data.

This dual bar chart shows the data for each week in a different colour:

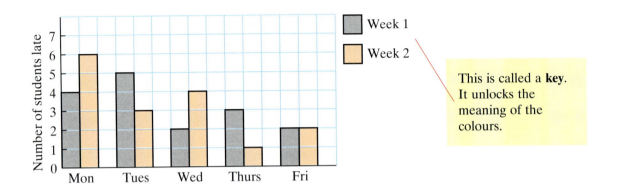

This is called a **key**. It unlocks the meaning of the colours.

### Exercise 15D

**1** This dual bar chart shows the number of hours of sunshine one week in Margate and Brighton.

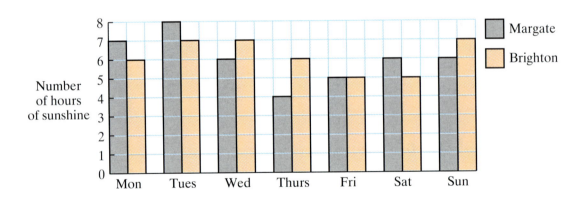

(a) How many hours of sunshine were there in Margate on Saturday?

(b) On how many days were there six hours or more of sunshine in (i) Margate (ii) Brighton?

(c) Which day did both resorts have the same number of hours of sun?

(d) On which day did one town have two hours' more sunshine than the other?

(e) Which town had the most sunshine during the whole week?

**2**   This table shows how many fan letters two boy bands received one week:

|  | Mon | Tues | Wed | Thur | Fri | Sat |
|---|---|---|---|---|---|---|
| Boys unlimited | 5 | 8 | 2 | 11 | 6 | 10 |
| Boys 'r' us | 7 | 3 | 9 | 4 | 12 | 7 |

**(a)** Draw a dual bar chart to represent this data.
**(b)** On which day were most letters received?
**(c)** How many letters were received altogether?

**3**   The table shows Judy and Iris' test scores. The tests were marked out of 20.

|  | English | Maths | Science | History | Geography | French | Art |
|---|---|---|---|---|---|---|---|
| Judy | 16 | 14 | 10 | 15 | 19 | 6 | 8 |
| Iris | 12 | 18 | 18 | 7 | 11 | 14 | 10 |

**(a)** Draw a dual bar-chart to compare their results.
**(b)** Use information from your chart to write *two*
sentences comparing their results.
**(c)** If anyone scored less than 10 they had to do the test
again. Which tests did Judy have to do again?

**4**

The chart shows the maximum and minimum temperatures in New York:

|  | Jan | Feb | Mar | Apr | May | Jun | Jul | Aug | Sep | Oct | Nov | Dec |
|---|---|---|---|---|---|---|---|---|---|---|---|---|
| Max | 37 | 38 | 45 | 57 | 68 | 77 | 82 | 80 | 79 | 69 | 51 | 41 |
| Min | 24 | 24 | 30 | 42 | 53 | 60 | 66 | 66 | 60 | 49 | 37 | 29 |

**(a)** Draw a dual bar chart to show this data.
**(b)** In which month was the difference between the
maximum and minimum temperature greatest?
**(c)** Write down three observations from your chart.

> An observation is
> something you notice,
> like a pattern in the
> data.

**5** This dual bar chart shows the number of cars sold by two garages:

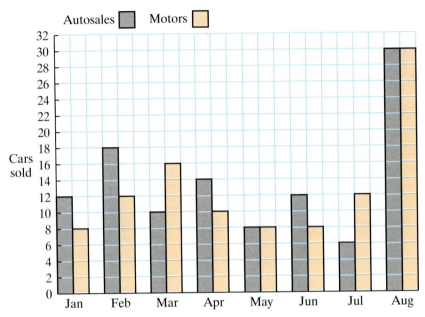

(a) Which garage sold most cars in March?

(b) Autocars sold more cars than Motors did in June.
How many more cars did they sell?

(c) Which garage sold most cars altogether?

(d) Copy and complete this table using data from the
dual bar chart:

|           | Jan | Feb | Mar | Apr | May | Jun | Jul | Aug |
|-----------|-----|-----|-----|-----|-----|-----|-----|-----|
| Autosales | 12  |     |     |     | 8   |     | 6   |     |
| Motors    | 8   | 12  |     | 10  |     |     |     |     |

## 15.5 Pie charts

■ **A pie chart is a way of displaying data to show how something is shared or divided.**

This pie shows how much market share different soap powders have.

The larger the angle the more the sector represents.

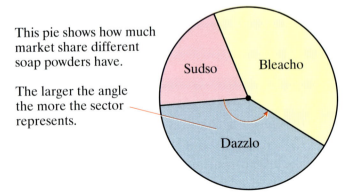

**Example 2**

Denzil counted the number of birds he saw in his garden one morning.

Draw a pie chart to show this data.

| Bird | Frequency |
|------|-----------|
| Sparrow | 9 |
| Blackbird | 3 |
| Starling | 5 |
| Robin | 1 |
| Total | 18 |

Here is how to calculate the angles of the sectors:

18 birds are represented by  $360°$

1 bird  is  represented by  $\dfrac{360}{18} = 20°$

| Bird | Frequency | Angle |
|------|-----------|-------|
| Sparrow | 9 | $9 \times 20 = 180°$ |
| Blackbird | 3 | $3 \times 20 = 60°$ |
| Starling | 5 | $5 \times 20 = 100°$ |
| Robin | 1 | $1 \times 20 = 20°$ |

To find the angle for a sector multiply the number of birds it represents by $20°$

Now draw the pie chart using a protractor:

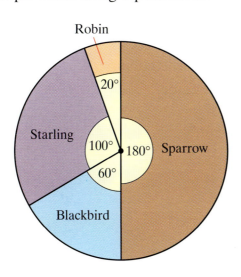

Check that the angle total is $360°$:

$180 + 60 + 100 + 20 = 360$

Mark in the angles.
Write in what each sector represents.

**Example 3**

This pie chart shows how 36 pupils usually come to school:

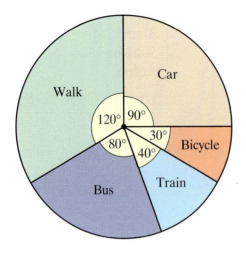

How many pupils walk to school?

The angle of the Walk sector is 120°.

The fraction of pupils who walk to school is $120 \div 360 = \frac{1}{3}$

The number of pupils is $\frac{1}{3}$ of the total

$$\frac{1}{3} \text{ of } 36 \quad \text{is} \quad 36 \div 3 = 12$$

So 12 pupils walk to school.

## Exercise 15E

1   This pie chart shows 20 pupils' favourite colours.
  (a)  What is the angle of the Red sector?
  (b)  How many pupils chose Red?
  (c)  How many pupils chose Green?

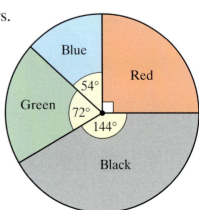

**2**  Karen earns £30 per week
baby sitting.
The pie chart shows how
she spent it last week.

Copy and complete this table.

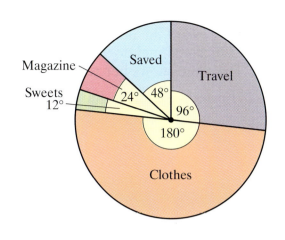

| Item | Angle | £ |
|------|-------|---|
| Travel | | |
| Clothes | | |
| Sweets | | |
| Magazines | | |
| Saved | | |

**3**  The table shows the number of vehicles in a car park.
Copy and complete the table.

| Type | Number | Angle |
|------|--------|-------|
| Car | 45 | |
| Lorry | 2 | |
| Motorcycle | 3 | |
| Van | 10 | |

Display this information on a pie chart.

**4**  This pie chart shows how many letters Vijay
received last week.

Measure the angles using a protractor and
copy and complete the table.

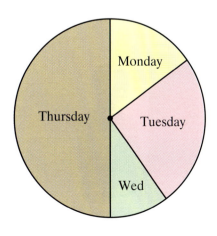

| Day | Angle | Number of letters |
|-----|-------|-------------------|
| Monday | 54° | 3 |
| Tuesday | | |
| Wednesday | | |
| Thursday | | |

**5** Amy asked the 30 pupils in her class 'Which channel do you watch the most?' The table shows her results.

Draw a pie chart to illustrate this data.

| Channel | Frequency |
|---------|-----------|
| BBC1 | 10 |
| BBC2 | 1 |
| ITV | 15 |
| Channel 4 | 2 |
| Channel 5 | 2 |

## 15.6 Different types of data

Some data can be counted:

There are 8 people in this room

There are 15 sheep in the pen

20 red cars pass the school in one hour

■  **Data you can count is called discrete data.**

Some data needs to be measured:

The distance around the tree trunk is 86 cm

Sue is 1.54 m tall

The temperature is 15.4 °C

■  **Data you measure is called continuous data.**

## Exercise 15F

Use one of the words ┃Discrete┃ or ┃Continuous┃
To describe each of these forms of data:

1  The length of a field
2  The number of hairs on a person's head
3  The number of budgies in an aviary
4  The ages of your classmates
5  The amount of water in a jug
6  The weights of turkeys in a supermarket
7  The cost of an ice cream
8  The shoe sizes of your classmates
9  The width of a person's foot
10  The time it takes to run 100 metres

# 15.7 Line graphs

So far all the data shown in charts has been discrete.

■  **You can show continuous data in a line graph.**

**Example 4**

Verity recorded the temperature in her garden every hour
from 8 am to 5 pm.

| Time | 8 am | 9 am | 10 am | 11 am | 12 pm | 1 pm | 2 pm | 3 pm | 4 pm | 5 pm |
|---|---|---|---|---|---|---|---|---|---|---|
| Temp (°C) | 7 | 9 | 12 | 16 | 22 | 22 | 21 | 20 | 20 | 18 |

(a) Draw a line graph to show this data.
(b) Describe any pattern you see.
(c) Use your graph to estimate the
    temperature at 11:30 am.

(a) First plot all the points.
    Then join them up.
(b) The line graph shows that
    the temperature rises then
    starts to fall.
(c) At 11:30 am the temperature
    is approximately 19 °C.

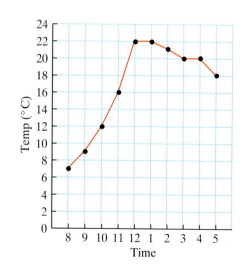

Joining the points on a line graph helps you estimate values in between them.

You cannot do this for discrete data. There are no values 'in between'. For example, there can be 3 people in a car or 4 people, but not 3.7 people.

## Exercise 15G

1   A hospital nurse recorded a patient's temperature in degrees Celsius every hour.
The results are shown in this table.

| Time | 0600 | 0700 | 0800 | 0900 | 1000 | 1100 | 1200 | 1300 |
|---|---|---|---|---|---|---|---|---|
| Temperature (°C) | 33 | 37 | 39 | 45 | 42 | 43 | 40 | 37 |

(a) Draw a line graph to show this data.
(b) What might the patient's temperature have been at
    (i) 0730   (ii) 1130
(c) What time was the highest temperature recorded?
(d) Describe what happened to the patient's temperature between 0900 and 1200.

2   Joe kept a record of the mileage on his car as it got older.
His data is shown in the table:

| Age (years) | 0 | 1 | 2 | 3 | 4 | 5 | 6 |
|---|---|---|---|---|---|---|---|
| Miles ('000) | 0 | 12 | 20 | 30 | 41 | 57 | 65 |

(a) Display the data on a line graph.
(b) Estimate how many miles the car had done when it was $4\frac{1}{2}$ years old.

3   The maximum and minimum temperatures in °F in Llangrannog last year were:

|  | Jan | Feb | Mar | Apr | May | Jun | Jul | Aug | Sep | Oct | Nov | Dec |
|---|---|---|---|---|---|---|---|---|---|---|---|---|
| Max | 45 | 48 | 52 | 55 | 60 | 66 | 72 | 75 | 67 | 56 | 49 | 42 |
| Min | 34 | 32 | 36 | 39 | 40 | 42 | 44 | 45 | 39 | 37 | 33 | 30 |

(a) On the same axes draw line graphs to represent this data.
(b) Make a comment on your results.

**4**   The table shows the number of ferries leaving
Fishguard before noon for the last 10 months.

| Month | Jan | Feb | Mar | Apr | May | Jun | Jul | Aug | Sept | Oct |
|-------|-----|-----|-----|-----|-----|-----|-----|-----|------|-----|
| Ferries | 34 | 32 | 38 | 40 | 40 | 45 | 45 | 48 | 44 | 36 |

Draw a diagram to represent this data.
Why should you *not* draw a line graph?

## 15.8 Scatter graphs

Ken is a used car salesman.
He has 10 cars for sale.

He makes a table of the miles
travelled and the age of each
car:

| Age (years) | 3 | 5 | 2 | 3 | 1 | 4 | 6 | 6 | 7 | 2 |
|-------------|---|---|---|---|---|---|---|---|---|---|
| Miles ('000) | 27 | 40 | 15 | 37 | 12 | 58 | 70 | 48 | 80 | 32 |

He plots all the points on a **scatter graph**:

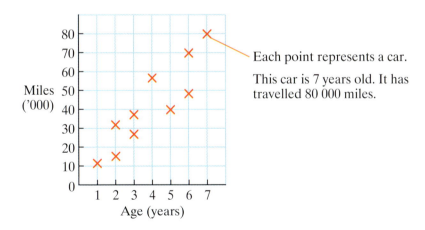

Each point represents a car.

This car is 7 years old. It has
travelled 80 000 miles.

There seems to be a relationship between the age of a car
and the number of miles it has travelled.

In general the number of miles travelled increases as the
age of the car increases.

Ken also makes a table of the value of the car and its age:

| Age (years) | 3 | 5 | 2 | 3 | 1 | 4 | 6 | 6 | 7 | 2 |
|---|---|---|---|---|---|---|---|---|---|---|
| Value (£) | 7400 | 3500 | 8200 | 6100 | 9900 | 3000 | 3000 | 4200 | 2200 | 8500 |

The scatter graph looks like this:

In general, the price of a car decreases as the age of the car increases.

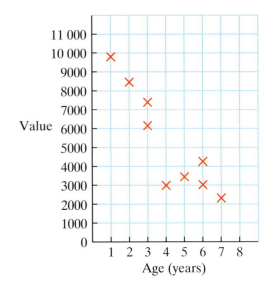

■ **A scatter graph (or diagram) can be used to show whether two sets of data are related.**

■ **The relationship between two sets of data is called a correlation.**

You need to be able to recognize different types of relationships between two sets of data. Look at these scatter graphs:

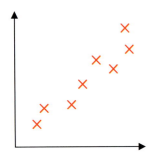

As one value increases the other one also increases. There is a **positive correlation**.

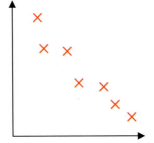

As one value increases the other decreases. There is a **negative correlation**.

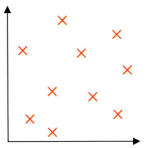

The points are randomly and widely spaced out. There is **no correlation**.

## Exercise 15H

**1**   Twelve Year 7 pupils took a reading test and a spelling test.
Their scores out of 100 are shown in the table:

| Reading | 52 | 60 | 82 | 75 | 90 | 30 | 25 | 48 | 63 | 71 | 38 | 20 |
|---|---|---|---|---|---|---|---|---|---|---|---|---|
| Spelling | 48 | 60 | 76 | 70 | 74 | 25 | 24 | 51 | 62 | 65 | 43 | 15 |

(a) Draw a scatter graph to illustrate this data.
    Put spelling on the *x*-axis and reading on the *y*-axis.
(b) Comment on any correlation you see.

**2**   Owen sells new cars.
The table shows the value and the engine size of 10 new cars.

| Value (£'000) | 7 | 9.5 | 12 | 9.8 | 11 | 17 | 16.5 | 15 | 19 | 24 |
|---|---|---|---|---|---|---|---|---|---|---|
| Engine size (litres) | 1 | 1.1 | 1.6 | 1.1 | 1.4 | 2.2 | 1.8 | 1.6 | 2 | 2.5 |

(a) Draw a scatter graph to show this data.
(b) Comment on the correlation.

**3**   The average fuel consumption (in miles per gallon) and the engine size (in litres) of 12 cars is shown in the table:

| mpg | 30 | 45 | 40 | 32 | 35 | 38 | 28 | 18 | 22 | 36 | 48 | 60 |
|---|---|---|---|---|---|---|---|---|---|---|---|---|
| litres | 2 | 1.1 | 1.5 | 1.2 | 1.6 | 1.1 | 1.6 | 3 | 2.5 | 1.4 | 1 | 1.1 |

(a) Draw a scatter graph to show this data.
(b) Comment on the correlation.

**4**   In a fitness competition 10 men did as many press-ups as they could in 1 minute. The table shows the number of press-ups each man managed and his age.

| Age | 40 | 30 | 62 | 21 | 38 | 54 | 31 | 28 | 45 | 58 |
|---|---|---|---|---|---|---|---|---|---|---|
| Press-ups | 31 | 52 | 8 | 60 | 35 | 20 | 41 | 63 | 18 | 12 |

(a) Plot this data on a scatter graph.
(b) Comment on the correlation.

# Summary of key points

1 Another word for information is **data**.

2 You can use a tally chart (or frequency table) to collect and organize data.

3 A pictogram uses pictures or symbols to show data.

4 A bar chart uses bars, blocks or lines to show data.

5 Dual bar charts are used to compare two sets of similar data.

6 A pie chart is a way of displaying data to show how something is shared or divided.

7 Data you can count is called discrete data.

8 Data you measure is called continuous data.

9 You can show continuous data in a line graph.

10 A scatter graph (or diagram) can be used to show whether two sets of data are related.

11 The relationship between two sets of data is called a correlation.

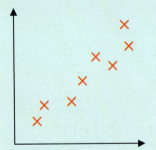

As one value increases the other one also increases. There is a **positive correlation**.

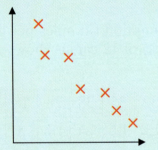

As one value increases the other decreases. There is a **negative correlation**.

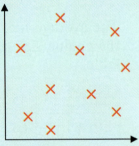

The points are randomly and widely spaced out. There is **no correlation**.

# 16 Percentages

## 16.1 Understanding percentages

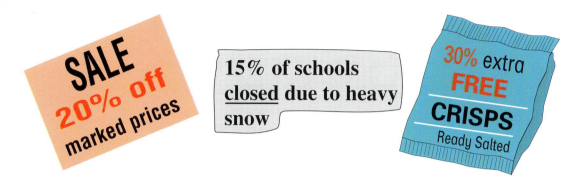

The symbol % means 'per cent'.
Per cent means 'in every 100'.

3% means 3 in every 100.
3% is called a **percentage**.

100% of something is all of it.

I want 100% commitment. That means total commitment

There are 5 pieces of
chocolate in this bar.
Each piece is 100 ÷ 5 = 20%
of the whole.

There are 4 slices of pizza.
Each slice is 100 ÷ 4 = 25%.
3 slices will be 3 × 25% = 75%

### Exercise 16A

1   A rod is cut into five equal pieces. What percentage of
    the rod is each piece?

2   A pie is cut into ten equal pieces. What percentage of
    the pie is each piece?

**3** What percentage of each shape is shaded?

(a)

(b)

(c)

(d)

(e)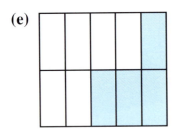

(f)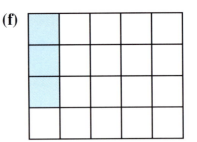

(g)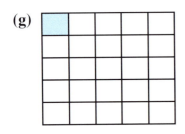

(h)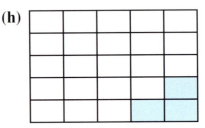

(i)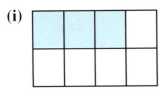

(j)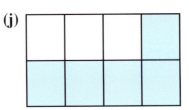

## 16.2 Writing percentages as fractions

You can write a percentage as a fraction.

3% means 3 out of 100. As a fraction this is $\dfrac{3}{100}$

Notice that the denominator is 100

3% and $\dfrac{3}{100}$ represent the same amount.

■ **You can write a percentage as a fraction with the denominator 100.** For example:

$$23\% = \frac{23}{100}$$

These hundred squares show some more fractions and percentages:

$\frac{1}{4}$ shaded

| 1 | 2 | 3 | 4 | 5 | 6 | 7 | 8 | 9 | 10 |
|---|---|---|---|---|---|---|---|---|---|
| 11 | 12 | 13 | 14 | 15 | 16 | 17 | 18 | 19 | 20 |
| 21 | 22 | 23 | 24 | 25 | 26 | 27 | 28 | 29 | 30 |
| 31 | 32 | 33 | 34 | 35 | 36 | 37 | 38 | 39 | 40 |
| 41 | 42 | 43 | 44 | 45 | 46 | 47 | 48 | 49 | 50 |
| 51 | 52 | 53 | 54 | 55 | 56 | 57 | 58 | 59 | 60 |
| 61 | 62 | 63 | 64 | 65 | 66 | 67 | 68 | 69 | 70 |
| 71 | 72 | 73 | 74 | 75 | 76 | 77 | 78 | 79 | 80 |
| 81 | 82 | 83 | 84 | 85 | 86 | 87 | 88 | 89 | 90 |
| 91 | 92 | 93 | 94 | 95 | 96 | 97 | 98 | 99 | 100 |

25 parts shaded.
25% shaded.

$\frac{1}{2}$ shaded

| 1 | 2 | 3 | 4 | 5 | 6 | 7 | 8 | 9 | 10 |
|---|---|---|---|---|---|---|---|---|---|
| 11 | 12 | 13 | 14 | 15 | 16 | 17 | 18 | 19 | 20 |
| 21 | 22 | 23 | 24 | 25 | 26 | 27 | 28 | 29 | 30 |
| 31 | 32 | 33 | 34 | 35 | 36 | 37 | 38 | 39 | 40 |
| 41 | 42 | 43 | 44 | 45 | 46 | 47 | 48 | 49 | 50 |
| 51 | 52 | 53 | 54 | 55 | 56 | 57 | 58 | 59 | 60 |
| 61 | 62 | 63 | 64 | 65 | 66 | 67 | 68 | 69 | 70 |
| 71 | 72 | 73 | 74 | 75 | 76 | 77 | 78 | 79 | 80 |
| 81 | 82 | 83 | 84 | 85 | 86 | 87 | 88 | 89 | 90 |
| 91 | 92 | 93 | 94 | 95 | 96 | 97 | 98 | 99 | 100 |

50 parts shaded.
50% shaded.

$\frac{3}{4}$ shaded

| 1 | 2 | 3 | 4 | 5 | 6 | 7 | 8 | 9 | 10 |
|---|---|---|---|---|---|---|---|---|---|
| 11 | 12 | 13 | 14 | 15 | 16 | 17 | 18 | 19 | 20 |
| 21 | 22 | 23 | 24 | 25 | 26 | 27 | 28 | 29 | 30 |
| 31 | 32 | 33 | 34 | 35 | 36 | 37 | 38 | 39 | 40 |
| 41 | 42 | 43 | 44 | 45 | 46 | 47 | 48 | 49 | 50 |
| 51 | 52 | 53 | 54 | 55 | 56 | 57 | 58 | 59 | 60 |
| 61 | 62 | 63 | 64 | 65 | 66 | 67 | 68 | 69 | 70 |
| 71 | 72 | 73 | 74 | 75 | 76 | 77 | 78 | 79 | 80 |
| 81 | 82 | 83 | 84 | 85 | 86 | 87 | 88 | 89 | 90 |
| 91 | 92 | 93 | 94 | 95 | 96 | 97 | 98 | 99 | 100 |

75 parts shaded.
75% shaded.

**Example 1**

Write these percentages as fractions in their simplest form:

**(a)** 20%          **(b)** 5%          **(c)** 40%

**(a)** 20% means $\frac{20}{100}$     **(b)** 5% means $\frac{5}{100}$     **(c)** 40% means $\frac{40}{100}$

$$\frac{20}{100} \overset{\div 20}{\underset{\div 20}{=}} \frac{1}{5}$$

$$\frac{5}{100} \overset{\div 5}{\underset{\div 5}{=}} \frac{1}{20}$$

$$\frac{40}{100} \overset{\div 20}{\underset{\div 20}{=}} \frac{2}{5}$$

Remember: to find the simplest form, you divide the top and the bottom by the same number.

■ **Remember these percentages and their equivalent fractions:**

$$50\% = \frac{1}{2} \qquad 25\% = \frac{1}{4} \qquad 75\% = \frac{3}{4}$$

Equivalent means they represent the same amount.

## Exercise 16B

**1** For each hundred square, write down
- the fraction shaded
- the percentage shaded

**(a)**

| 1 | 2 | 3 | 4 | 5 | 6 | 7 | 8 | 9 | 10 |
|---|---|---|---|---|---|---|---|---|---|
| 11 | 12 | 13 | 14 | 15 | 16 | 17 | 18 | 19 | 20 |
| 21 | 22 | 23 | 24 | 25 | 26 | 27 | 28 | 29 | 30 |
| 31 | 32 | 33 | 34 | 35 | 36 | 37 | 38 | 39 | 40 |
| 41 | 42 | 43 | 44 | 45 | 46 | 47 | 48 | 49 | 50 |
| 51 | 52 | 53 | 54 | 55 | 56 | 57 | 58 | 59 | 60 |
| 61 | 62 | 63 | 64 | 65 | 66 | 67 | 68 | 69 | 70 |
| 71 | 72 | 73 | 74 | 75 | 76 | 77 | 78 | 79 | 80 |
| 81 | 82 | 83 | 84 | 85 | 86 | 87 | 88 | 89 | 90 |
| 91 | 92 | 93 | 94 | 95 | 96 | 97 | 98 | 99 | 100 |

**(b)**

| 1 | 2 | 3 | 4 | 5 | 6 | 7 | 8 | 9 | 10 |
|---|---|---|---|---|---|---|---|---|---|
| 11 | 12 | 13 | 14 | 15 | 16 | 17 | 18 | 19 | 20 |
| 21 | 22 | 23 | 24 | 25 | 26 | 27 | 28 | 29 | 30 |
| 31 | 32 | 33 | 34 | 35 | 36 | 37 | 38 | 39 | 40 |
| 41 | 42 | 43 | 44 | 45 | 46 | 47 | 48 | 49 | 50 |
| 51 | 52 | 53 | 54 | 55 | 56 | 57 | 58 | 59 | 60 |
| 61 | 62 | 63 | 64 | 65 | 66 | 67 | 68 | 69 | 70 |
| 71 | 72 | 73 | 74 | 75 | 76 | 77 | 78 | 79 | 80 |
| 81 | 82 | 83 | 84 | 85 | 86 | 87 | 88 | 89 | 90 |
| 91 | 92 | 93 | 94 | 95 | 96 | 97 | 98 | 99 | 100 |

**(c)**

| 1 | 2 | 3 | 4 | 5 | 6 | 7 | 8 | 9 | 10 |
|---|---|---|---|---|---|---|---|---|---|
| 11 | 12 | 13 | 14 | 15 | 16 | 17 | 18 | 19 | 20 |
| 21 | 22 | 23 | 24 | 25 | 26 | 27 | 28 | 29 | 30 |
| 31 | 32 | 33 | 34 | 35 | 36 | 37 | 38 | 39 | 40 |
| 41 | 42 | 43 | 44 | 45 | 46 | 47 | 48 | 49 | 50 |
| 51 | 52 | 53 | 54 | 55 | 56 | 57 | 58 | 59 | 60 |
| 61 | 62 | 63 | 64 | 65 | 66 | 67 | 68 | 69 | 70 |
| 71 | 72 | 73 | 74 | 75 | 76 | 77 | 78 | 79 | 80 |
| 81 | 82 | 83 | 84 | 85 | 86 | 87 | 88 | 89 | 90 |
| 91 | 92 | 93 | 94 | 95 | 96 | 97 | 98 | 99 | 100 |

**2** Write these percentages as fractions.
Write the fractions in their simplest form.

| | | | |
|---|---|---|---|
| **(a)** 1% | **(b)** 29% | **(c)** 26% | **(d)** 40% |
| **(e)** 42% | **(f)** 48% | **(g)** 44% | **(h)** 60% |
| **(i)** 12% | **(j)** 10% | **(k)** 8% | **(l)** 28% |
| **(m)** 55% | **(n)** 90% | **(o)** 45% | **(p)** 25% |

## 16.3 Writing percentages as decimals

You can also write a percentage as a decimal:

$$3\% \quad \text{means} \quad \frac{3}{100} \quad \text{means} \quad 3 \div 100 = 0.03$$

■ **To change a percentage to a decimal divide by 100.**
For example: 23% means $23 \div 100 = 0.23$

Remember: to divide by 100 move every digit 2 places to the right.

### Example 2

Write these percentages as decimals:
**(a)** 37%     **(b)** 70%

**(a)** $37\% = 37 \div 100 = 0.37$
**(b)** $70\% = 70 \div 100 = 0.70 = 0.7$

## Exercise 16C

Change these percentages to decimals:

| | | | | | | | |
|---|---|---|---|---|---|---|---|
| **1** 12% | | **2** 29% | | **3** 66% | | **4** 25% |
| **5** 8% | | **6** 35% | | **7** 42% | | **8** 3% |
| **9** 17% | | **10** 1% | | **11** 5% | | **12** 82% |
| **13** 99% | | **14** 7% | | **15** 16% | | **16** 80% |

**17** Copy and complete this table of equivalent percentages, fractions and decimals.

| Percentage | Fraction | Decimal |
|:---:|:---:|:---:|
| 80% | $\frac{4}{5}$ | 0.8 |
| 70% | | |
| 10% | | |
| | $\frac{1}{100}$ | |
| | $\frac{1}{2}$ | |
| | | 0.25 |
| | $\frac{3}{4}$ | |
| 100% | | |

Hint: to change a fraction to a decimal you divide the top by the bottom, for example
$\frac{3}{5} = 3 \div 5 = 0.6$

## 16.4 Finding a percentage

■ **You can find a percentage of a number by changing the percentage to a decimal. Then multiply the decimal by the number.**

**Example 3**

Find:

**(a)** 20% of £30

**(b)** 15% of 60 kg

**(a)** $20\% = 20 \div 100 = 0.2$

**(b)** $15\% = 15 \div 100 = 0.15$

$$20\% \quad \text{of} \quad £30$$

$$15\% \quad \text{of} \quad 60 \text{ kg}$$

$$= \quad 0.2 \quad \times \quad 30 = £6 \qquad 0.15 \quad \times \quad 60 = 9 \text{ kg}$$

Remember to give units in your answer.

## Exercise 16D

Find:

| | | | |
|---|---|---|---|
| **1** | 10% of £35 | **2** | 20% of £15 |
| **3** | 50% of 17 kg | **4** | 25% of 240 g |
| **5** | 17% of £28 | **6** | 6% of £22.50 |
| **7** | 53% of £36 | **8** | 12% of 165 kg |
| **9** | 15% of 75 kg | **10** | 30% of 15 m |
| **11** | 5% of 4.2 m | **12** | 75% of 18 kg |
| **13** | 8% of 17.5 kg | **14** | 13% of £62 |

**15** A Hi-Fi system costs £179. Wes wants to buy the Hi-Fi system on credit. The shopkeeper asks for a 15% deposit.
How much deposit must Wes pay?

**16** There are 30 pupils in Class 7M. 60% of them are girls. How many girls are there in Class 7M?

**17** The 75 boys in Year 7 were asked to choose their favourite sport. 84% of the boys chose football. Work out how many boys chose football.

**18** Of the 950 pupils in Peak School 6% usually cycle to school and 22% usually travel to school by bus. Find:
   **(a)** the number of pupils who usually cycle to school,
   **(b)** the number of pupils who usually travel to school by bus.

**19** There are 55 seats in a coach. 40% of the seats are vacant. How many seats are vacant?

**20** A school raises £2400 during a summer fair. The school gives 35% of the money to charity. How much money is left?

## 16.5 Percentage increase and decrease

Increases and decreases are often given in percentages.

House prices increased by 5.2% in March

SALE 20% off marked prices

$33\frac{1}{3}$% EXTRA FREE!

Which car? magazine reports that on average a car depreciates in value by **16%** each year.

### Example 4

Jane earns £800 per month.
Next month she will get a pay rise of 5%.

**(a)** How much is her pay rise?

**(b)** What will she earn next month?

**(a)** Her pay rise will be 5% of £800

5% is $5 \div 100 = 0.05$

So 5% of £800 is $0.05 \times 800 = £40$

**(b)** Next month she will earn $£800 + £40 = £840$

### Example 5

In a sale all prices are reduced by 15%

Find the sale price of a dress that originally cost £24

15% is $15 \div 100 = 0.15$

The dress is reduced by $0.15 \times 24 = 3.6$
$$= £3.60$$

So the sale price is $£24 - £3.60 = £20.40$

■ **To increase an amount by a percentage:**
  • **find the percentage of the amount**
  • **add it to the original amount**

■ **To decrease an amount by a percentage:**
  • **find the percentage of the amount**
  • **subtract it from the original amount**

### Exercise 16E

**1**  Dara left £150 in her savings account for one year. She was paid interest of 7% per year.

(**a**) Calculate the amount of interest paid to Dara.

(**b**) How much did she have altogether?

**2**  In a sale *Music Corner* reduced the prices of CDs by 5%. Robert bought a CD which usually cost £12. Work out:

(**a**) the reduction in the price

(**b**) the new price of Robert's CD

**3**  A shopkeeper buys polo shirts for £8.40 each and sweatshirts for £12.80 each. He sells them for 45% more than he buys them for. Work out the price at which he sells:

(**a**) a polo shirt          (**b**) a sweatshirt

**4**  In his job as a salesman John is paid a basic rate of £5.20 per hour and a 15% commission on sales. How much is John paid in a week when he works 28 hours and makes sales of £540?

**5**  Ramana is paid at a basic rate of £3.80 per hour. The hourly rate for overtime is 30% more. During a particular week Ramana worked a basic 40 hours and then four hours overtime. Calculate:

(**a**) the hourly rate for overtime

(**b**) the total amount Ramana earned that week

# Summary of key points

1  You can write a percentage as a fraction with the denominator 100. For example:

$$23\% = \frac{23}{100}$$

2  Remember these percentages and their equivalent fractions:

$$50\% = \tfrac{1}{2} \qquad 25\% = \tfrac{1}{4} \qquad 75\% = \tfrac{3}{4}$$

Equivalent means they represent the same amount.

3  To change a percentage to a decimal divide by 100. For example: 23% means $23 \div 100 = 0.23$

4  You can find a percentage of a number by changing the percentage to a decimal. Then multiply the decimal by the number.

5  To increase an amount by a percentage:
   • find the percentage of the amount
   • add it to the original amount.

6  To decrease an amount by a percentage:
   • find the percentage of the amount
   • subtract it from the original amount.

# 17 Averages

You often see or hear the word average.
Here are some examples:

- The average number of children in a family is 2.4
- The average rainfall in Britain in June is 50 mm.
- 12-year-olds in Britain spend 4 hours a day watching TV on average.

This box holds 38 matches on average. The number of matches may vary slightly.

The word average means that something is typical, or describes something that typically happens.

In mathematics an average is a single value that is typical of a set of data. It can be used to make general statements about the data.

There are three different averages:

- the mean
- the mode
- the median

This unit describes each average and shows you how to find them.

## 17.1 The mean

When people use the word average they often mean the **mean**.

- **The mean of a set of data is the sum of the values divided by the number of values.**

$$\text{mean} = \frac{\text{sum of the values}}{\text{number of values}}$$

Ian got these marks for his last 8 Geography homeworks:

7, 5, 8, 3, 1, 8, 10, 6

His mean mark is worked out like this:

$$\frac{7+5+8+3+1+8+10+6}{8} = \frac{48}{8} \quad \text{— add up all the values}$$
$$\text{— divide by the number of values}$$
$$= 6$$

Ian's mean mark was 6.

### Exercise 17A

**1** Calculate the mean of each set of values:
  **(a)** 5, 9, 4, 6, 8, 4
  **(b)** 8, 5, 6, 7, 4, 9, 3, 6, 7, 5
  **(c)** 15, 18, 13, 16, 14, 12, 17
  **(d)** 21, 34, 26, 40, 22, 44, 35, 30
  **(e)** 18, 45, 23, 27, 33, 41, 36, 28, 16, 33

**2** Here are 8 people's heights:
  172 cm,  178 cm,  170 cm,  171 cm,
  175 cm,  177 cm,  173 cm,  172 cm
  **(a)** What is their mean height?
  **(b)** How many people were taller than the mean height?

**3** Here are the weekly wages of 15 professional footballers:
  £200, £200, £210, £220, £220, £250, £250, £250,
  £280, £280, £300, £350, £400, £410, £500
  Work out their mean wage.

**4** Ben and Amy did a survey to see how many books pupils in their class had read in the last two months. Here are their results:
  2, 3, 1, 0, 1, 2, 1, 2, 3, 4, 0, 1, 0, 3,
  5, 1, 0, 2, 6, 1, 0, 2, 3, 1, 0, 0, 3, 2
  Work out the mean number of books read.

  This is the average number of books read by each pupil.

**5** Gordon worked during his holidays and was paid:

|          | Mon   | Tues  | Wed   | Thurs | Fri   | Sat    |
|----------|-------|-------|-------|-------|-------|--------|
| Week 1   | £5.60 | £6.20 | £2.40 | £6.30 | £8.60 | £10.30 |
| Week 2   | £4.40 | £6.20 | £4.00 | £7.24 | £8.60 | £12.40 |

  Calculate:
  **(a)** His mean daily wage for week 1.
  **(b)** His mean daily wage for week 2.
  **(c)** Gordon's mean daily wage for the two weeks.

  Hint: you need to find the mean of **all** the values.

**6** The average test mark for a group of ten pupils was 42.5

   **(a)** How many marks did the group get altogether?

   **(b)** Two new pupils took the test and joined the group. One scored 33 and the other scored 6. Calculate the new mean for the group.

Hint: if you know the mean and the number of values, how do you find the sum of the values from

$$\text{mean} = \frac{\text{sum of values}}{\text{number of values}}$$

**7** Work out the mean mark for your last ten:

   **(a)** Maths homeworks

   **(b)** English homeworks.

**8** Peter's and Karen's marks in a series of tests were:

| Peter | 25 | 36 | 34 | 45 | 37 | 42 |
|-------|----|----|----|----|----|----|
| Karen | 31 | 28 | 43 | 35 | 39 | 28 |

   **(a)** Who had the higher mean mark and by how much?

   **(b)** If Peter scores 26 in the next test, how many marks must Karen get to have the same mean mark as Peter?

## 17.2 The mode

■ **The mode of a set of data is the value which occurs most often.**

Ian's marks for his last 8 Geography homeworks were:

   7, 5, 8, 3, 1, 8, 10, 6

He scored 7, 5, 3, 1, 10 and 6 once each.
He scored 8 twice.

The mode was 8. You can say the modal mark was 8.

**Example 1**

Find the mode of each set of data:

**(a)** 1, 5, 3, 2, 7, 4, 3, 2

**(b)** 23, 43, 25, 66, 41, 24

**(c)** 11, 13, 11, 13, 14, 15, 11

(a) 1, 5, 7 and 4 all occur once.
2 and 3 occur twice.
There are two modes: 2 and 3.

(b) Each value occurs only once.
There is no mode.

(c) 14 and 15 occur once.
13 occurs twice.
11 occurs three times.
The mode, or modal value, is 11.

## Exercise 17B

**1** Find the mode of each set of data:

(a) 5, 2, 8, 2, 6, 8, 4, 2, 6, 9

(b) 7, 3, 3, 6, 8, 1, 4, 7, 5, 2, 7, 8

(c) 6, 8, 2, 7, 3, 7, 5, 2, 4, 7, 3, 2, 6

(d) 13, 16, 11, 14, 17, 15, 10, 19, 12, 11,
17, 15, 19, 17, 14, 18, 13, 10, 15, 17,
10, 18, 14, 12, 15, 10, 16, 12, 19, 16,
12, 15, 11, 13, 18, 16, 15, 13, 11, 14

**2** Rachel asked the girls in her class what size shoes they wore. The results were:

5, 3, 3, 4, 3, 4, 6, 4, 3, 5, 5, 4, 6, 4

(a) What is the mode of this data?

(b) Give a reason why a shoe shop will be interested in the mode size.

**3** These are the numbers of hours of sunshine at a seaside resort on each day one June.
Find the mode for the numbers of hours of sunshine.

```
 6  10  8  7  5  7  1   0  2  5
 7   8  6  6  2  2  0   1  7  9
10   0  4  7  8  7  9  10  5  6
```

**4** Find the mode of the shoe sizes for your class.

**5** There are 30 pupils in class 7A.
Their marks in last week's science test are shown on
the bar chart.

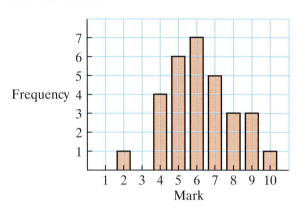

Which mark was the mode?

## 17.3 The median

The third kind of average is the median.
It is the middle value of a set of data.

To find the middle value you must arrange the data in
order of size.

**Example 2**

Find the median of each set of data:
**(a)** 1, 3, 2, 6, 5, 8, 4, 3, 3
**(b)** 4, 8, 3, 5, 6, 3, 5, 7, 6, 3
**(c)** 20, 26, 82, 40, 32, 64

**(a)** Arrange the values in size order:

1, 2, 3, 3, 3, 4, 5, 6, 8

The middle value is 3.
The median is 3.

**(b)** Arrange the values in size order:

3, 3, 3, 4, 5, 5, 6, 6, 7, 8

There are two middle values: 5 and 5.
They are the same.
The median is 5.

**(c)** Arrange the values in order of size:

20, 26, 32, 40, 64, 82

There are two middle values: 32 and 40.
They are not the same.
The median is the average (mean) of the two middle
numbers:

$$\text{median} = \frac{32 + 40}{2} = \frac{72}{2} = 36$$

The median is 36.

> Notice that this median value is not in the original list.
>
> Because there is an even number of marks there are two 'middle' values.
>
> The median is calculated from these.

■ **The median of a set of data is the middle value when
the data is arranged in size order.
When there is an even number of values the median is
the average (mean) of the middle two values.**

## Exercise 17C

**1** Find the median of the following sets of data:

(a) 6, 2, 9, 1, 4, 8, 5, 9, 7
(b) 12, 18, 10, 14, 17, 13, 12, 18, 15
(c) 31, 45, 16, 38, 36, 42, 29, 40, 37
(d) 8, 3, 5, 11, 4, 9, 4, 7
(e) 26, 16, 23, 14, 18, 22, 25, 10

**2** The number of people sitting in the first nine rows of a
cinema were:

on Tuesday:  15, 26, 19, 32, 36, 25, 30, 17, 23
on Friday:   17, 11, 28, 34, 23, 32, 19, 20, 16

(a) Find the median for (i) Tuesday  (ii) Friday.
(b) Find the median for both days together.

**3** A class of 30 pupils was asked to estimate the length of
an exercise book (in pages). Here are their results:

65, 70, 80, 50, 80, 75, 95, 60, 45, 65, 60,
85, 100, 90, 95, 95, 90, 60, 80, 100, 45,
50, 65, 85, 90, 70, 75, 65, 80, 85

Find their median estimate.

## 17.4 The range

Ian's Geography homework marks were:

  7, 5, 8, 3, 1, 8, 10, 6

His highest mark was 10. His lowest mark was 1.

The range of his marks was: $10 - 1 = 9$

■  **The range of a set of data is the difference between the highest and lowest values:**

  **range = highest value − lowest value**

### Exercise 17D

1  Calculate the range for each set of data:
   (a) 6, 8, 3, 9, 7, 2, 5, 5, 3
   (b) 12, 6, 13, 21, 9, 16, 8, 15, 11
   (c) 21, 18, 15, 26, 17, 11, 14, 23, 19
   (d) 36, 23, 41, 17, 45, 19, 31, 26, 35
   (e) 53, 27, 72, 54, 33, 25, 34, 70, 49

2  Here are Ailsa's times in minutes for her journeys to and from school one week.

  22, 21, 24, 28, 23, 24, 21, 26, 23, 25

   Find the range of her times.

3  The range of a set of data is 12.
   If the smallest value is 33, what is the largest value?

4  The average daily sales for 3 car showrooms are shown in the table.

|            | Jan | Feb | Mar | Apr | May | Jun | Jul | Aug | Sep | Oct | Nov | Dec |
|------------|-----|-----|-----|-----|-----|-----|-----|-----|-----|-----|-----|-----|
| Quicksale  | 12  | 15  | 23  | 11  | 21  | 18  | 14  | 48  | 23  | 18  | 24  | 20  |
| Motormove  | 24  | 27  | 10  | 15  | 18  | 22  | 14  | 38  | 21  | 16  | 19  | 18  |
| Carseller  | 17  | 19  | 16  | 34  | 26  | 18  | 22  | 52  | 30  | 25  | 19  | 24  |

   Calculate the range for each month.

5  Six tennis racquets are priced as follows:

  £85, £72, £106, £80 and ?

   If the range is £38 what could ? be?

## 17.5 Average and range from frequency tables

Data is often shown in a frequency table.
You can use the table to work out the mean, mode and range of the data.

There is more about collecting data in frequency tables on page 234.

**Example 3**

This frequency table shows the number of pets the students in class 7B own:

| Number of pets | Frequency |
|----------------|-----------|
| 1 | 1 |
| 2 | 16 |
| 3 | 10 |
| 4 | 3 |

Find the mean, mode and range of this set of data.

The table shows that   1 student owns 1 pet
16 students own 2 pets
10 students own 3 pets
3 students own 4 pets

### The mean

The mean number of pets is:    $\text{mean} = \dfrac{\text{total number of pets}}{\text{total number of students}}$

You could work it out like this:

$$\frac{1+2+2+2+2+2+2+2+2+2+2+2+2+2+2+2+2+3+3+3+3+3+3+3+3+3+3+4+4+4}{30}$$

But it is quicker to see that

$$\text{Mean} = \frac{1\times1 \ + \ 16\times2 \ + \ 10\times3 \ + \ 3\times4}{30} = \frac{75}{30}$$

$$= 2.5$$

The mean number of pets is 2.5

## The mode

The mode is easy to spot.
It is the number of pets with
the highest frequency.
The modal number of pets is 2.

A common mistake is to say the mode
is 16 because it is the largest number.
Here the highest frequency shows you
which **number of pets** is the mode.

## The range

The range of pets is:

range = highest number of pets – lowest number of pets

The highest number of pets is 4
The lowest number of pets is 1
The range is $4 - 1 = 3$

### Exercise 17E

1   The number of goals scored by
    teams in the Premier League one
    week is shown in the table:

| Number of goals | Frequency |
|:---:|:---:|
| 0 | 6 |
| 1 | 2 |
| 2 | 8 |
| 3 | 3 |
| 4 | 1 |

(a) Work out the mean number of goals scored.
(b) What was the modal number of goals scored?
(c) Find the range of this data.

2   The ages of 100 students in a primary school are given
    in the table.

| Age | 4 | 5 | 6 | 7 | 8 | 9 | 10 | 11 |
|:---|:---:|:---:|:---:|:---:|:---:|:---:|:---:|:---:|
| Frequency | 10 | 12 | 13 | 11 | 14 | 16 | 14 | 10 |

(a) Work out the mean age.
(b) What is the modal age?

**3**  The table shows the weekly wages of people working in a garage:

| Job | Number of people | Wage |
|---|---|---|
| Owner | 1 | £850 |
| Foreman | 1 | £250 |
| Mechanic | 5 | £175 |
| Clerk | 2 | £150 |
| Cleaner | 1 | £135 |

**(a)** Calculate:  (i) the mean wage  (ii) the range.

Each person is given £100 per week pay rise.

**(b)** Calculate the new mean and range.

**(c)** Comment on the new results.

## 17.6 Making comparisons

You can use the average and range to compare two or more sets of data.

Jenny and Aleisha are both Goal Shooters in Netball.

In her last 5 games, Jenny scored 4, 11, 12, 8 and 10 goals.
Aleisha scored 12, 12, 0, 11, 0 in her last 5 games.

Which player should be picked for the school team?

Their average scores are:

Jenny:  $\dfrac{4 + 10 + 12 + 8 + 10}{5} = \dfrac{35}{5} = 7$

Aleisha:  $\dfrac{12 + 12 + 0 + 11 + 0}{5} = \dfrac{35}{5} = 7$

Both players score an average of 7

Jenny's range is $12 - 4 = 8$
Aleisha's range is $12 - 0 = 12$

Jenny's range is lower: her results are less spread out.
Aleisha has some high scores but also some 'no scores'.
Jenny is probably the best choice for the school team.

**Exercise 17F**

1  The students in class 7D took a spelling test.

The mean mark for the girls was 12.
The range of marks for the girls was 10.

The mean mark for the boys was 10.
The range for the boys was 12.

Overall who did better in the test, the boys or the girls? Justify your answer.

> Justify means give a reason to support your answer.

2  A politician said that the average wage in England is higher than the average wage in Germany.
Does this mean the English are better off than the Germans?
Explain your answer.

3  Make up a set of data to show that left handed people are better at darts than right handed people.

## Summary of key points

1  The mean of a set of data is the sum of the values divided by the number of values.

$$\text{mean} = \frac{\text{sum of the values}}{\text{number of values}}$$

2  The mode of a set of data is the value which occurs most often.

3  The median of a set of data is the middle value when the data is arranged in size order.
When there is an even number of values the median is the average (mean) of the middle two values.

4  The range of a set of data is the difference between the highest and lowest values:

$$\text{range} = \text{highest value} - \text{lowest value}$$

# 18 Using and applying mathematics

This unit shows you how to use mathematics to **investigate** a problem.

## 18.1 The problem

### Hop and Step

Lucy and her friends are playing a game called Hop and Step.

They have put a green hoop and a red hoop on the floor with some blue hoops in between.

To play the game, Lucy starts in the green hoop. She must finish in the red hoop.

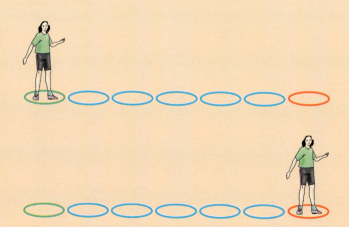

There are three rules to the game:

**Rule 1**  She can only move forwards towards the red hoop.

**Rule 2**  She can take a step. This moves her one hoop forward.

**Rule 3**  She can take a hop. This moves her two hoops forward.

Investigate the number of different ways of getting from the green hoop to the red hoop as the number of blue hoops changes.

## 18.2 Understand the problem

The first thing to do is make sure you understand the problem.
The best way to do this is just have a go.

### Example 1

Suppose there are four blue hoops.
Find three different ways of getting from the green hoop to the red hoop.

Remember to follow the rules.

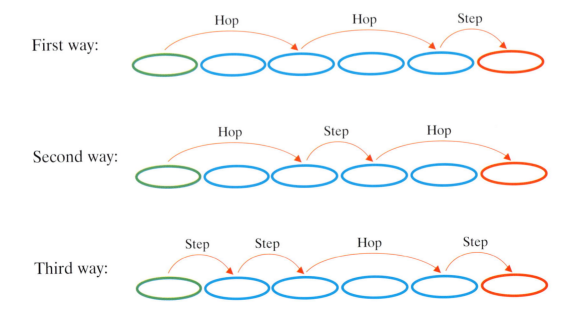

Show that there are 8 different ways of getting from the green to the red hoop when there are 4 blue hoops.

## 18.3 Make the problem as simple as you can

Once you understand the problem try to make it as simple as you can.

The simplest game is when there are **zero** blue hoops:

There is only one way of getting to the red hoop: one step.

The next simplest game is when there is **one** blue hoop:

There are two ways of getting to the red hoop: one hop or two steps.

**Exercise 18B**

1   Put two blue hoops between the green and red hoops.
   **(a)** List all the ways of getting from the green to the red hoop.
   **(b)** How many different ways are there of getting from the green to the red hoop?

2   Put three blue hoops between the green and red hoop.
    Show that there are five different ways of getting from
    the green to the red hoop.

## 18.4  Organize your approach

As the number of blue hoops increases, you need to
organize your approach to be sure you find all the ways of
getting from the green to the red hoop.

An organized approach to a problem is called a **strategy**.

Here is one strategy you could use:

Do as many hops as you can.

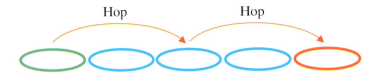

Reduce the number of hops by one.

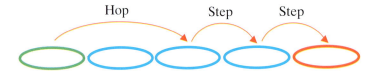

Reduce the number of hops by one again.

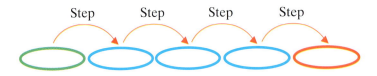

Using a strategy means you are more likely to find **all** the
ways of getting from green to red.

You can shorten the words like this:

Let  S  stand for Step

And H  stand for Hop.

The moves for three blue hoops are:

HH      2 Hops      0 Steps

HSS ⎫
SHS ⎬ 1 Hop      2 Steps
SSH ⎭

SSSS    0 Hops      4 Steps

When there are three blue hoops there are
5 different ways of getting from green to red.

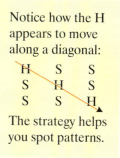

Notice how the H
appears to move
along a diagonal:

H    S    S
S    H    S
S    S    H

The strategy helps
you spot patterns.

---

**Exercise 18C**

Use your strategy to show that there are 8 different ways of
getting from the green to the red hoop when there are
4 blue hoops.

## 18.5 Record your results

So far you should know that the number of ways of getting
from the green to the red hoop is:

1 when there are 0 blue hoops

2 when there is   1 blue hoop

3 when there are 2 blue hoops

5 when there are 3 blue hoops

8 when there are 4 blue hoops

A good way to keep your results is in a table:

| Number of blue hoops | Number of ways of getting from green to red |
|:---:|:---:|
| 0 | 1 |
| 1 | 2 |
| 2 | 3 |

**Exercise 18D**

Copy and complete the table:

| Number of blue hoops | Number of ways of getting from green to red |
|:---:|:---:|
| 0 | 1 |
| 1 | 2 |
| 2 | 3 |
| 3 | |
| 4 | |

## 18.6 Make predictions

Once you have some results and have recorded them in a table you can try to predict what will happen next.

Use your table of results to see if you can spot a pattern:

| Number of blue hoops | Number of ways of getting from green to red |
|:---:|:---:|
| 0 | 1 |
| 1 | 2 |
| 2 | 3 |
| 3 | 5 |
| 4 | 8 |

You should be able to see that:

**The number of ways increases as the number of blue hoops increases.**

You can predict that there will be more than 8 ways when there are 5 hoops.

If you just look at the number of ways you might spot that there is a pattern:

| Number of blue hoops | Number of ways of getting from green to red | Even or odd? |
|:---:|:---:|:---:|
| 0 | 1 | Odd |
| 1 | 2 | Even |
| 2 | 3 | Odd |
| 3 | 5 | Odd |
| 4 | 8 | Even |

You can predict that the pattern will continue like this:

Odd, Even, <u>Odd, Odd, Even,</u> Odd, Odd, Even, Odd, Odd, Even …

This part repeats.

Your prediction could be:
There are an odd number of ways when there are 5 hoops.
There are an odd number of ways when there are 6 hoops.

### Exercise 18E

Predict whether there will be an odd or an even number of ways when there are:

(a)  7 blue hoops    (b)  10 blue hoops   (c)  20 blue hoops

## 18.7  Try to predict the next number

The point of making a prediction is to find the number of ways without having to play the game.

You can predict that there is an odd number of ways when there are 5 blue hoops.
But the best prediction is exactly how many ways there are.

To predict how many ways there are with 5 blue hoops you need to find a pattern in the numbers.

It helps to write the number of ways like this:

1          2          3          5          8          ?

You need to spot that:
To find the next number in the sequence, add the previous two numbers together.

The pattern suggests that the number of ways when there are 5 blue hoops is 13.

You can predict that there are 13 ways when there are 5 hoops.

## 18.8 Test your prediction

Now you have a prediction, you must test it to see if it works.

This means you use your strategy to show there are 13 ways when there are 5 blue hoops.

### Exercise 18F

1   Show that there are 13 ways of getting from the green to the red hoop when there are 5 blue hoops.

2   Make and test a prediction for the number of ways when there are 6 blue hoops.

## 18.9 Make a generalization

Once you have tested your prediction and it works, you can use your prediction to generalize.
This means giving a rule that always works.

The rule for this sequence of numbers is:

To find the next number in the sequence, add the previous two numbers together.

You can use this generalization to make further predictions if you are still unsure:

Remember: this sequence is called a Fibonacci sequence. You can find out more on page 55.

| Number of blue hoops | Number of ways of getting from green to red |
|:---:|:---:|
| 0 | 1 |
| 1 | 2 |
| 2 | 3 |
| 3 | 5 |
| 4 | 8 |
| 5 | 13 |
| 6 | 21 |
| 7 | 34 |

$8 + 13 = 21$

$13 + 21 = 34$

## Exercise 18G

Use your generalization to work out the number of ways when there are:

**(a)** 8 blue hoops      **(b)** 9 blue hoops

**(c)** 10 blue hoops      **(d)** 15 blue hoops

Now use all the steps again to play this version of Hop and Step:

Lucy plays a new game of Hop and Step.
This time the rules are the same except:

a hop takes her 3 hoops forward.

● Investigate the number of different ways of getting from the green hoop to the red hoop as the number of blue hoops changes.

● Try to find a new generalization.

● Use your generalization to find the number of ways when there are 10 blue hoops.

## Summary of key points

For any investigation

● Understand the problem – have a go.
● Make the problem as simple as you can
● Organize your approach – use a strategy
● Record your results – use a table
● Make predictions – try to predict the next number
● Test your prediction
● Make a generalization

# 19 Calculators and computers

This unit shows you some ways of using scientific calculators, graphical calculators and computers to help solve mathematical problems.

The examples will work on Casio calculators and most computers. Your teacher will tell you if you need to change any of the instructions.

## 19.1 Using your memory

You can use the memory on a scientific calculator to help you with money or lists.

### Example 1

Janet's money box contains twenty three 1p coins, seventeen 2p coins, nine 5p coins, and thirteen 10p coins. How much money has she saved?

Press

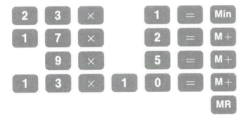

Answer:   232 pence which is £2.32

### Exercise 19A          Scientific calculator

1   Lucy buys these stamps from the Post Office:   8 second class stamps at 20p, 22 first class stamps at 26p, 3 stamps at 37p, and 2 stamps at 43p. Find the total cost and the change she receives if she pays with a £10 note.

2   In one week a school tuck shop sold 83 bars of chocolate at 42p each, 229 cans of squash at 35p each and 355 packets of crisps at 15p each. Find the total takings for the week.

**3** Michael bought 17 Christmas cards at 5p each, 12 cards at 9p each and 5 cards at 14p each. How much did he spend on Christmas cards?

**4** Suwani does a 6 mile sponsored walk. Twenty nine people sponsor her at 2p per mile, thirteen people at 5p per mile, and twelve people at 10p per mile. How much will she collect if she completes the whole distance?

## 19.2 Square numbers and number chains

You can find square numbers using the key $x^2$

> The $x^2$ key multiplies a number by itself.
>
> Multiplying a number by itself gives a **square number**
>
> $5 \times 5 = 25$
>
> A short way to write $5 \times 5$ is $5^2$
>
> You say '5 squared'

**Example 2**

Find   **(a)** $5^2$   **(b)** $7^2$   **(c)** $13^2$

**(a)** Press [5] [$x^2$] [=]     Answer: 25

**(b)** Press [7] [$x^2$]     Answer: 49

**(c)** Press [1] [3] [$x^2$]     Answer: 169

### Exercise 19B

**1** Calculate $9^2$

**2** Calculate $12^2$

**3** Calculate $17^2$

**4** Calculate $5^2 + 12^2$

**5** Calculate $6^2 + 8^2$

### Number chains

You can make a number chain by using a simple rule.

## Example 3

Start with 44      Follow this rule:
'square and add the digits of the previous number'

$$44 \rightarrow 4^2 + 4^2 = 16 + 16 = 32$$
$$32 \rightarrow 3^2 + 2^2 = 9 + 4 = 13$$
$$13 \rightarrow 1^2 + 3^2 = 1 + 9 = 10$$
$$1 \rightarrow 1^2 = 1 \quad \text{STOP when you get a number which is already in the chain}$$

This chain becomes a circle unless you stop.

Number chain:  $44 \rightarrow 32 \rightarrow 13 \rightarrow 10 \rightarrow 1$

## Exercise 19C

1   Square and add the digits starting with 19

2   Square and add the digits starting with 49

3   Square and add the digits starting with 82

4   Square and add the digits starting with 15

## 19.3  Ordering whole numbers and decimals using random numbers

Most calculators and computer programs can produce **random numbers**. These are usually decimals with three digits. For example:

$$0.348 \qquad 0.846 \qquad 0.962 \qquad 0.137$$

sometimes they have fewer digits:

$$0.7 \qquad 0.86 \qquad 0.29 \qquad 0.04$$

Find out how to make your calculator produce random numbers.

**Random** means all numbers have an equal chance of being produced.

## Exercise 19D      Scientific calculator

1   Find the  Rn#  or  Ran#  key.
You may have to press  INV  or  SHIFT  first.
Produce 20 random decimal numbers and write them down.

**2** **A game for two players** Each player draws this number grid:

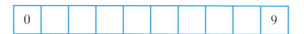

- Take turns to produce a random number.
- Look at the last digit.
- Write it in the right place on your grid.

The first person to collect all the digits from 0 to 9 wins.

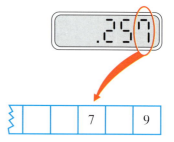

**3** Repeat the game using this grid:

- Collect the last **two** digits of each random number.
- Write them on your grid.

The first person to fill their grid wins.
**But** all the numbers must be in order:

| 0 | 15 | 28 | 41 | 49 | 52 | 68 | 74 | 81 | 99 |
|---|----|----|----|----|----|----|----|----|----|

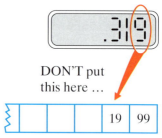

DON'T put
this here …

… or every number
to its left must
be less than 19!

**4** Repeat the game using this grid:

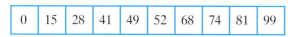

- Use **all three** digits of each random number, including the decimal point

Remember: **0.428** is less than **0.43** is less than **0.5**

## Random numbers by computer

You can write a computer program in BASIC to produce random decimal numbers. One of these programs should work on your computer:

```
10 REPEAT              DO
20 PRINT RND           PRINT RND
30 LET Z = GET         LET Z = GET
40 UNTIL FALSE         LOOP
50 END                 END
```

Press the *Space bar* to see the next random number.

Press *Escape* or *Ctrl·Break* to stop the programs.

## Exercise 19E        BASIC

**1**  Type and save the program on your computer.

**2**  Produce 10 random decimal numbers by running the program. Write them down.

**3**  Edit the program so the line:

```
PRINT RND
```

becomes:

```
PRINT INT(10*RND)
```

Run the new program to produce 20 random whole numbers between 0 and 9.

Write your numbers down.

**4**  Repeat the game from question 3, page 288 but use the BASIC program with the line:

```
PRINT INT(100*RND)
```

This produces random whole numbers from 0 to 99.

**5**  Repeat the game using this grid:

| 0 | | | | | | | | | 1 |
|---|---|---|---|---|---|---|---|---|---|

Use the BASIC program with this line:

```
PRINT (INT(100*RND))/100
```

This produces random two-digit decimal numbers. Use all the digits and the decimal point. For example:

| 0 | .17 | .2 | .39 | .61 | .69 | .7 | .88 | .97 | 1 |
|---|-----|-----|-----|-----|-----|-----|-----|-----|---|

## 19.4 Multiplication tables practice

The next page shows some ways to practise your times tables using random numbers:

## Exercise 19F    Scientific calculator

**1    Seven times table**

- Press the `Rn#` or `Ran#` key and write down the *last digit* of your random number.
  Ignore 0 or 1 when they occur.
- *Without using a calculator* multiply this random digit by 7 and write down your result.
- Repeat this 20 times, then check your answers using the calculator.

| 7 times table | | |
|---|---|---|
| random number | my result | check |
| 7 | 49 | ✓ |
| 2 | 14 | ✓ |
| 4 | 27 | ✗ |
| 5 | 40 | ✗ |

**2    Now try other multiplication tables.**

## Exercise 19G    Graphical calculator

**1    Six times table**

- Produce a random whole number from 2 to 12 by pressing the keys:

  `Int`  `1`  `1`  `Ran#`  `+`  `2`  `EXE`

  and write it down.
- *Without using a calculator* multiply this random number by 6 and write down your result.
- Keep pressing `EXE` to repeat this 20 times, then check your answers using the calculator.

| 6 times table | | |
|---|---|---|
| random number | my result | check |
| 10 | 60 | ✓ |
| 3 | 18 | ✓ |
| 12 | 60 | ✗ |
| 5 | 30 | ✓ |

**2    Now try other multiplication tables.**

## Exercise 19H    BASIC

**1    Type and save this program on your computer:**

```
10 FOR X=1 TO 20
20 PRINT INT(11*RND+2);" x 8 = ?"
30 LET Z=GET
40 NEXT X
50 END
```

## 2   Eight times table

- Run the program and write down the random number it produces.
- *Without using a calculator*, multiply this random number by 8 and write down your result.
- Keep pressing the *Space bar* to repeat this 20 times, then check your answers using a calculator.

| |
|---|
| 2 × 8 ? |
| 10 × 8 ? |
| 12 × 8 ? |
| 7 × 8 ? |
| 3 × 8 ? |

**3**   Now try other multiplication tables.

---

### Exercise 19I      Spreadsheet

**1**   Type this formula into cell A1 of a new spreadsheet:

`=INT(11*RAND()+2)`

This will display a random whole number from 2 to 12. Write this number down.

- *Without using a calculator*, multiply this random number by 9 and write down your result.
- Do a manual recalculation of the spreadsheet to repeat this 20 times, then check your answers using a calculator.

**2**   Now try other multiplication tables.

**3**   Start a new spreadsheet. Follow these instructions carefully:

In cell A1 type the formula `=INT(11*RAND()+2)`
Copy cell A1 down column A as far as cell A15

In cell B1 type the letter "x"
Copy cell B1 down column B as far as cell B15

In cell C1 type the formula `=INT(11*RAND()+2)`
In cell C2 type the formula `=C$1`
Copy cell C2 down to column C as far as cell C15

In cell D1 type " ="
Copy cell D1 down column D as far as cell D15

Move to a column which you cannot see at the moment, for example column K
In cell K1 type the formula `=A1*C1`
Copy cell K1 down column K as far as cell K15

> Most spreadsheets are set up to do automatic recalculation.
>
> Find out how to make your spreadsheet do manual recalculation.
>
> Then it will only do calculations when you press a key (like F9 in Excel).

> Put a *space* before the *equals* sign

Move back to column A so that you cannot see the numbers in column K

Now you are ready to begin!

- Do a manual recalculation of the spreadsheet. It will show times table questions:

Do another manual recalculation and repeat the process.

| | A | B | C | D | E | F | G | H | I | J | K |
|---|---|---|---|---|---|---|---|---|---|---|---|
| 1 | 5 | x | 12 | = | | | | | | | 60 |
| 2 | 2 | x | 12 | = | | | | | | | 24 |
| 3 | 9 | x | 12 | = | | | | | | | 108 |
| 4 | 3 | x | 12 | = | | | | | | | 36 |
| 5 | 8 | x | 12 | = | | | | | | | 96 |
| 6 | 9 | x | 12 | = | | | | | | | 108 |
| 7 | 6 | x | 12 | = | | | | | | | 72 |
| 8 | 7 | x | 12 | – | | | | | | | 84 |

- *Without using a calculator*, work out the answers and type them in column E

- Move to column K to check your answers

Clear column K then have another go!

## 19.5 Recycling machines and number sequences

This recycling machine adds 2 to each input number.

If the first input is 1 the output is 3.

Then 3 is the second input and the output is 5.

The **sequence** of numbers produced in this way begins 1, 3, 5, 7, 9 ... (the odd numbers).

You can use the constant function on your calculator to produce number sequences like this.

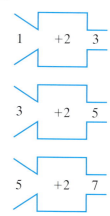

## Exercise 19J    Scientific calculator

Write down the first five numbers in each of these sequences:

1  [2] [+] [+] [1] [=] [=] [=] ...        (add 2)

2  [3] [+] [+] [4] [=] [=] [=] ...        (add 3)

3  [2] [×] [×] [3] [=] [=] [=] ...        (multiply by 2)

4  [5] [−] [−] [6] [0] [=] [=] [=] ...    (subtract 5)

5  [2] [÷] [÷] [6] [4] [=] [=] [=] ...    (divide by 2)

This two step recycling machine multiplies by 2 then subtracts 3.

If the first input is 4 the output is 5.

Then 5 is the second input and the output is 7.

This sequence begins    4,  5,  7,  11,  19 ...

You can use the answer memory on a graphical calculator to produce these number sequences.

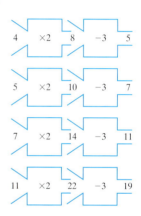

## Exercise 19K    Graphical calculator

Write down the first five numbers in each of these sequences:

1  [4] [EXE] [Ans] [×] [2] [−] [3] [EXE] [EXE] ...

2  [2] [EXE] [Ans] [×] [3] [+] [1] [EXE] [EXE] ...

3  [7] [EXE] [Ans] [×] [2] [−] [1] [EXE] [EXE] ...

4  [7] [8] [4] [EXE] [Ans] [÷] [2] [÷] [8] [EXE] [EXE] ...

5  What two step machine produces the sequence:
   5,  13,  29,  61,  125  ... ?

6  What two step machine produces the sequence:
   13,  21,  37,  69,  133  ... ?

# 19.6 Symmetry in LOGO

You can use the computer program LOGO to help you understand rotational symmetry and line (reflective) symmetry.

First type the following three procedures:

```
TO SQUARE
REPEAT 4[FD 50 RT 90]
END
```

```
TO RFLAG
FD 50 SQUARE BK 50
END
```

```
TO LFLAG
FD 50 LT 90 SQUARE RT 90 BK 50
END
```

> Find out which version of LOGO you are using.
>
> The instructions given here are written for MSWLogo

### Example 4

Type CS HT PD REPEAT 4[RFLAG RT 90]
This shape has rotational symmetry of order 4.
There are no lines of reflective symmetry.

### Example 5

Type CS HT PD REPEAT 2[RFLAG LFLAG RT 180]
This shape has rotational symmetry of order 2.
There are 2 lines of reflective symmetry.

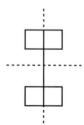

### Exercise 19L

Type the following LOGO commands on your computer then draw each shape in your book.

Write down whether each shape has rotational symmetry.

Draw any lines of reflective symmetry.

**1**   CS HT PD REPEAT 3[RFLAG RT 120]

**2**   CS HT PD REPEAT 8[RFLAG RT 90 LFLAG RT 90]

> Find out how to *save*, *load* and *edit* LOGO procedures

**3**  CS HT PD REPEAT 8[RFLAG RT 45]

**4**  CS HT PD REPEAT 3[RFLAG LFLAG RT 120]

**5**  CS HT PD REPEAT 4[SQUARE RT 90]

**6**  CS HT PD LFLAG SQUARE

**7**  CS HT PD REPEAT 2[LFLAG SQUARE RT 90]

**8**  CS HT REPEAT 8[PU FD 50 PD SQUARE PU BK 50
     RT 45]

## 19.7 Angles practice in LOGO

You can use the computer program LOGO to help you draw
and estimate angles. You will need the following three
short procedures Q, H and A:

```
TO Q
MAKE "B RANDOM  90 CS HT PD
MAKE "A RANDOM 360 SETH :A
MAKE "D SIGN (180 . :a)
SETPC [255 0 0]
FD 120  BK 120
REPEAT  :B [FD 30 BK 30 RT :D]
FD 120  BK 120
END


TO H
SETPC [0 255 0]  SETH :A
REPEAT 12 [FD 60 BK 60 RT 30]
END


TO A
SHOW :B
END
```

> Find out which
> version of
> LOGO you are
> using.
>
> The instructions
> given here are
> written for
> MSWLogo

Procedure Q draws a *new angle* for you to estimate. If you
need *help* use procedure H. The *answer* is given by
procedure A.

> Find out how to
> *save*, and *load*
> LOGO
> procedures.

## Exercise 19M

1  Type and save the procedures Q, H and A.

2  Use procedure Q to draw a new angle, then try to estimate the size of the angle in degrees. Write down your estimate. If you need help use procedure H. Check your estimate with procedure A. Write down the computer's answer. Repeat this for another 9 angles.

3  Edit procedure Q so that the line

```
          MAKE "B RANDOM   90 CS HT PD
becomes   MAKE "B RANDOM  180 CS HT PD
```

Now repeat question 2.

> Find out how to *edit* procedures in LOGO

4  Edit procedure Q so that the line

```
          MAKE "B RANDOM  180 CS HT PD
becomes   MAKE "B RANDOM  270 CS HT PD
```

Now repeat question 2.

## 19.8 Charts and graphs from data using a spreadsheet

Computer spreadsheets can produce a selection of different charts and graphs, so it can be very useful to use a spreadsheet for storing your data.

> Find out how to produce bar charts and line graphs from data in your computer spreadsheet.
>
> Look for horizontal bar charts, vertical bar charts and line graphs.

## Exercise 19N

1  The daily temperature (minimum and maximum) and monthly rainfall figures for Monkey Bay in Malawi are shown below. Type this data into your spreadsheet and save it.

|   | A | B | C | D |
|---|---|---|---|---|
| 1 | **Month** | **Min Temp °C** | **Max Temp °C** | **Rainfall mm** |
| 2 | Jan | 23 | 28 | 325 |
| 3 | Feb | 22 | 28 | 315 |
| 4 | Mar | 21 | 29 | 400 |
| 5 | Apr | 20 | 29 | 140 |
| 6 | May | 18 | 26 | 40 |
| 7 | Jun | 16 | 25 | 10 |
| 8 | Jul | 15 | 25 | 5 |
| 9 | Aug | 16 | 26 | 2 |
| 10 | Sep | 18 | 29 | 3 |
| 11 | Oct | 21 | 32 | 5 |
| 12 | Nov | 24 | 32 | 60 |
| 13 | Dec | 23 | 30 | 225 |

**2** Display the
   rainfall data
   in a line graph
   like this:

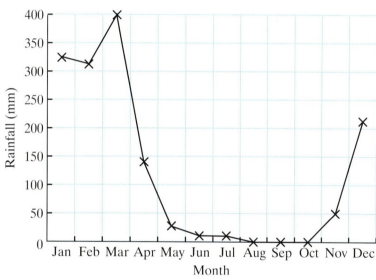

**3** Display the
   temperature data
   in a bar chart like this:

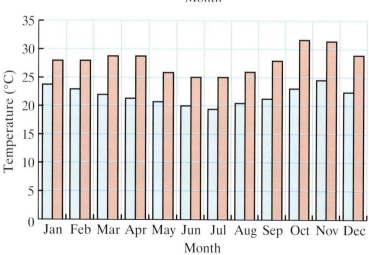

# Index